Leading Hybrid Organi

Hybrid working on a large scale arrived suddenly with the COVID-19 pandemic. And it's here to stay. Going beyond the quick-fix solutions that emerged during the transition, this book takes a deeper, systems approach to leading a hybrid organisation to help managers understand the real, 'beneath the surface' issues in hybrid working.

Established ways of managing everyday problems, such as workflow, communication and performance management, now seem inadequate when some members of staff are in the office and others are working remotely. In addition to day-to-day management tasks, there are also more complex challenges such as developing a cohesive team and organisational culture and a strong attachment to the organisation. Drawing on contemporary management theory, behavioural science, psychoanalysis and social psychology, the book explains the impacts and how to address areas such as: team and organisational identity; recruitment and retention of talent; personality and hybrid working; team dynamics; performance management; security and insider risk; well-being, burnout and engagement; diversity equality and inclusion; ESG; and handling conflict.

This engaging book empowers leaders and managers by enabling them to understand the dynamics of hybrid working, and giving them the tools to influence these processes to improve their effectiveness in the organisation.

Michael Drayton is a leadership expert, clinical psychologist, executive coach and author. He coaches senior leaders on the Executive MBA and other leadership development programmes at Saïd Business School, University of Oxford. He is the author of three books on the psychology of leadership.

"*Leading Hybrid Organisations* offers a well-researched and engagingly written analysis of the leadership and psychological challenges in hybrid organisations. Its informative and interesting perspective provides leaders with practical tools and strategies for ensuring team well-being and productivity in diverse work settings."

Professor Sue Dopson, *Professor of Organisational Behaviour, Saïd Business School, University of Oxford*

"Do you want your workplace to be a magnet for your employees? This book will help managers and leaders understand the importance of communication styles, push and pull factors, creating identity and connection to the organisation, and ensuring there is a distinction between working at home and working in the office that motivates employees to return and thrive."

Ranjit Dhindsa, *Employment Partner, Board member, Business Leader, Office Leader and Special Advisor to a social enterprise business, FieldFisher LLP*

"As an occupational health physician, I have observed the evolving dynamics of hybrid work during the pandemic. Many organizations have struggled to adapt to this new way of working. This book addresses these challenges head-on. It is evidence-based yet easy to read, offering practical insights and strategies for success with lots of examples, from the Titanic to Project Aristotle by Google. An essential business read."

Dr. med. Kai Haas, *Head of Occupational Health, Salzgitter AG, Germany*

Leading Hybrid Organisations

How to Build Trust, Collaboration and a High-Performance Culture

Michael Drayton with
Elsine van Os

Routledge
Taylor & Francis Group
LONDON AND NEW YORK

Designed cover image: Getty Images/FilippoBacci

First published 2024
by Routledge
4 Park Square, Milton Park, Abingdon, Oxon OX14 4RN

and by Routledge
605 Third Avenue, New York, NY 10158

Routledge is an imprint of the Taylor & Francis Group, an informa business

© 2024 Michael Drayton

The right of Michael Drayton to be identified as author of this work has been asserted in accordance with sections 77 and 78 of the Copyright, Designs and Patents Act 1988.

All rights reserved. No part of this book may be reprinted or reproduced or utilised in any form or by any electronic, mechanical, or other means, now known or hereafter invented, including photocopying and recording, or in any information storage or retrieval system, without permission in writing from the publishers.

Trademark notice: Product or corporate names may be trademarks or registered trademarks, and are used only for identification and explanation without intent to infringe.

British Library Cataloguing-in-Publication Data
A catalogue record for this book is available from the British Library

Library of Congress Cataloging-in-Publication Data
Names: Drayton, Michael, 1960– author.
Title: Leading hybrid organisations : how to build trust, collaboration and a high-performance culture / Michael Drayton.
Description: New York, NY : Routledge, 2024. | Includes bibliographical references and index.
Subjects: LCSH: Flextime. | Flexible work arrangements. | Personnel management. | Teams in the workplace—Management. | Multinational work teams.
Classification: LCC HD5109 .D73 2024 (print) | LCC HD5109 (ebook) | DDC 331.25/724—dc23/eng/20240212
LC record available at https://lccn.loc.gov/2023056949
LC ebook record available at https://lccn.loc.gov/2023056950

ISBN: 978-1-032-47223-2 (hbk)
ISBN: 978-1-032-48138-8 (pbk)
ISBN: 978-1-003-38760-2 (ebk)

DOI: 10.4324/9781003387602

Typeset in Sabon
by Apex CoVantage, LLC

This book is dedicated to Angela, my wonderful wife, who has been my rock and biggest supporter throughout this journey.

To Jenny and Guy, for your love and support. I hope this book makes you proud.

To Geoff, my dear friend who inspired me to start this project in the first place.

And to my editor, Charlie Wilson. Your insight and guidance were invaluable, and your thoughtful comments pushed me to improve my thinking and writing. I am grateful for your partnership in shaping this book.

Finally, to leaders everywhere guiding their organisations through these uncharted waters of hybrid work – may this book provide insights and tools to help you create thriving cultures, no matter where your people are. Thank you for your commitment to leading with care, curiosity and courage.

Contents

	Notes on Contributors	ix
	Preface	x
1	What This Book Is about and Why It's Important MICHAEL DRAYTON	1
2	How to Build a Group Identity in the Hybrid Organisation MICHAEL DRAYTON	20
3	Why Do Some People Love Coming into the Office and Others Hate It? Personality and the Hybrid Organisation MICHAEL DRAYTON	38
4	Communicating in the Hybrid Organisation MICHAEL DRAYTON	56
5	Evolving Workplaces and Hybrid Organisations MICHAEL DRAYTON	73
6	Security in the Hybrid Organisation ELSINE VAN OS	89
7	Well-being, Burnout and Engagement in the Hybrid Workplace MICHAEL DRAYTON	117
8	Leading the Hybrid Organisation: From Leader as Explorer to Leader as Healer MICHAEL DRAYTON	135

9 The Only Way Is Ethics: ESG and the Hybrid
  Organisation   156
  MICHAEL DRAYTON

10 The Future of Hybrid: How to Make a Hybrid Company
   Where You Want to Work   172
   MICHAEL DRAYTON

   Index   189

Contributors

Michael Drayton is a leadership expert, clinical psychologist, executive coach and author. He coaches senior leaders on the Executive MBA and other leadership development programmes at Saïd Business School, University of Oxford. He is the author of three books on the psychology of leadership.

Elsine van Os is an intelligence specialist and clinical psychologist recognised for her insider-risk management expertise. She has spearheaded high-profile security projects for the Dutch government and Shell across 50+ countries, especially high-risk regions. In 2016, she founded Signpost Six, an insider-risk consultancy.

Preface

In the summer of 2022, I was chatting with my friend Geoff at a barbecue. Geoff is a senior leader of a complex organisation. He was telling me about the headaches of managing a hybrid team. He said he hadn't met many of his new direct reports in person and worried they weren't forming an attachment to the organisation. Geoff talked about how difficult innovation was with half the team in the office and the other half at home. That interesting conversation sparked the idea that this would be a good topic for a book. And here it is.

Managing a hybrid workforce is one of today's most difficult challenges for leaders. While some books provide advice and tips, deeper questions remain. This book takes a more in-depth approach grounded in systems thinking and psychology to provide guidance on leading sustainable hybrid models.

We will look at management theory, psychoanalysis and social psychology to uncover the underlying issues and keys to effective leadership in hybrid organisations.

New leadership mindsets are required for hybrid working. Our experiences shape our mindsets, but what worked in the past may not work now. Running a reconfigured hybrid organisation requires us to update our leadership thinking and models to reflect new realities. We will examine rigorous research on how to best manage change, foster a sense of belonging and build trust; these are critical hybrid leadership challenges.

This book provides the in-depth understanding needed to develop the mindset and skills required to harness the potential of hybrid working and build successful hybrid organisations.

1 What This Book Is about and Why It's Important

Michael Drayton

This book is about how to lead a successful hybrid organisation. There are books on the market that tell you what to do to make the transition to hybrid working a success. The situation is still quite new, evolving and unsettled. As a result, these cookbook methods are hit or miss. The ideas may work for some organisations while being disastrous for others.

To figure out how to successfully develop your hybrid organisation, you need a much deeper understanding, a method that goes back to first principles. If you run an investment bank, you must understand how markets operate rather than simply following tips. This book takes a deeper first-principles psychological and systems approach to understanding and leading a hybrid organisation.

Leading any organisation, especially a hybrid organisation, is difficult because it requires you to consider not only individual and group/team factors, but also larger systemic factors such as your organization's culture and the larger economic and political forces affecting your organisation. After all, it was not a clever culture change initiative or a particularly insightful and persuasive article in the *Harvard Business Review* that sparked hybrid working in the first place, but the harsh medical, social and political realities of the pandemic.

We will look at contemporary management theory, psychoanalysis and social psychology. My aim is to get you thinking about the real, beneath-the-surface issues in hybrid working. Only there will you find the key to understanding and effectively leading a successful hybrid organisation.

Hybrid working is the biggest single issue facing leaders

In a 2022 *Financial Times* article, Gillian Tett described facilitating two discussions with C-suite executives: one at the New York Stock Exchange about inflation, and the other at Ernst & Young about macroeconomics. In each group, the topics of inflation and macroeconomics were quickly forgotten in favour of an emotional, enthusiastic and presumably more pressing and meaningful discussion

DOI: 10.4324/9781003387602-1

about how they should manage hybrid working in their respective organisations. '"It's the biggest single issue," the boss of a Midwest industrial group forlornly admitted' (Tett, 2022).

The pandemic forced the rapid adoption of hybrid working in most, if not all, organisations. It was a remarkable shift in how we work. Within the space of a few weeks, whole departments moved from working in traditional office environments to working from home, using new and unfamiliar (for most of us) teleconferencing software like Zoom.[1] My own working pattern and life changed enormously. Before the pandemic, I would spend a couple of nights away from home most weeks and a few days abroad every couple of months. After the pandemic, my working life moved lock, stock and barrel into my little home office at the bottom of my garden (where I am now writing this book). The change has been personally great for me in so many ways, but there are lots of things I miss from my old life – but more on that later.

Now that the pandemic is over, hybrid working is the norm for most organisations. My day-to-day interactions with executives have led me to the conclusion that not much thought has been given to what makes a successful hybrid organisation. Established ways of managing everyday problems, such as workflow, communication and performance management, now seem inadequate when some members of staff are in the office and others are working remotely. In addition to these bread-and-butter tasks, there are far more complex challenges, such as developing a cohesive team and organisational culture and a strong attachment to the organisation when some people like coming into work and others avoid the office. This whole thing is a huge challenge for most leaders.

Most of us, myself included, have just muddled along and done our best. We responded to problems as they arose. For example, the Wi-Fi signal in my office at the bottom of the garden isn't great, so I joined a long queue to have an electrician install an Ethernet cable, which solved that problem. That's how most organisations managed the move to working from home – pragmatically and let's say tactically, by addressing issues as they came up. There's nothing wrong with this approach in the short term, but it's neither proactive nor strategic. A very significant change in structure and culture has been forced on most organisations, but the strategic direction and leadership skills needed to manage this change still feel a bit muddled.

Leading a hybrid organisation requires a new mindset

Hybrid working is different to what's gone before, and making it work requires a new and different leadership mindset.

A mindset is the collection of assumptions and underlying beliefs that your mind holds about various aspects of the world. You have a mindset about relationships, morality and, of course, work. Your mindset developed from past experiences of what seems to have worked in life, given your personality and circumstances. Your mindset has got you to where you are now. We all have all kinds of mindsets about all kinds of different things. In this book, I'll focus on work.

Your mindset about work is constructed from three factors: your personality, and I'll talk more about that in Chapter 3; your personal circumstances (let's say your environment); and your personal experiences of things that have worked.

Your *current* mindset about work has its roots in your experience of running a successful, traditionally structured, probably office-based organisation. Now most organisations have changed, with some employees in the office and some at home. Some want to get back to the office and others are resisting. The old mindset isn't congruent with the new situation. The traditional mindset that has served you so well in the past is no longer the optimal mindset for the new situation. In the words of Marshall Goldsmith, one of the best executive coaches in the business, 'What got you here won't get you there' (Goldsmith & Reiter, 2007). To create and run this new, reconfigured hybrid-business structure, you will need a new mindset. Metaphorically, you will need a software upgrade. The question is, after all these years working in a particular way, how do you go about getting one?

You could just muddle through and learn from the inevitable mistakes you will make. That is not a bad way to learn, but I believe there is a better way, or at the very least a route that will make the journey shorter and less exhausting. We return to first principles. Rather than reinventing the wheel, let us look at some serious peer-reviewed research that describes what people have learned in the past about how people change and how to develop trust between managers and employees. After all, these will be two of the biggest challenges in creating and leading an effective hybrid organisation.

A pause

As you read about these ideas, I suggest that, from time to time, you pause and ask yourself if the ideas seem to make sense. Do they fit with your experience of the real world of work? Do they help to make sense of past workplace events and the characters you have known? Maybe the ideas I'm about to describe will give you a fresh and new perspective on things that have happened in the past. Maybe they will give you a new way of making sense of work and a new way of telling your story.

If these ideas can help you understand and explain the past, they might also be able to help you predict how events will unfold in the future. They might be able to give you some ideas about the best types of actions to take to increase the likelihood of a positive outcome. Later in this chapter, we will look at how Kodak's failure to change its leadership mindset did not end well.

How people change

How do people change?

We had to change a lot during the lockdown in order to survive. One minute we were happily commuting to our office, where we would do work stuff before heading home again. The next moment, we were sitting in front of a webcam talking to people on Zoom. Work was spread out on the kitchen table, or in the spare bedroom, the one that had to be quickly converted into a home office.

We changed because the environment demanded it. It was more difficult for some than others, but most people managed and quickly became accustomed to working from home.

Working from home now feels normal, and having to return to the office feels strange, like a change, and like a major disruption to our now settled and orderly life.

Peter's story: 'Why should I come back to the office?'

'Peter, you have to come into the office at least twice a week.'

'Why should I? What's the point?'

Everybody likes Peter. He is one of those contrarian, eccentric, likeable people. He works hard, cares about what he does and looks after his team. His crankiness is endearing rather than annoying. He's been working from home since the pandemic, and people miss him. A few days ago, the CEO issued an edict that everybody has to spend a minimum of two days in the office. Some people grumbled, but everyone returned – everyone, that is, except Peter. Now, it's your job to persuade Peter that he has to show his face, and the task is proving difficult.

'Peter, it's not me. If it were down to me, you could work from home, but it's company policy now – the big boss says you have to be in for at least two days a week.'

'I'm not bloody five years old. I'm not going to do something just because a "grown-up" says I should. Give me a good reason and I might think about it.'

'Okay, the team wants to see you face to face.'

'I see their ugly mugs all the time on Zoom, and there are no complaints. It would be nice to meet up – but it's too much hassle.'

You go on to provide some other reasons why Peter needs to come back, all of which he firmly rejects as being 'nonsense'.

Rolling his eyes, Peter eventually says, 'Look, my work is pretty good and I can do it better working from home than in the office. I can manage my team perfectly well over Zoom, and they're happy enough, aren't they?'

Well, yes, Peter's work is excellent, and his team is functioning well.

'I love working here. I love the work, the challenge and all the people. But if you aren't happy with the way I work, maybe I should look around for something else?'

The psychology of change

> It ought to be remembered that there is nothing more difficult to take in hand, more perilous to conduct, or more uncertain in its success, than to take the lead in the introduction of a new order of things. Because the innovator has for enemies all those who have done well under the old conditions and lukewarm defenders in those who may do well under the new. This coolness arises partly from fear of the opponents, who have the laws on their side, and partly from the incredulity of men, who do not readily believe in new things until they have had a long experience of them.
>
> (Machiavelli, 1988)

Nikolai Machiavelli's thoughts about change, written in 1513, are as true today as they were in Renaissance Italy. They perfectly describe the conflicting psychological forces generated by the prospect of change.

The key to understanding Peter and change in general is the word ambivalence.

It's not that people don't want to change; it's that usually they are in two minds. A part of them wants to change, and another part doesn't. Part of them is drawn to change; for most of us there is a natural human instinct to grow and develop. However, another part is scared, often terrified, of changing. This is because change also means loss. It means leaving behind something that feels safe and familiar. The past and present feel settled, but the future, the change, feels unsettled and uncertain, and there is threat in uncertainty.

If you have to talk to somebody about change, rather than trying to persuade them to change, a more constructive way of framing the conversation is to say, 'Maybe there is part of you that would like to change and part that doesn't?' This opens up a dialogue rather than an argument.

Kurt Lewin and change

Back in 1948, the social psychologist Kurt Lewin came up with an idea that is useful in understanding change and figuring out the best thing to do to make change happen. He called it Force Field Analysis (Lewin, 1947, 1997).

Imagine for a moment that you are out shopping and you buy a new desk for your study, which happens to be in your attic. A few days later, it arrives, but the delivery people leave it in your hallway, saying that they are not paid to carry it up the stairs. What do you do?

The desk is too heavy for you to move. You could get some strong friends to help you move it. Maybe you could go to the gym and lift weights for six months so you become strong enough to move it yourself. You might be able to move the desk a little at a time if you took out the drawers and unscrewed and removed the desktop

This is an analogy for Kurt Lewin's model of change. You want to change your study with a nice new desk. Your desire to get the desk to the study is what Lewin calls a driving force. Unfortunately, other forces are conspiring to prevent your desired change and thwart your driving force: namely, the force of gravity, the weight of the desk and your own puny physique. These are what Lewin termed restraining forces.

If you want to change something, you have to strengthen the driving forces or weaken the restraining forces, or ideally a mixture of both. Using our desk analogy, you can strengthen the driving forces by recruiting your mates to move the desk or going to the gym to get stronger so you can move the desk by yourself. Or you can start to weaken the restraining forces by removing the drawers and desk top to make it lighter and moving the desk one piece at a time.

Lewin knew that driving forces are in a constant struggle with forces that want to restrain and prevent change. Social and psychic cohesion is maintained when there is an equilibrium between these opposing forces. However, Lewin didn't see this as a linear process like a tug of war. The forces acting on the change are all around, not just pushing and pulling. In the case of transforming your organisation to a hybrid organisation, you will need to consider not only the forces driving and restraining change but other peripheral forces such as transport (is it easy for Peter to get to the office?), status (are those who work from home seen as higher or lower status in the organisation?) and technology (does Peter have a good internet connection?).

Lewin also made the point that change is dynamic, in that if you remove one small restraining force, it has the potential to rapidly accelerate change and open up new opportunities. Let's say you successfully lure Peter back to the office with the idea that he runs a two-hour ideas development meeting with his team. And let's say the team comes up with a breakthrough idea in that meeting. Neither the idea nor meeting would have existed without the change that came from the Force Field Analysis.

What This Book Is About

Kurt Lewin developed these ideas in the aftermath of World War II – a time of social change. In 1948, he wrote:

> A culture is not a painted picture; it is a living process, composed of countless social interactions. Like a river whose form and velocity are determined by the balance of those forces that tend to make the water flow faster, and the friction that tends to make the water flow more slowly, the cultural pattern of a people at a given time is maintained by a balance of counteracting forces.
>
> (Lewin, 1997)

Organisations are currently caught up in the fast-flowing river to hybrid working. To negotiate the river, you will need to figure out the various forces at play. It's these conflicting forces generated by the change to hybrid working that are the beneath-the-surface, driving forces of Peter's reluctance to return to the office. It's not just about Peter's stubbornness; it's also the wider social and economic forces finding expression in his behaviour.

What can you do?

To get Peter back to the office, the first step is to understand the conflicting forces. Don't just bombard him with the reasons why he should return (driving forces) but ask him about why he is reluctant to return (restraining forces). In Lewin's words, you should do a Force Field Analysis.

When you've done that, start to figure out how you can weaken the restraining forces and strengthen the driving forces. For example, you might say to Peter, 'I can see why you don't want to come in and do the sort of work you can do just as well from home – makes sense. We want to use the two days in the office for more creative and strategic problem-solving with you and your team, which is a lot more effective face to face than online. We also want to build in some social and team-building time.' You get the idea?

The process of change

Kurt Lewin figured out what triggers change and what it takes to make change happen, but he didn't stop there. He went on to study and write about how change develops and moves forward. According to Lewin, any change, be it individual, team or organisational, has distinct stages, which he called freeze – unfreeze – move – refreeze. Think of a block of ice as a metaphor for change. It's impossible to force the block of ice into a new shape without shattering it. If you want to change the block of ice into a new shape, you need to melt it (unfreeze), pour the water into, say, an ice cube tray (move) and refreeze it.

Freeze

When a person, team or organisation is in a state of freeze (or is frozen), they are in equilibrium with the forces that drive change and restrain change equally balanced. Of course, people and organisations (which are really groups of individual people) never remain static or entirely frozen. However, using Lewin's idea, when we are in a state of freeze, life seems stable and change, although possible, seems a long way away. In a state of freeze, change is something that we think about and talk about rather than do. You might think to yourself, 'I must cut down on my drinking', as you reach out for your third glass of red wine and lift it to your lips . . . That's the state of freeze.

Unfreeze

People, teams or organisations move into the unfreeze stage when the forces that want to change start to outweigh the forces that do not want to change. Slowly, the ice melts and the transformation into something else – in this case, water – begins. When people, teams and organisations unfreeze, the source of the 'heat' is social, political and economic pressure – the force driving change. It is easy to see how the pandemic's social, political and economic pressures drove dramatic changes in how work was done. In the case of the red wine drinker, the pressure might come from a doctor ('you have liver disease') or a worried spouse, which causes the person to stop drinking. Change is not a single event but rather a series of events that lead up to the abrupt change event. When asked how he became bankrupt, Mike Campbell, a character in Ernest Hemingway's 1926 novel *The Sun Also Rises*, replies, 'Two ways . . . Gradually and then suddenly' (Hemingway, 2006). That's a good description of Lewin's model and how change happens. It's the ice turning into water.

Move

Move is when change starts to happen. This is when people are at their most anxious. It's a bit like the moment a baby is born. It's exciting, because a new life is there to be seen, a new human life full of potential and possibilities. Translated into organisational language, something new has been created. Using Lewin's words, there has been a transition from one state to another, with a new property emerging that is full of possibility. At the same time there is always tremendous anxiety.

Following childbirth, mother and baby are at their most vulnerable. Similarly, the organisation is at its most vulnerable when it changes significantly. Imagine standing on a diving board and looking down at the pool, which looks a long way away. You feel apprehensive as you step forward because you know that as soon as you launch yourself off that diving board, there is no going back. Big organisational change can feel a bit like that: once you have committed yourself, it's very hard to go back. Change is unsettling for most people.

How did the sudden change to working from home during the pandemic feel for you? I guess that you felt ambivalent. Part of you may have felt apprehensive, maybe a bit scared that nothing would work. But maybe there was another part that felt excited? Working from home was a bit of a novelty, and as they say, a change is as good as a rest. But whatever the dominant emotion was, you probably felt unsettled.

After a while, though, things and feelings began to settle down a bit and maybe you began to think, 'Well, this isn't so bad – I could get used to this working from home stuff.' You may have saved hours not having to commute and because of that you were able to make time for a daily walk. It wasn't all roses and you did get tired of the back-to-back Zoom meetings, but hey, you can't have everything, can you?

This is assuming that you have a white-collar professional job that transfers fairly easily to home working. You might live in a decent-sized house with plenty of space and a garden. If that was you, then working from home was probably okay. But what was lockdown like for those whose job couldn't be done remotely? What was it like for the average dentist, electrician or hairdresser, for example? Or what was lockdown like for people whose circumstances weren't as comfortable as yours? What about the single parent with two young children living in a small flat with no access to a garden or childcare? Well, remote working was hard and not very pleasant if that was your situation.

For most of us, though, working from home turned out to be alright. There is a range of 'alright', but most people made the adjustment and got used to what became known as the 'new normal'. That was the point when, to use Lewin's term, society and organisations began the slow process of re-freezing.

Refreeze

Refreezing happens when the forces driving change and those restraining change start to balance out. Things settle down in the new situation and it starts to feel normal rather than new. Of course there are, and always will be, changes, but these feel more like minor adjustments rather than a major upheaval.

Currently, most people who have been working from home for a while are used to it and most quite like it. In fact, the newspapers are full of stories of battles between organisations who want to get their people back into the office and the people – the employees – who are actively resisting going back. The 'new normal' is now just . . . normal. The situation is beginning to freeze up again. Society and organisations are refreezing into a new shape. That's why now is the time to proactively consider what a 'refrozen organisation' – your refrozen organisation – could look like. How could it be moulded into a shape that's best for the organisation and the people who make up that organisation? That is essentially the topic of this book.

Using Lewin's change framework to achieve success

Lewin's ideas about the process of change and how it is either driven forward or restrained by the interaction of opposing forces are both simple and profound. His ideas give us a framework for understanding past change and the forces at play that will determine the direction of future change – and how leaders can influence those forces and the direction of change. We will return to Lewin's ideas throughout this book.

Seeing change as a property that emerges from the struggle of opposing forces is important because it enables you to understand and influence those forces. This way of understanding is different to the traditional way of seeing change, and leads to a different approach to creating change. The more traditional approach will give the employee loads of reasons why change is good, but will usually fail to address (and weaken) the restraining factors. It will fail to ask employees why they *don't* want to change and what worries them about change. And that is one of the main reasons that change initiatives often flounder or fail.

People need good rational and emotional reasons why they should change. But they also need to have the reasons that they don't want to change – their fearfulness of change – acknowledged, understood and addressed. In other words, don't just keep piling on the reasons why the proposed change is a good thing (after a little while most people know them), but also talk about what you can do to help with their fears – the reasons for wanting to avoid or resist change. These reasons might seem unreasonable to you, but they are entirely logical and reasonable to the people who hold them.

Pause for a second and reflect on how you might practically apply Lewin's ideas to the thorny problems of getting employees back to the office when they are reluctant to come. At the end of the chapter, we will explore how to do a Kurt Lewin Force Field Analysis that will help you figure out the issues in your own organisation or team.

Trust and the hybrid organisation: The X and Y of leadership

Making changes will be much more difficult if there is a lack of trust in your organisation. Let us not get too abstract here, because trust is not an abstract concept – trust is something that happens in the relationship between individual human beings; in this case, between manager and employee. What can social psychology teach us about trust in a changing organisation? Actually, quite a lot.

When people work from home, some managers and some employees become preoccupied with trust. The manager wonders whether they can trust their direct reports to get on with the work in the absence of their supervision and guidance. Paradoxically, some employees feel guilty about working from home. They feel paranoid that their manager suspects that they are skiving and so they overcompensate by working twice as hard as they would at the office. The organisation might well encourage them to take care of their health by, for example, going out for a walk at lunchtime. But they don't do this, for fear of being spotted and reported strolling through the park when they should have been working. Of course, these attitudes span a wide continuum. A lot of employees work hard and at the same time manage to look after their well-being, and a lot of managers trust their employees to get on with things without being micromanaged. But there are many employees who struggle to prioritise their health over the demands of work, and there are many managers who struggle to trust and see the best in those they manage.

Trust has always been a hot topic in the relationship between manager and employee. The advent of working from home has just exacerbated all of the emotions around trust. Trust is important in a well-functioning, high-performance organisation, especially in a hybrid organisation where people don't see each other quite so much.

In one of the most influential management books of the twentieth century, *The Human Side of Enterprise* (McGregor, 1960), Douglas McGregor, a US management professor, examined trust, management style and performance. In the book he described two distinct and opposing management styles which he called Theory X and Theory Y. He used the word 'theory' not so much to indicate that it was his theory but more to suggest that X and Y were descriptions of the psychological theories used by managers to understand the behaviour and motivation of those they manage. He used the letters X and Y to avoid making any value judgements between the two styles, because he did not want to imply that one was good and the other bad. As we will see, both have their place dependent on context.

According to McGregor, every manager will hold a set of underlying assumptions about the general character and motivation of the average employee. These assumptions can be entirely conscious, or they might be semiconscious, under the surface but influencing the manager's behaviour.

McGregor grouped generally authoritarian, cynical and suspicious management attitudes into what he termed 'Theory X' and participative, trusting and empowering attitudes as being informed by 'Theory Y'.

The dominant management style, both in the individual manager and in the overall culture of the organisation, will have a profound influence on the level of trust in the organisation and the consequent success, or otherwise, of the move to hybrid working. Let's look in more detail at the two management styles.

The authoritarian management style of Theory X

If your management style is influenced by Theory X, you believe that your employees dislike work and will do everything possible to avoid it. You know in your heart that they are inherently lazy and want to do as little as possible for as much money as they can get out of the company. To do a reasonable job, most employees require clear direction as well as constant prompting and supervision. Employees will avoid accepting responsibility for their work, especially when things go wrong.

Theory X is a deeply held belief that is usually hidden beneath a thin veneer of modern management jargon. This veneer will quickly start to split when pressure at work increases. Micromanagement and criticism are invariably the result of Theory X beliefs. Any good work or effort is frequently ignored ('they are only doing what they are paid for') or rewarded with monetary bonuses rather than genuine thanks and recognition. I remember someone once describing their workplace as 'the sort of place where if you do a good job, it isn't even noticed, never mind appreciated, but if you make a mistake, they are down on you like a ton of bricks'.

Without a doubt, most managers would strongly deny being a Theory X manager if they were asked. Only an idiot would openly espouse Theory X beliefs and values in the modern workplace. Despite this, I am sure you have met a lot of Theory X managers in your career. Because of the pressure to change, you will see a lot of Theory X emerge in the process of transforming your organisation into a successful hybrid organisation, especially if you are aware of it and on the lookout for it. Theory X management attitudes will sabotage your best efforts.

Theory Y's participative management style

If Theory Y informs your underlying management beliefs, you believe that employees are generally trustworthy and want to do their best at work. Because the employee genuinely wants to do their best, all you, as a good manager, need to do to ensure high performance is to support, help and nurture the employee; and when you are not doing that, you should just stay out of their way and let them get on with it. Of course, these assumptions result in very different management behaviours and a very different manager-employee relationship – one infused with trust, as opposed to the Theory X relationship, which is infused with mistrust and suspicion.

How to use McGregor's management ideas

The power of McGregor's idea is in its simplicity. It gives us a framework to understand what is beneath the surface of managers' observable behaviour. If we accept that behaviour isn't fixed, that behaviour is influenced by the environment and organisational culture, and that management style is on a continuum rather than being categorical, then McGregor's ideas become a practical tool that helps us both to understand and change management behaviour.

Behaviour can change

People's behaviour changes all the time. If we understand Kurt Lewin's Force Field Analysis, we understand what causes behaviour to change. Think back to Force Field Analysis and how our behaviour is influenced by opposing forces in the environment. For a moment, reflect on just how quickly and dramatically behaviour changed because of the pandemic. Even the most extreme X manager had to learn to manage their teams remotely.

All behaviour is determined by three factors:

- The person: the personality, skills and past experiences of the individual.
- The team or immediate social environment in which the individual exists. We are influenced by those around us far more than we realise.
- The wider system, by which I mean the organisation's dominant culture and the wider social, political and economic forces in the world.

Management style exists on a continuum between X and Y and all competent managers adjust their management style depending on the demands of the situation and environment. Some managers are more flexible than others and these are the more effective managers. In reality it isn't a case of, 'Stan and Philip are X managers and Stephen and Joseph are Y managers.' Maybe Joseph has a preference for Y-type management, but in a recession when the company starts losing money and there is a demand for more production with fewer resources, Joseph will quickly adapt by becoming a full-on Stalinist X manager.

In other words, management style and mindset are the product of an interaction between:

- an individual manager's personality and preferences
- the culture and pressures exerted by the manager's immediate social group and the wider social, political and economic forces at play in the world

Leading the hybrid organisation: Trust and change

What has all this got to do with leading the hybrid organisation?

Lewin wrote that change is a dynamic process, the result of a struggle between opposing forces, one driving change and the other restraining change. If your aim is to strengthen the driving forces, then the people whom you want to change will have to have a reasonable degree of trust in you and those managing the change.

Managers, according to McGregor, have two broad underlying assumptions that manifest in their management style: Theory X and Theory Y. The former results in authoritarian management, while the latter results in more participative management. To build trust in an organisation, the participative management style is usually the best, although there will be situations that call for a more directive, firm, 'command and control' style of management.

I have been coaching C-suite leaders for 20 years, and one of the most difficult challenges I have encountered is an awkwardness and, at times, a reluctance in most senior managers and leaders to assert their authority. Objectively, these people are very senior in organisations, but they just don't feel that senior. This perception/feeling results in two things:

- a reluctance or awkwardness to give firm direction or guidance when the situation demands it
- fear of conflict, even when the conflict is necessary and constructive.

The story of Kodak: Leadership mindset versus the real world

The history of the corporate world is full of examples of how a leadership mindset failed to keep pace with an evolving business environment: Nokia, Woolworths and Blockbuster to name just three. But it's hard to beat the story of the demise of Kodak because it's both dramatic and nuanced.

It's a story of how one of America's corporate giants went from hero to zero in a comparatively short time. Within this big drama were many nuanced and subtle scenes that built on each other until the climax and the curtain fell on Kodak. Throughout the drama, leaders at Kodak were, for at least some of the time, doing the right things – well, at least superficially. Kodak came very close to surviving. But as we know from that wonderful thing hindsight, Kodak didn't survive and went bust in 2012.

The story of Kodak is an interesting one because it isn't a story of obvious mistakes. Kodak's leaders weren't stupid, incompetent, complacent or even particularly arrogant. What failed was their mindset, which was rooted in the past and not open to new possibilities.

Kodachrome: Life just isn't the same in black and white

In the spring of 1973, Paul Simon's song 'Kodachrome' made it to number two in the US charts. The song was all about our memories and how much brighter and better they appeared when photographed with Kodak's eponymous 35-millimetre colour print film (Simon, 1973).

When Paul Simon wrote this in the early 1970s, and for the preceding decades, Kodak meant photography, just like Hoover meant vacuum cleaners and Kleenex meant facial tissues. Contained in these lyrics was the idea that would have probably saved Kodak.

Right from its beginnings in 1886, Kodak had innovation in its DNA. Kodak's founder, George Eastman, had a remarkable vision to democratise photography by making cameras, films and processing cheap, portable and easy.

His big idea was to make small, easy-to-use cameras that were cheap. He then made big money from selling film to the camera owner and then processing and printing their photographs. You could buy a nice, leather-covered Kodak Brownie box camera, preloaded with a 100-exposure film, and when you'd taken your snaps, you sent the whole camera back to Kodak, who developed and printed your pictures. They would return them in an album along with your camera reloaded with a new film. It was a sensation and a great business model. Kodak also had an inspiring advertising slogan: 'You press a button, we do the work.'

Because of George Eastman and Kodak, photography became something for the general public, not just professional photographers and keen amateurs who could afford expensive equipment and had the technical skills and space needed to develop and print films.

George Eastman and Kodak revolutionised photography, and their business model created a captive market of consumers. In 1935, they released Kodachrome, which was produced right up until 2009.

Can you think of any other photographic film that has inspired a number-two hit record? By 1962, Kodak was making $3 billion in sales, which was a lot of money at the time. Twenty years later this had grown to $10 billion. Kodak was the Apple of the early twentieth century.

Like Apple, Kodak deeply understood the psychological and emotional needs of the consumer. Their 'Kodak Moments' advertising campaign changed the idea that photography was something for only special occasions, like weddings. Now, it was everyday moments, like a child's birthday party, that became precious. These were the Kodak Moments that had to be captured, or they would be lost forever.

Kodak was doing great. They were on a roll. So, what went wrong? The easy response would be to blame the emergence of digital technology and Kodak's failure, or perhaps slowness, to respond to this disruption. But that isn't true. As far back as 1975 the very first digital camera was invented by Kodak engineer Steve Sasson. Like the early mobile telephones, it was as big and as heavy as a brick and took ages to take an actual photograph.

Okay, you might say, Kodak invented the digital camera, but I bet they didn't invest in it, did they? Well, yes, they did. Kodak invested billions (at a time when a billion dollars was a lot of money) and created a range of half-decent user-friendly digital cameras. But, you may counter, didn't Kodak miss the boat when people began using smartphones to take pictures and share their photos online? Well, again, no. In 2001, Kodak acquired a photo-sharing website called Ofoto and rebranded it as Kodak EasyShare Gallery. They heavily promoted this as a way of sharing Kodak digital images online. Of course, their cameras could have done better and their internet photo-sharing service could have been slicker. But credit where credit is due: they did okay.

So, let's ask the question again: what went wrong with Kodak?

To answer this question, let's return to Kurt Lewin's Force Field Analysis.

Kurt Lewin's Force Field Analysis and Kodak's demise

You may recall that earlier I wrote that for an idea to have any value it has to be able to make sense of past events. If it can do this, then it also has predictive power to guide decisions about what is happening now and how things might develop in the future.

Let's see if Lewin's Force Field Analysis can make any sense of the demise of Kodak. In other words, how does the story of Kodak relate to Force Field Analysis.

According to Lewin, in order to effect change, driving forces must be strengthened while restraining forces must be weakened. Kodak's leaders did a good job of strengthening driving forces but not so much of weakening restraining forces. They were simply too attached to film- and photo-processing, too attached to the past. Kodak's demise was caused not by a lack of innovation or a dislike of emerging technology, but by Kodak's leadership's inability to break with the past. Kodak manufactured and processed film. That was what they had done for decades, and it was what had made them one of the world's wealthiest and most powerful corporations. They simply could not give it up. It would have been a bit like Steve Jobs deciding not to develop the iPhone, 'because Apple is a computer company, not a telecoms company'.

Paul Simon understood something about Kodak that the company's leadership did not. He recognised that Kodak was not in the photography chemicals business, but rather in the memories business. They did not sell film, but rather memories; their real product was 'Kodak Moments', not cameras or Kodachrome.

Until the 1980s, those Kodak Moments had been preserved and shared using analogue photographs. People would have multiple prints made of their kid's birthday party and share them with relatives and friends (which was great business for Kodak). With the emergence of Facebook and the like, people began to share these images digitally online. Kodak adapted to this, but remained stubborn in seeing their core business as being photographic film and printing photographs.

Society and their customers' move to digital was Kodak's *driving force* for change, but holding on to the belief that their core business was photographic film was their big *restraining force*. And that is what did it for Kodak. They had one foot on the accelerator and the other on the brake.

Part of Kodak's mission statement read, 'We will derive our competitive advantage by delivering differentiated, cost-effective solutions – including consumables, hardware, software, systems and services – quickly and with flawless quality.' When Steve Jobs started Apple, his mission statement was, 'To make a contribution to the world by making tools for the mind that advance humankind.' There is the problem. Apple makes 'tools for the mind'. Kodak makes 'consumables'. Apple was future focused, but Kodak was rooted in the past. Steve Jobs' mindset was to look for new ways to build tools for the mind. Kodak wanted to do what it had always done, but better. Because of this, the forces restraining change eventually triumphed, and Kodak went bust.

Kodak, mindset and hybrid organisations

The story of Kodak is a dramatic example of how important it is to give serious thought to your underlying assumptions – your mindset – about the primary task of your organisation and how this can adapt to changes in the business environment. Kodak was a company that was too big to fail, but it did fail. It didn't fail because of a lack of good people, money or innovation; it failed because of the failure in leadership mindset.

Questions to reflect on

If you are feeling stuck about the move to hybrid, here are some questions to reflect on:

1. What are the forces driving change? Write down at least three.
2. What are the forces restraining change? Write down at least three.
3. Write down at least three things you could do to strengthen the driving forces.
4. Write down at least three things you could do to weaken the restraining forces.
5. What forces are driving and restraining change in you? Do your own personal Force Field Analysis.
6. What is the primary task of your organisation?

Here are some further questions that I have adapted from an excellent article in the *Harvard Business Review* by Scott Anthony, clinical professor at Dartmouth College (Anthony, 2016).

1. What business are you in today? Try not to answer the question in terms of things you make, technology or industry/profession (avoid saying 'We make washing machines' or 'We are lawyers'). Instead, try to figure out what problem you are actually solving for your customers. Why do they buy stuff or services from you? That was the difference between Kodak seeing itself as a chemical film company, an imaging company or a moment-sharing company.
2. What new opportunities does hybrid working open up?
3. What capabilities do you need to implement to make the best of these opportunities?

Key points

- Change is dynamic, not linear.
- The prospect of change generates feelings of ambivalence.
- Change results from the struggle between driving forces and restraining forces.
- To make change happen, you have to understand what the forces are, and strengthen the driving forces and weaken the restraining forces.

Note

1 Zoom was a pandemic success story. In January 2020, its stock price was around $76 per share. By the following September, when the pandemic was at its worst, it had risen to over $470.

References

Anthony, S. D. (2016). 'Kodak's Downfall Wasn't About Technology'. *Harvard Business Review*, 15 July. https://hbr.org/2016/07/kodaks-downfall-wasnt-about-technology.

Goldsmith, M. & Reiter, M. (2007). *What Got You Here Won't Get You There: How Successful People Become Even More Successful*. New York: Hyperion Books.

Hemingway, E. (2006). *The Sun Also Rises*. New York: Simon & Schuster. (Original work published 1926.)

Lewin, K. (1947). 'Frontiers in Group Dynamics: Concept, Method and Reality in Social Science; Social Equilibria and Social Change'. *Human Relations*, 1, 5–41.

Lewin, K. (1997). *Resolving Social Conflicts/Field Theory in Social Science*. Washington DC, American Psychological Association, p. 46. (Original work published 1948.)

Machiavelli, N. (1988). *Machiavelli: The Prince*. Cambridge: Cambridge University Press. (Original work published 1513.)

McGregor, D. (1960). *The Human Side of Enterprise*. New York: McGraw Hill.

Simon, P. (1973). 'Kodachrome'. Track 1 on *There Goes Rhymin' Simon*. CD. New York: Sony CMG.

Tett, G. (2022). 'Why CEOs Are So WTF about WFH'. *Financial Times*, 13 July. https://www.ft.com/content/8a3f1fa7-8c0c-4068-b0d9-f12c84f0b8d6.

2 How to Build a Group Identity in the Hybrid Organisation

Michael Drayton

Think for a moment about a successful Premier League football team. The players have a high level of skill and fitness and they know what's expected of them on the football pitch. The word 'goals' is used a lot in organisations, but in football it has a real, tangible meaning. Players know their respective roles: defenders defend, midfielders get the ball from their half of the pitch to the opposition's half, and the goalkeeper's job is to stop the ball from going into the net, not to score goals. However, all players have flexibility to step out of their role if the situation demands it. Nobody will complain if the goalkeeper does score a goal.

One of the most important attributes of a successful football team is that they play as a team, rather than just a collection of talented individuals. For example, a striker facing two defenders in the opposition's penalty area must decide whether to try to beat the defenders and go for the goal, or pass to a teammate with a clear shot on goal. In a good team, the striker will choose to pass and forgo individual glory. Getting a group of talented, well-paid and sometimes prima donna-ish individuals to work together as a team and put the needs of the team before their individual desire for glory is the manager's job. Managers like Manchester United's Sir Alex Ferguson play such an important role in a team's success. They may not even touch a football, but they excel at getting the team to play like a team, rather than just a collection of individuals. A good manager can train the team, motivate them and even yell at them, but ultimately, when they are on the pitch playing against the opposition, success is down to the players. The team must be its own coach during the game.

Teams are assembled based on the members' technical skills, not on how well they get along with each other. However, the ability to get along with each other, to feel connected and attached, and to feel a sense of belonging is important for the quality of performance, whether you are a football team or the marketing team of a pharmaceutical company.

People form attachments not only to other people and groups but also to places and things. If you are a football fan, you know how

DOI: 10.4324/9781003387602-2

attached you are to your team's home ground. You may even feel more at home in your seat with familiar people around you if you have a season ticket. It's the same at work. It's easy to become attached to the building and places in it where you and your team work. If you have a desk, or even your own office, you may want to personalise it and make it your own. If you have to work at a different desk, it just doesn't feel the same.

This chapter discusses how people form attachments and connections to one another, to groups (teams) and to places. It is about the psychology of how people bond and work together to form a team, rather than just a group of individuals assigned to a similar task. This is important to understand because the pandemic lockdown and working from home have all disrupted this process for many workplace teams, particularly those that have formed or had a significant number of members join since working from home became the norm. Psychologists have been studying how people form attachments to other people, groups and places for decades. If you want to understand how to create a strong sense of identity in your team, you must first understand the process.

How do people form attachments?

> All of us, from cradle to grave, are happiest when life is organised as a series of excursions, long or short, from the secure base provided by our attachment figures.
>
> (Bowlby, 1944)

These words, written over 30 years ago by John Bowlby, capture the essence of attachment theory. In the 1930s, Bowlby was working as a child psychiatrist in the East End of London, helping children with emotional problems. One of his early observations was the link between early separation from the mother and later juvenile delinquency. In his research study, '44 Juvenile Thieves' (Bowlby, 1944), he compared a group of 44 young thieves to a group of 44 other young people who had emotional problems but did not steal or harm others. He discovered something fascinating. Seventeen of the forty-four juvenile thieves had been separated from their mother for an extended period of time before the age of five, while only two of the non-thieves group had been separated. Bowlby also discovered that 32 per cent of the juvenile thieves exhibited 'affectionless psychopathy', which means they had no emotional connection with other people. This led Bowlby to make the connection between early childhood separation from the caregiver (usually the mother) and later serious emotional disturbance. This was the root of his famous attachment theory.

Bowlby said that our need to form attachments to others is evolutionary and genetic. We are pre-programmed to form close bonds with others to ensure our survival in a hostile world, and the need is active from the moment we are born until the moment we die. When this process is interrupted, problems ensue.

Attachment theory is a spatial theory. It describes how people's emotional states are influenced by how close or far they are to the person to whom they are attached. Jeremy Holmes, a psychotherapist, put it succinctly:

> 'I feel tense when my mummy goes out of the room so I must keep a good eye out for her and scream if necessary', or, 'when my mummy comes so close to me while I am playing I feel uncomfortable, so I'll try to move away a bit, without discouraging her so much that she loses interest.'
>
> (Holmes, 2014)

Adults in the workplace go through the same process. You would probably prefer a boss who is present – who knows you, may offer praise when you do a good job and is available to help you when you need it. In contrast, if your boss is either absent or micromanages your work and constantly looks over your shoulder, you are likely to feel anxious and uneasy. That is attachment theory in the workplace.

Our need to form attachments is a deep-seated instinct in all of us. To feel safe and secure, we are compelled to form bonds – to connect with people, groups or places. We will feel intense anxiety if they are too distant or untrustworthy, or too intense and suffocating. If these bonds are broken for an extended period of time, we tend to detach and look for someone or something else with whom to form a bond. This is why understanding Bowlby's attachment theory is useful when establishing an effective high-performance hybrid organisation with low staff attrition.

Attachment to groups and places

How many times have you said, 'I really loved the holiday, but it's always nice to get home'? This is after opening the front door of your house and struggling in with your suitcases having arrived home following a really nice holiday.

Thus far, our examination of attachment has focused mainly on individual people, such as loved ones and friends. But what about work? Do we develop similar attachments to the teams we work with, and to the physical workplace itself, or the office where we spend our working hours? Our environment, including the buildings we live and work in and the people we work with, provides a safe haven, a secure base where we feel safe to explore situations that feel less safe and secure. We experience a sense of belonging – a place and people we can retreat to if life or work isn't going well.

When we are separated from a person we feel attached to, we think about them. We might feel uncomfortable or a sense of unease when they are away, and relief when they are back. This can also apply to a building – our house. Similarly, if you have a good attachment to work, you will enjoy a business trip but feel relieved to get back to the familiarity of your office and those you work with.

When you are ill, upset or in distress, you will want to be with your loved ones or friends. They are a safe place where you can retreat to recharge and problem-solve. The same applies to the workplace and team. You might have had a difficult interaction with a customer or supplier and felt better after returning to your office and colleagues and offloading.

If you are unwillingly separated from your loved ones for a prolonged period of time, you may become anxious and depressed. In the clinical literature, this is called separation distress. Bowlby described this as a process that gradually develops from protest to despair and eventual detachment.

This also applies to work. You become attached to the organisation that employs you. The organisation meets (at least sometimes) your needs for mental stimulation, purpose and meaning. It also meets your emotional needs for belonging, security and well-being. When work starts to fail to meet your needs, you might begin the process of emotionally detaching. Work might start getting boring and not meeting your need for mental stimulation; you might not see the point of what you do and lack a sense of meaning and purpose; you might not feel safe to speak your mind at work and feel resentful. That's when you detach and leave the organisation.

The following section offers an example of how one company used the principles of Bowlby's attachment theory to overcome a problem they had with high staff turnover.

Creating a sense of belonging to the organisation

WIPRO is an information technology and consultancy company. Its call centre in Bangalore has won an award for being one of the nicest places to work in India. Wages are competitive, and there are numerous employee benefits available, including a good staff restaurant, free transportation to and from work, and company-sponsored social clubs and events. The company treats its employees well.

Despite this, WIPRO had a big problem with staff attrition. Between 50 and 70 per cent of new hires would leave before the end of their first year. When asked why they wanted to leave, they always said the same thing: 'I just want a better job.' The staff who left didn't particularly criticise WIPRO, but neither did they express a sense of connection to the company.

WIPRO's leadership team was extremely concerned about the high level of staff turnover and decided to take action. They initially tried all the obvious things, such as raising salaries and improving perks. Despite this, WIPRO continued to lose quality employees at an alarming rate. All of the positive changes implemented by the company had made no difference.

In 2010, feeling frustrated and stuck, the WIPRO senior leadership team brought in a team of psychologists to try to figure out what to do. They came up with a novel and interesting way of approaching the problem and an equally interesting way of testing out their ideas. Their approach was based on the ideas of John Bowlby.

The team of psychologists led by Bradley Staats believed that the root cause of employee turnover at WIPRO was not a lack of tangible workplace qualities, as all of the basic necessities were already in place. Instead, they believed that the issue was caused by more subtle and intangible, psychological factors related to employees' sense of connection and belonging within the organisation (Cable et al., 2013). Employees who chose to leave did not have particularly negative feelings towards WIPRO; rather, they simply did not care. They did not feel connected to the organisation.

To put this theory to the test, the researchers divided hundreds of new hires into three groups. The first group received standard onboarding and technical training, as well as an hour of company culture training. During this hour, a 'star performer' from the company spoke to the group about the company's identity, and the group had the opportunity to ask questions. The first group received a sweatshirt embroidered with the company name and logo at the end of the training.

The second group also received the standard onboarding and technical training, as well as the additional hour of input. However, the focus of this hour was on the trainees themselves, rather than the company. They were asked to talk about their talents and interests and how they could contribute to the company. They were also asked questions like, 'What is unique about you that leads to your happiest times and best performance at work?' At the end of the training, the second group received a sweatshirt like the first group, but this time it was embroidered with their name next to the company name.

The third group, the control group, received the standard onboarding and did not receive the sweatshirt.

Now, consider what you know about attachment theory. Do you think the experiment had any impact on retention? If so, which group had the highest retention rate?

When the new hires were followed up seven months later, the senior leadership team at WIPRO and the researchers were astounded to find that the trainees in group two were 250 percent more likely than those in group one and 157 percent more likely than those in the control group to still be working at WIPRO. This means that the one extra hour of training significantly increased staff retention by 250 percent. The researchers called the onboarding process that group two received 'personal identity socialisation'. They concluded:

> Socialization is serious business for organizational leaders. The process of recruiting, hiring and training new employees is expensive and time-consuming. High turnover is one of the most obvious consequences of unsuccessful socialization. However, by making relatively small investments in socialization practices, we have found that companies can make significant improvements in employee retention and engagement. Newcomers develop a more positive view toward the organization and inject greater quality and purpose into their work.
>
> (Cable et al., 2013)

Business writer Daniel Coyle discusses the WIPRO research in his book *The Culture Code* (Coyle, 2018), and attributes the success of the experiment to the sense of belonging that the new hires in group two felt as a result of the personal identity socialisation during onboarding. Coyle explains:

> The group two trainees... received a steady stream of individualized, future-oriented, amygdala-activating belonging cues. All these signals were small – a personal question about their best times at work, an exercise that revealed their individual skills, a sweatshirt embroidered with their name. These signals didn't take much time to deliver, but they made a huge difference because they created a foundation of psychological safety that built connection and identity.
>
> (Coyle, 2018)

I agree with Daniel Coyle's analysis and would add that the most powerful effect of the intervention was activating the innate desire for attachment in the personal identity socialisation group. The questions and exercises sent the message that the company was interested in them and wanted them to be a part of WIPRO for the long term. The two-way dialogue of the questions and exercises helped to build a relationship (while the control group's interactions with the company were largely one-way, with the trainees being the passive recipients of information from the company). This sense of belonging was further reinforced by the trainee's name being embroidered on the sweatshirt *next to* the company's name.

The 'great resignation' and 'quiet quitting' have become common phrases in the business world since the shift to remote work. These phenomena are symptoms of a lack of attachment between the employee and the organisation. When people don't feel a sense of belonging or connection with their organisation, the relationship becomes purely transactional. In this case, it is rational for employees to leave for a company that offers more money or perks. On the other hand, if an employee feels like they belong at their company, if they enjoy and respect their colleagues and feel liked and respected in turn, they are much less likely to leave, as the WIPRO research demonstrated.

Attachment theory and the hybrid team

Here are a few ideas from attachment theory to help you improve attachments and thus performance in your hybrid team.

Principle one: Bring the whole team together face to face at least once a week

It's hard (I'd say impossible) to form any sort of meaningful attachment to a person you've never or rarely actually met physically. If you accept this, then it logically follows that if you want to build a high-performing hybrid team, there have to be times when the team members actually meet physically, face to face.

Once a week is an arbitrary timescale – I'd actually recommend a minimum of two days a week together. Of course, timescale will depend on the nature of your business.

People who are used to working from home for weeks on end will most likely be resistant. I recall coaching a CEO about her employees' reluctance to return to work. This was shortly after the end of lockdown, and while some employees were eager to return to the office, others were digging in their heels. She decided to hold firm and tell all of the company's employees that they had to be in work for a minimum of three days a week. She took a lot of heat for this, with long-serving employees threatening to resign. Nevertheless, she stuck to her guns and people came back to work. People did moan and groan at first, but after a while, she would look around the office and see people happily chatting with one another, having coffee together and generally enjoying the social aspects of working. It was as if the pandemic and lockdown never occurred. Often, it's the anxious apprehension about returning to the workplace rather than the actual experience of returning to work that puts people off. It is the change that they dislike, not the office. Once things had calmed down, the CEO was able to relax and allow people to come in for two days a week of more flexible work if they felt strongly about it and could justify it. Despite the difficulty of her decision, she felt it was the right one. I agreed with her.

Principle two: Encourage informal social activities

The comments section of an article about hybrid working in the *Financial Times* caught my eye. One person said that they enjoyed coming into work three days a week mainly because they enjoyed going out for a pint after work on Thursdays with their colleagues.

Before lockdown, I coached one very talented director who was brilliant at this. He was very good at making sure people took their lunch breaks, and he would regularly organise lunchtime walking groups and after work social events. He would also arrange monthly 'cocktail and curry' evenings. These informal social events really helped the people he managed to get to know each other.

A high-performing team works as a team rather than a group of individuals. In order for them to form themselves into a team, you have to put them together for extended periods of time in the same place and in an environment where they feel they can relax and be themselves. That's just not going to happen using teleconferencing.

Principle three: Help people to become attached to the workplace

To encourage a sense of place attachment, you can allocate each employee their own individual space in the office and encourage them to personalise it. In the era of 'hot desking', having an individual desk is unusual in many organisations, but I believe this is a mistake. People enjoy having their own space where they can add personal touches like family photos and plants, bringing a piece of themselves into the office and strengthening their connection and sense of belonging to the organisation.

Principle four: Encourage a sense of shared identity with the organisation

Engage in a dialogue – a conversation – with the employee. Ask them what their signature strengths are, and ask them what they feel they can bring to the organisation. This is different from the approach of many organisations that see this sort of conversation as one-way traffic, with the organisation force-feeding the employee information about the company's culture and how things are done in the organisation.

Use tangible objects to reinforce the sense of shared identity. At WIPRO they gave new recruits a sweatshirt with the company name and logo next to the new entrant's name. This might not be appropriate in your organisation, but you could consider other objects bearing the organisation's name and the employee's name such as notebooks or coffee mugs. Organisations have been using this approach for years; for example, think of the army, the legal profession or airlines, all of which use uniforms.

How proximity improves performance

Two teams of people with similar qualifications and experience are both working to solve hard problems. One of the teams is excellent; they are competent and quick at getting to the answer. The other team is mediocre at best. What factor separates the excellent team from the mediocre team?

This was the problem given to Thomas Allen to solve. Allen was a professor of management at the Massachusetts Institute of Technology (MIT). He had an unusual background for a management school academic. He was a working-class boy made good with degrees in computer science, engineering and management. Before his academic career, he had served with the US Marines in the Korean War and worked for big corporations such as Boeing. He was a perfect choice to lead the project.

This was the 1970s, when the Cold War between the Soviet Union and the West was driving much government research, particularly in the US. These were the years leading up to Ronald Regan's 'Strategic Defence Initiative', nicknamed his Star Wars programme. Government and a few private-sector technology companies were working on really difficult problems such as how satellites communicate with each other in a nuclear attack early-warning system.

There was a big difference between the effectiveness and efficiency of teams that at least on paper looked equally qualified. This difference puzzled and concerned the US government, and they commissioned Thomas Allen and his team to find out what was going on.

Allen set about this challenge by finding what he called 'twin projects'. These were projects of equal complexity being worked on by research and development (R&D) teams who were as much as possible equally matched in terms of qualifications and experience. He then looked at the overall quality of each team's work, considering how creative or innovative their solutions were, how practical they were and how long it had taken each team to come up with their ideas. Allen then went on to look for any common factors shared by the successful teams (Allen, 1977).

The big stand-out factor in the successful teams was how well the individuals in that team worked together. The great teams had chemistry. They frequently talked to each other, and they helped and at times robustly challenged each other. There was a degree of conflict but an absence of hard feelings. Allen said that the factor that separated the successful R&D teams from the mediocre R&D teams was the quality and frequency of communication between team members.

The next question Allen set out to answer was why some teams communicated well and others didn't. After all, the team members in the successful and less successful groups looked at least on paper to be very similar people.

First he looked at the obvious common-sense factors. Were the successful teams, on average, younger? Did they have more/fewer female members? Were they better qualified or had the team members attended more prestigious universities? Were they more experienced (what was the average number of years of postgrad experience?).

None of these factors made any difference. Essentially, the members of the successful and least successful teams were more or less identical. Talent – meaning education, qualifications and experience – made no difference in how well the teams communicated and the outcomes they produced.

Having ruled out human factors, Allen then turned his attention to environmental factors. And it was here where he found the answer. The reason why teams communicate well or not is a simple one, and one that I'm guessing Allen least expected.

The only factor that made a difference was the distance between the team members' desks! Allen found a very strong correlation between physical proximity and frequency and quality of communication. The

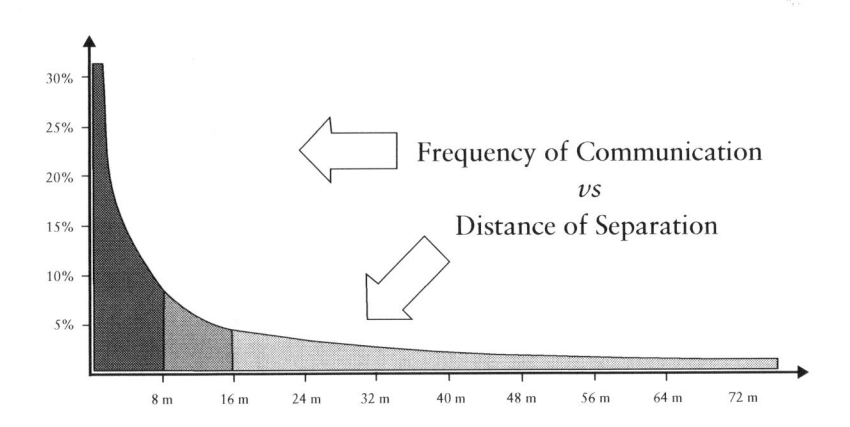

Figure 2.1 The Allen Curve

Source: Allen, T. J. (1977). Managing the Flow of Technology: Technology Transfer and the Dissemination of Technological Information within the R&D Organization. Cambridge MA: MIT Press.

closer somebody is to us, the more we talk to them and have richer, more meaningful conversations.

When Allen plotted the frequency of communication against proximity, he came up with a curve that looks like the letter J on its side. This is what eventually became known as the Allen Curve (Figure 2.1).

If your team members are six metres apart, the frequency and quality of communication goes through the roof. If team members are 50 metres apart, they become strangers. If your R&D team is spread over different floors, you may as well pack up and go home. 'It turns out that vertical separation is a very serious thing. If you're on a different floor in some organizations, you may as well be in a different country, Allen remarked' (Coyle, 2018).

The Allen Curve and the hybrid team

Thomas Allen's work was done back in the 1970s with engineers who worked in open-plan offices. How might it be relevant to leading a hybrid team?

The Allen Curve is consistent with the attachment theory literature. Attachment theory is a theory of proximity. The closer we are to those we feel attached to, the happier we are. It's a reasonable assumption to make that if teams feel happy or relaxed, they might talk more and 'play' more – in other words feel free to be creative.

It would seem that hybrid working would throw a spanner in the works of the Allen Curve. How can Thomas Allen's findings be relevant to a team disrupted and disconnected by hybrid working?

Allen anticipated this question back in 2007, when the development of the internet allowed some people in the corporate world to occasionally work from home. He used data from studies of email use and from his own earlier research on communication across different sites in a manufacturing company. He said the Allen Curve predicted communication just as it did with the engineers in the open-plan office. He explained:

> We do not keep separate sets of people, some of whom we communicate with by one medium and some by another. The more often we see someone face-to-face, the more likely it is that we will also telephone that person or communicate by another medium.
> (Allen & Henn, 2007)

In other words, if you have a colleague working at a different company site, you are far more likely to communicate with that person by phone or email if you have actually met them, face to face. That seems very relevant to leading hybrid teams.

A tale of two teams

I recently completed a project in a large corporation. As part of this project, I spent time observing two teams, which I will refer to as Team A and Team B. The members of each team were very similar in terms of competence, qualifications and experience, as in Thomas Allen's research, and they both had similarly difficult tasks to complete. And, as in Allen's study, one team excelled while the other struggled.

Here's what I noticed. In the poorly performing team, Team A, members hardly spoke. They were in a large open-plan room but sat apart in small sub-groups, which I'd describe as silos. At the start of the day, the seniors sat in the same room as the larger team, but as soon as they realised a meeting room, which was off the main room, was unoccupied, they moved in there. The only exception was the most senior leader, who seemed to be making a valiant attempt to move around the big room and talk (and, more importantly, listen) to members of the team.

In contrast, the members of the high-functioning team, Team B, sat closer together and faced each other. They frequently moved around the room, forming small groups with changing membership. I'd see the members of these small groups talking in an animated manner (these are what Thomas Allen would probably describe as clusters of high communicators). The seniors remained in the room and at the centre of things. Every hour or so, they would stand and initiate a group 'huddle', where the team were given an update on the progress of the project and asked if they'd encountered any problems. The general atmosphere in this team was light, calm, but at the same time energised. It was an atmosphere highly conducive to creative thinking. The atmosphere in Team A was very different. I'd describe it as tense, oppressive and slightly manic.

Team A didn't feel like a team. It felt broken and disconnected. It felt like a group of individuals or perhaps sub-groups of the team getting on with their own thing, and any communication was more concerned with competition than cooperation.

Something else I noticed in Team B was frequent displays of vulnerability. One of the team had to write something and felt stuck. Rather than suffer in silence, he approached a colleague and asked, 'Can you help me with this?' The exchange ended with the colleague saying, 'If you need any more help, just ask.'

Team B was just a much nicer team to be around. It was energising, not energy sucking like Team A. More importantly, Team B's performance and outcomes were stellar, while the performance and outcomes of Team A were at best mediocre.

It struck me that Team B had a strong sense of identity, coherence and belonging. Hell, I felt like I belonged there, and I'd only been with them for a day.

Attachment theory and the Allen Curve research go a long way in unpacking the factors that made Team B creative and effective and Team A mediocre.

The thing that accounted for much of the team cohesiveness was the closeness – in terms of physical proximity but also emotional and psychological closeness. Members of Team B seemed to slip seamlessly from being vulnerable to being expert and back again.

Tribes, coffee machines and collisions

If you want to lead an effective hybrid team, the elements of physical proximity and psychological/emotional closeness seem to matter. Both of these factors present an obvious challenge for hybrid teams.

If you think back to the WIPRO study, the main thing that made the difference in whether people stayed or left the company was their sense of belonging or attachment. In other words it was their awareness of being a part of a cohesive and clearly identifiable social group. The new recruit saw him- or herself as a part of the group and the others in the group saw the new recruit as a part of their group. There is two-way traffic in group membership – I see myself as being in the group and I am aware that the group sees me as a member. That daily social interaction is what makes group membership such a powerful force. When it works well, it means that it's sometimes difficult to leave – people get attached; hence the success of the WIPRO study.

When you join a company with a strong sense of identity, you do not just join a company; you join a tribe. Seth Godin, the well-known popular science writer, defined a tribe as follows:

> A tribe is a group of people connected to one another, connected to a leader, and connected to an idea. For millions of years, human beings have been part of one tribe or another. A group needs only two things to form a tribe: a shared interest and a way to communicate.
>
> (Godin, 2008)

You want your hybrid team to form a 'tribe', one that will be difficult to leave. According to Thomas Allen's research, simply being in the same location as a group of people for a couple of days a week improves performance significantly, but only if there is a high volume and quality of communication. If your team members are working together but are socially isolated, sitting at desks that are too far apart or in silos, not talking to one another, they might as well be working from home.

The Alan Curve, and my anecdotal experience, tells us that it's not just where your team is at any given point that matters; it's what they are doing and, more importantly, how they are interacting. This leads on to thinking about what tasks your team members perform when they're in the office (if they are sitting by themselves, responding to emails or on Zoom calls, they may as well be at home), but this is a discussion for later.

If you bring your team members in to spend time together for a couple of days a week, you should give serious thought to how your workspace is configured (again, we are going to more detail about this later). People need to be in an environment where they can mingle, talk, share ideas and generally get to know each other.

Think about how the desks are arranged. Maybe consider having meetings where people are standing up in groups rather than sitting around a conference table. Encourage members of the team to have coffee breaks and lunch breaks at the same time. Essentially, think about what you can do to encourage people to talk to each other as much as possible.

A decade ago, Bank of America was experiencing high levels of burnout in its call centre teams. To address this issue, they brought in Ben Waber, a scientist from MIT who specialises in using social-sensing technology, to conduct an analysis. Waber found that the employees were indeed highly stressed and many were on the verge of burning out. His analysis suggested that the best way to alleviate this workplace stress was by building systems and an environment that encouraged employees to spend time together away from their desks. He recommended that the company arrange team schedules so that they could all take a 15-minute coffee break together every day. In addition, Waber suggested that the company invest in high-quality coffee machines and place them in convenient gathering spaces to encourage interactions between team members. These changes had a significant impact: productivity increased by 20 per cent and staff attrition decreased from 40 per cent to 12 per cent. Waber's study also found that replacing four-person tables with ten-person tables in the staff restaurant resulted in a 10 per cent boost in productivity. The takeaway from Ben Waber's work is that creating spaces that encourage interactions between employees dramatically improves team performance (Waber, 2013).

Waber also looked at how the performance of remote-working teams could be improved. For example, is it worth getting everybody in a remote team together, even if that means the cost of travel and hotels, before starting a project? Does the additional expense, in terms of money and time, have a significant return on investment? Following his analysis, Waber concluded with an enthusiastic yes! After having a face-to-face meeting, the remote team saw significant improvements in their understanding of each other and, more importantly, an increase in mutual trust, as well as their ability to collaborate effectively. As a result, both the quantity and quality of communication within the team significantly improved after the team resumed the project working online (Waber, 2013).

The takeaway for hybrid teams from all of this research is that when team members are in the office, you need to maximise physical proximity and social interactions between them. The business writer Daniel Coyle calls these interactions 'collisions', a term he takes from Tony Hsieh (pronounced 'Shay'), the founder of the wildly successful company Zappos. Coyle writes:

> Beneath Hsieh's unconventional approach lies a mathematical structure based on what he calls collisions. Collisions – defined as serendipitous personal encounters – are, he believes, the lifeblood of any organisation, the key driver of creativity, community, and cohesion. He has set a goal of having 1,000 'collisionable hours' per year for himself and a hundred thousand collisionable hours per acre for the Downtown Project. This metric is why he closed a side entrance to Zappos headquarters, funnelling people through a single entrance.
>
> (Coyle, 2018)

Finally, in a hybrid organisation, the core principles we talked about above stress how important it is to help team members feel like they belong, are attached and have an identity. To thrive, a hybrid team should strive to become a close-knit 'tribe', with physical proximity and quality communication serving as key performance drivers. Strategic use of face-to-face meetings for remote teams, as well as thoughtful workspace design that encourages interaction and shared experiences, can significantly improve collaboration and productivity. Furthermore, the concept of 'collisions' emphasises the importance of chance personal encounters as a catalyst for creativity, community and cohesion. In the evolving landscape of hybrid work, these insights offer a roadmap for building thriving and connected teams that ultimately contribute to the success of the entire organization.

Developing from a group of individuals to a team

Let's move on to look at what psychology can tell us about how groups form and the power of group dynamics.

When a new recruit joins your organisation, they are likely to be joining an already existing team with a team culture – a tribe, to use Seth Godin's term. By 'culture' I mean a set of beliefs summarised in the phrase 'how we do things in this team'. That culture will have developed and changed over time. Like children, teams don't just arrive fully formed; they have to pass through a number of developmental stages.

The organisational psychologist Bruce Tuckman studied and identified these stages back in the 1960s and developed a model that became the best-known and most widely used – even today – way of understanding how teams develop a sense of cohesion (Tuckman, 1965). To achieve this a team has to successfully navigate five stages. He called these forming, storming, norming, performing and adjourning (sometimes called mourning):

- **Forming:** This is the honeymoon phase, when the members of the team are getting to know each other and are sounding each other out. Members are figuring out who they get along with and trust, and also who they don't like. At this stage most people are focused on being accepted, and to achieve this they will go out of their way to avoid conflict.
- **Storming:** The storming phase kicks in once people have got to know each other and are feeling safe within their role and have established some friends (and allies). Boundaries have become clearer, and inevitably some team members begin testing those boundaries and conflict starts happening. Silos can start to form in the storming phase. This is a tricky phase for the leader to manage; the conflicts from earlier can escalate and undermine the team's performance. Some members of the team can become more concerned with office politics than getting on with the job.
- **Norming:** If the leader manages the storming phase well, the team will move into what Tuckerman calls the norming phase. This is where the true boundaries have been established, people know where they are in the team's pecking order (or dominance hierarchy) and the team has a shared understanding of the primary task of the team. The group of individuals begins working as a team rather than a group of individuals with a shared goal. The team is now in the face of what Tuckman calls the performing phase.
- **Performing:** The team is stable, everyone has clear responsibilities and any conflict is about how best to perform the task rather than personalities or office politics. Different perspectives are experienced as being creative rather than destructive. Most of the time the team's motivation is intrinsic and they get on with things with minimal supervision. The group of individuals has evolved into a high-performance team.

This is a model of team development that is familiar to anyone who manages people. What does Tuckman's model mean in the context of hybrid teams? What can it tell us about what important or even essential things might be missing in a hybrid team?

Tuckman's model is a stage model, and if any of the stages get missed, the team will need at some point to revisit that stage, and the experiences associated with that stage, before they can develop into a high-functioning team. For example, you can't consider yourself a real team if you haven't experienced the '*Sturm und Drang*' of the storming stage.

It's hard to see how the performing and storming phases can be done in a team that only meets virtually. Without negotiating these phases, you'll end up with the group of individuals working together but not as a team.

Any group of people brought together to perform a task will produce something. What they produce might not be the best, but it will probably be okay. Earlier in this chapter I recounted an anecdote about two teams I observed. In one team, performance was optimal. The outcome was good. They got to the solution quickly and made minimal mistakes. The other team's outcome was, at best, mediocre. They took ages to get to a less-than-optimal solution and made lots of errors on the way. They weren't performing to the level you might expect given their skills and experience – the team wasn't achieving its potential.

It's exactly the same with a hybrid team. A hybrid team that hasn't met face to face or managed to negotiate Tuckman's stages is unlikely to meet its potential. For a hybrid team to perform well, it has to meet face to face for varying lengths of time at various stages in its life cycle. If it is a newly formed team, it will need to be together for a few days a week for a few weeks to get through the forming and storming phases at the very least. Similarly, when a new member joins an established team, the amount and frequency of face-to-face working should be increased to allow the new person to get to know people (to form), and also to push the boundaries, to find out the limits of those boundaries (storming).

Tuckman's model fits nicely with the attachment theory research and also the Alan Curve. What is crucial in making a hybrid team work is the quality of the relationships in that team. Furthermore, what determines that quality, to a large degree, is physical proximity.

Questions to reflect on

Here are some questions to reflect on when considering your hybrid team's sense of identity:

1. How well connected do the members of your team feel with each other?
2. Do your team members feel a sense of connection to the organisation?
3. Do your team members have the opportunity to talk about their individual unique skills?
4. How can they contribute to the future of the organisation?
5. Does your team have regular out-of-work social events?
6. Do you meet regularly, face to face, as a whole team?
7. When you do meet, is there an opportunity for vigorous discussion and debate?

8. Does the layout of your workspace encourage team interactions ('social collisions')?
9. Has your hybrid team negotiated Tuckman's team development stages?

Key points

- Teams are constructed based on skills, not people's ability to perform well together.
- The ability of the team to function as a team (not a collection of individuals sharing a task) determines the success of that team.
- High-performance teams are characterised by their members having secure attachments to each other and to the organisation.
- Establishing the secure attachments (shared identity, sense of belonging) is a challenge in the hybrid team.
- To establish secure attachments, hybrid teams should strive to:
  - Meet face to face at least one day a week, preferably two.
  - Enjoy regular out-of-work social activities together.
  - Share a workspace that encourages interaction ('social collisions').
  - Negotiate Tuckman's stages of team development (for example, in regular away days or offsites).

References

Allen, T. & Henn, G. (2007). *The Organization and Architecture of Innovation*. Routledge.

Allen, T. J. (1977). *Managing the Flow of Technology: Technology Transfer and the Dissemination of Technological Information within the R&D Organization*. Cambridge MA: MIT Press.

Bowlby, J. (1944). 'Forty-four Juvenile Thieves: Their Characters and Home-life (II)'. *International Journal of Psycho-Analysis*, 25, 107–28.

Cable, D. M., Gino, F. & Staats, B. R. (2013). 'Reinventing Employee Onboarding'. *MIT Sloan Management Review*, Spring, 1–10.

Coyle, D. (2018). *The Culture Code: The Secrets of Highly Successful Groups*. London: Penguin Random House.

Godin, S. (2008). *Tribes: We Need You to Lead Us*. London: Penguin Random House.

Holmes, J. (2014). *John Bowlby and Attachment Theory*. Abingdon: Routledge.

Tuckman, B. W. (1965). 'Developmental Sequence in Small Groups'. *Psychological Bulletin*, 63 (6): 384–99.

Waber, B. (2013). *People Analytics: How Social Sensing Technology Will Transform Business and What It Tells Us about the Future of Work*. London: FT Press.

3 Why Do Some People Love Coming into the Office and Others Hate It?
Personality and the Hybrid Organisation

Michael Drayton

On 16 May 2022 readers of the *Daily Mail* were confronted with the following headline: 'British workers lead the world in REFUSING to return to the office: UK tops the table of nations with the most staff clinging to post-pandemic WFH lifestyle . . . with women at the vanguard of flexidus'. The article continued: 'Nearly quarter of British workers say they would rather quit or find a new job rather than go back to the office' (Robinson, 2022).

While it's always good to see British workers leading the world, this particular achievement has proved to be a headache for many leaders.

The rather alarmist headline was a pretty accurate summary of an interesting report by the think tank The WFH group (Aksoy et al., 2022). They carried out a comprehensive survey and found, unsurprisingly, a large shift to working from home resulting from the pandemic. The researchers surveyed full-time workers in 27 countries between mid-2021 and early 2022. They then compared results across countries while controlling for age, gender, education and industry.

The research team found that on average people worked from home 1.5 days per week, but this varied widely across countries. Employers preferred people to work from home an average of a half-day per week after the pandemic, while workers wanted to carry on working from home 1.7 days per week.

Women, people with children and those with longer commutes valued the option to work from home two to three days per week even more than the average, and they were willing to sacrifice 5 per cent of their pay for this option.

Many employees were pleasantly surprised by their productivity while working from home. As a result, employers who observed higher productivity levels among their remote workers during the pandemic were more likely to plan for them to continue working from home in the future.

These findings were used by the researchers to explain the significant shift towards remote work and to explore its potential impact on workers, organisations, cities and the pace of innovation.

This research is interesting because it neatly sums up much of the ambivalence around hybrid working. On the one hand, many employees and employers acknowledge that working from home seems to have a positive impact on performance productivity. Yet there still seems to be some guerrilla warfare, with most employers wanting to encourage employees back to the office while most employees want to hang on to working from home – at least a day and a half a week.

This reluctance of some (not all) employees to return to the office following the end of lockdown is a recurring theme in many of the conversations I have had with leaders over the past year.

One CEO I know – let's call him James – decided to put his foot down. He sent a memo to all his employees telling them in no uncertain terms that they were required to work in the office between Tuesday and Thursday from the beginning of the following month. 'I thought that was very reasonable,' he told me. 'They're still getting the opportunity for a long weekend, after all!'

I asked him how things turned out. He said, 'A few – or more than a few – moaned and complained. A few even hinted that they might start looking around for another job if they had to come into the office three days a week. Things were, I'll admit, pretty unsettled and a bit tense for a few weeks.'

'How did things work out once people had settled down and accepted the change?' I asked.

'Well,' he said, 'it was all very interesting. Nobody left in the end, thank God. People came back, and whined a bit, and some people looked out of sorts, but it was kind of okay after a couple of weeks. I noticed that even those who were initially moaning soon got back into the swing of things. I'd see them happily chatting to their colleagues over a cup of coffee. It was back to normal – like lockdown had never happened. We do have a few people who generally seem to struggle, and of course we were as flexible with them as we could be. Worked out well and it wasn't at all as traumatic as I expected.'

I thought that James's approach was sensible, but I guess it required a certain amount of courage on his part. And, of course, a lot of patience and persistence.

Most executives I talk to, though, tended to avoid James's admittedly direct approach and sidestepped the problems and potential conflict. They turned a blind eye to their corporate refuseniks and hoped the issue would resolve itself. Well, that was a possibility, but the probability was that it wouldn't. If you have read the previous chapter, you will know that these leaders soon began to notice a drop in team performance and engagement as well as a rise in employees leaving the organisation. Ignoring the problem is the easy solution in the short term but certainly not the best solution for the long term. Having half your staff in the office and half working from home isn't ideal for team performance and cohesion.

This issue of some employees being reluctant or even refusing to return to the office is a major challenge for leaders in a hybrid organisation.

Who is this subset of employees who find it difficult to return to work?

Most people are ambivalent about change. And returning to the office after working from home for a couple of years is a change. Even those who are eager to return will miss some aspects of their lives while working from home. Everyone has a preference, and the majority have a strong preference. This issue, like most others, is not black and white.

What is the main factor that makes the difference? Who are they, this sub-group who find it hard to return to the office? What characteristics define them and differentiate them from their colleagues who are happy to return? Well, there are lots of reasons (family circumstances, length of commute, size of accommodation), but by far the most important factor is personality. Some people prefer to be with others, and some prefer to be alone. Some people like to be left to get on with their work, while others prefer clear direction and guidance. Some people are very focused and orderly, others are easily distracted and so on.

In this chapter I will describe the psychology of personality. We'll discuss what personality is and how personality influences your employees' attitudes to work, and in particular their attitude to returning to the office.

Why is this important to leading the hybrid organisation?

Having some knowledge of personality theory can help you understand and guide the people you lead. It's also good to think about how your own personality affects your feelings and actions, especially regarding hybrid working.

Defining personality

Let's define our terms. What precisely do I mean by 'personality'? If you pause and think about that question, you'll soon realise that it's a hard one to answer. Personality is complex.

Personality theory is a rather arcane branch of academic psychology. Most people do not know much about personality theory, because most of us lack the technical language (otherwise known as jargon) to really describe personality. This limits what we can see. We say that so-and-so has a pleasant personality, that someone is a little lazy, outgoing or a worrier. People do not think much about 'personality' if someone seems normal and does not do anything out of the ordinary.

Often, we believe that we know someone well, but we are mistaken. This becomes clear when the person engages in extreme behaviour, such as committing a crime. It was 'out of character', as we say. In fact, we are mistaken: this is in character, because their behaviour is an expression of their personality, or at least a part of it that we have not noticed. The issue is that most people are unable to see and understand the complexity of personality. With a trained eye, though, you can observe the various facets of someone's personality and have the words and language to articulate them.

One of the reasons personality is difficult to define is that we see the world from the inside out. We observe the world through the distorting lens of our own personality. We then assume that our perception is the correct, rational, accurate and objective one (why would we think otherwise?). We then go on to assume that because our perception is right, the perception of others must be wrong, inaccurate or distorted. If we consider ourselves to be reasonable, rational and of average intelligence, we might assume that our understanding of the world is pretty accurate. However, this is not always the case. If everyone saw the world in the same way, there would be no disagreement on issues like politics or sports teams.

Our personality is like a filter that shapes the way we perceive and respond to the world around us. This is why two intelligent, well-educated and generally decent people can disagree so vehemently on a topic like Brexit. They are not seeing the same reality; instead, their perceptions are shaped by their own personalities.

Our personality is also the psychological equivalent of our immune system. Just as our physical immune system protects us from harmful pathogens, our personality protects our mental and emotional well-being by providing us with coping skills and the ability to adapt to stress and challenges, such as the changes involved in hybrid working. Some people have a personality that is better suited or equipped to handle the stress and pressure of everyday life. Others have a more sensitive personality, and consequently struggle to cope with life's challenges and might even become overwhelmed by stress and anxiety.

If we accept personality as a type of psychological immune system, the next question is: how do we explain why people differ? Why does a single stressful event, such as having to return to the office after working from home for a couple of years, cause anxiety in one person and joy in another?

The word 'personality' has a common, day-to-day meaning as well as a technical meaning. Psychologists use the term technically to describe and understand the patterns in our unique and long-lasting differences in thinking, emotion and behaviour.

Why is this important to leading a hybrid organisation?

> ### A brief history of personality
>
> People have been struggling to understand personality (or 'character') probably forever but certainly since the days of ancient Greece. The Greeks had several theories of personality, the two best known being:
>
> - **The four temperaments theory:** The philosopher and physician Hippocrates divided personality into four types based on the balance of four bodily fluids, or 'humours', which were blood, phlegm, yellow bile and black bile. The four temperaments were sanguine (optimistic and social), phlegmatic (calm and unemotional), melancholic (serious and introspective) and choleric (short-tempered and aggressive).
> - **Plato's tripartite soul theory:** The philosopher Plato divided the soul into three parts: rational, spirited and appetitive. The rational part was responsible for reasoning and decision-making, the spirited part was responsible for emotions and desires, and the appetitive part was responsible for basic bodily needs and instincts.
>
> These theories explained the complexities of human personality and behaviour in a way that was accessible and understandable to the ancient Greeks, and they still make sense today. While these theories are no longer considered scientifically valid, they have had a lasting impact on Western thought and continue to influence modern ideas about personality.
>
> In particular, these ideas from ancient Greece laid the foundations of what is probably the best-known theory of personality: Sigmund Freud's psychoanalysis. Freud said that an individual's behaviour and emotions are the result of unconscious conflicts and motives, many of which are rooted in early childhood experiences. According to Freud, the personality has three parts:
>
> - **Id**, representing unconscious and instinctual desires
> - **Ego**, representing the rational, practical and decision-making aspect of personality

- **Superego,** representing the moral and ethical component of personality

These three parts interact to form an individual's overall personality and behaviour.

The British psychologist Don Bannister pithily rephrased Freud's theory by describing the mind as 'a battlefield . . . a dark cellar in which a well-bred spinster lady and a sex-crazed monkey are locked in mortal combat, the struggle being refereed by a nervous bank clerk' (Bannister, 1966). In other words, we are all born with and continue to experience powerful biological drives. As we mature and become more socialised, we discover that such desires can get us into trouble and so we learn to deny, control or modify them so as to fit in with society. We are constantly engaged in a dynamic struggle between what we'd like to do, what we ought to do and what we can get away with. This ambivalence is the essence of psychoanalysis. Our observable personality and what we perceive to be 'us' is our ego. Modern personality theory describes this observable ego rather than the conflicts that go on beneath the surface.

The big five model of personality

The best and most up-to-date theory of personality is the big five (five-factor) model (McCrae & Costa, 2006; Soto et al., 2015). It's the one most widely accepted by the academic community.

The big five model was created through empirical test construction, which is a scientific process that uses rigorous mathematical analysis to define the complex nature of human personality. The model was developed by researchers McCrae and Costa, who began with a pool of words that could be used to describe personality, such as 'cheerful', 'easy going' and 'worrier'. They then gave these words to hundreds of individuals to use when describing themselves. Using a statistical technique called factor analysis, McCrae grouped the related traits into broad factors or dimensions. For instance, individuals who describe themselves as 'cheerful' are also likely to describe themselves as 'outgoing'. The descriptions of people's personalities ultimately fell into five broad factors – hence 'the big five'. This way of understanding and talking about personality was developed through a rigorous and scientific process and its accuracy has been demonstrated across cultures, with similar patterns of personality traits found in cultures. The big five model has strong predictive validity and can be used to anticipate various outcomes and behaviours, including job performance and mental and overall well-being.

Big five personality profile self-assessment[1]

I'd like you to pause here and do a quick personality self-assessment, having some knowledge about how your own personality affects your feelings and actions, especially regarding hybrid working. It will also help you understand and guide the people you lead.

Look at the following 30 questions and give yourself a score from 1 to 5 depending on how much you agree with the statements.

'I tend to . . .'

-	Strongly disagree Score 1	Disagree Score 2	Don't care either way Score 3	Agree Score 4	Strongly agree Score 5
1. Talk a lot					
2. Be compassionate and soft-hearted					
3. Be well organised					
4. Worry a lot					
5. Love art, music and literature					
6. Dominate and act as a leader					
7. Avoid being rude to other people					
8. Be good at starting new tasks					
9. Feel depressed or blue					
10. Be interested in abstract ideas					
11. Be full of energy					
12. Think the best of other people					
13. Be reliable and can always be counted on					

	Strongly disagree Score 1	Disagree Score 2	Don't care either way Score 3	Agree Score 4	Strongly agree Score 5
14. Be emotionally unstable and easily upset					
15. Be original and come up with lots of new ideas					
16. Be outgoing and sociable					
17. Try not to be cold and uncaring					
18. Keep things neat and tidy					
19. Be highly strung and frequently stressed					
20. Be creative and interested in art					
21. Like being in charge					
22. Treat other people with respect					
23. Be persistent and finish tasks that I start					
24. Feel insecure and uncomfortable with who I am					
25. Be a deep thinker and be interested in complicated ideas					
26. Be more active than most other people					
27. Avoid finding fault in other people					
28. Take care over things					
29. Be quite temperamental and emotional					
30. Be very creative					

Now find your score for each personality factor as follows:

- **Extroversion:** Add together your scores from questions 1, 6, 11, 16, 21 and 26. Write the total down here: [ ]
- **Neuroticism:** Add your scores from questions 4, 9, 14, 19, 24 and 29. Write the total down here: [ ]
- **Agreeableness:** Add your scores from questions 2, 7, 12, 17, 22 and 27. Write the total down here: [ ]
- **Openness:** Add your scores from questions 5, 10, 15, 20, 25 and 30. Write the total down here: [ ]
- **Conscientiousness:** Add your scores from questions 3, 8, 13, 18, 23 and 28. Write the total down here: [ ]

Next, put your total score for each factor in the table below:

Personality factor	Interpretation	My score
Extraversion	6 = low; 12 = med; 30 = high	
Neuroticism	6 = low; 12 = med; 30 = high	
Agreeableness	6 = low; 12 = med; 30 = high	
Openness	6 = low; 12 = med; 30 = high	
Conscientiousness	6 = low; 12 = med; 30 = high	

No value judgement is attached to being high or low on any of the factors. Being high or low on, say, openness brings both advantages and disadvantages.

Here is a summary of the five factors and how they apply at work:

1. **Openness:** Individuals who score high in openness are curious, imaginative and open to new experiences. They enjoy learning and exploring new ideas, and they may be more open to trying new technologies or approaches to problem-solving. In a hybrid team, individuals who score high in openness may be valuable contributors to brainstorming sessions or projects that require creative thinking. They may also be open to trying new communication tools or methods to facilitate collaboration.
2. **Conscientiousness:** Individuals who score high in conscientiousness are organised, reliable and responsible. They are likely to complete tasks on time and pay attention to detail. In a hybrid team, individuals who score high in conscientiousness may be reliable project leaders or team members, as they are likely to follow through on their commitments and pay attention to the details of a project.
3. **Extraversion:** Individuals who score high in extraversion are outgoing, energetic and assertive. They enjoy being around people

and may have a large social network. In a hybrid team, individuals who score high in extraversion may be effective at building relationships with team members and promoting team cohesion. They may also be effective at communicating ideas and leading group discussions.
4. **Agreeableness:** Individuals who score high in agreeableness are cooperative, kind and considerate. They are likely to prioritise the needs of the team over their own and may be skilled at resolving conflicts. In a hybrid team, individuals who score high in agreeableness may be valuable mediators and may be able to foster a positive and harmonious team dynamic.
5. **Neuroticism:** Individuals who score high in neuroticism are more likely to experience negative emotions such as anxiety, insecurity and vulnerability. They may be more sensitive to criticism or change. In a hybrid team, it may be helpful for managers to be aware of team members who score high in neuroticism and provide additional support or reassurance as needed.

The big five model and the hybrid organisation

Our personality is the main factor that influences our attitudes to hybrid working. And these attitudes will influence and in many cases determine our behaviour and day-to-day actions. It's therefore helpful to have at least a basic understanding of personality theory if you want to understand and effectively influence the behaviour of those you lead. Also, dare I say it, you might want to reflect on your own personality and how it influences your own attitudes and resultant behaviour around hybrid working.

A lot of our behaviour at work, particularly behaviour that causes problems (for instance, resisting returning to the office), is bound up with our overall attitude to authority. Are you someone who values and appreciates guidance, attention and direction from the boss? Do you like being told what to do? Or do you enjoy autonomy and sometimes feel resentful when you are told what to do? Can you sometimes be belligerent at work (you'd see it as standing up for yourself – not being pushed around)?

Your attitude to authority is largely determined by your personality. Let's go through the five personality factors and see how they influence attitudes to hybrid working and authority.

Openness

People who are high on openness are curious and creative, and because of this they tend also to be distractible. They have an idea, but then this idea is quickly replaced by another. If they find a task boring, they will really struggle to focus and persevere with it. They are likely to go off and find something more interesting to do. They'll get up to make a coffee, go for a wander or check their Twitter feed. Anything for stimulation. The one thing they hate most in the world is being bored.

In contrast, people who are low on openness really enjoy routine. They rarely get bored. They tend to be socially conservative people who find safety and comfort in conforming to a set routine. They positively enjoy tasks that are familiar and repetitive. They enjoy and thrive in a workplace that is steady, calm and predictable. The thing that they hate most in the world is change.

Encouraging your high-openness employees back to the office should be fairly easy. They are likely to welcome the stimulation of being with other people and the general buzz of the corporate environment. You might want to give some thought to the tasks that they do at the office. If these are routine tasks similar to the ones they are doing at home then you are not making best use of their talents. Use their office time for the more creative, innovative and 'solving hard problems in a group' type work.

People who are low on openness are likely to be more of a challenge. Remember, these folk really don't like change. They probably found the move to working from home a couple of years ago to be stressful and exhausting; but now they are used to it. Life has settled into a steady routine for them and now you are proposing to disrupt this steady routine by asking them to return to the office. You will more than likely experience resistance. The best way to minimise this resistance is to make the change – the return to part-time office working – as structured and predictable as you can. Don't expose them to the stress of having to return overnight. Maybe offer them a timetable that's clear about what is expected and when. In fact, this structured, predictable 'timetable' approach is probably the best approach to take with everybody.

Conscientiousness

People who are high on conscientiousness are industrious and orderly and will be at the front of the queue of employees wanting to get back to the office. They are likely to yearn for and benefit from the return to boundaries around their work life. One of the 'problems' that high-conscientious people experience is that they don't know when to stop. When they are working from home and nobody is there to prompt them, when it's time to stop working (people in the office closing down their computers and drifting off home), then their tendency to overwork can run riot.

Employees who are low on conscientiousness are laidback and disorganised and hate pressure. When you ask the low-conscientious person to return to working in the office, you are likely to get one of two responses:

- **Resistance:** For them it's much easier to avoid difficult tasks and dodge responsibility at home than in the office, where they are in full view of others and the boss. With this group your strategy should be to insist that they return in a firm but kind manner. This is the group of people most likely to whine and complain, so you will need to be strong and stick to your guns.
- **Acceptance:** Paradoxically, you might find that some of the low-conscientiousness group actually want to return to the office. These are the folk who have some insight and self-awareness. They understand that they find it hard to get organised and get things done. They also understand that this tendency might cost them their job and consequent income. This group actually values the structure and boundaries provided by a corporate environment. They might not like rules, but they realise that they need them and benefit from them. Work is the scaffolding that holds their life together and they know it. They need direction, supervision and support if they are to get anything done and hold on to their job and income. To get these low-conscientious folks back to the office, give them a structured timetable that clearly shows what is expected and by when.

Extraversion

Those employees who are high on extraversion will be hassling you to allow them to come back to the office. These employees get much of their energy from being around other people. Working from home will have been stressful for them – like a flower not getting enough water and sunshine. They will have missed their colleagues and friends and will be eager to return.

Employees who are low on extraversion ('introverts') are the ones most likely to experience significant problems when you ask them to return to the office. These employees are able to function perfectly well with other people, it's just that they find it stressful and exhausting. This, understandably, makes them genuinely anxious at the thought of returning to working in the office. They are much happier working from home, where they can quietly and diligently get on with things. These folks work hard and usually are more productive working from home rather than in the office.

You can make a good case for flexibility when deciding where the low-extraversion employee works. If they are productive working from home, and they seem anxious and reluctant to return to the office, maybe consider allowing them to do most of their hours at home. Forcing them back to the office will have little benefit for the organisation or the introverted individual.

The big drawback is that you will be greatly depleting the cognitive diversity of the team to which they belong. The value of a high-performance team is in the diversity of voices in that team. A good team needs its quiet introverts as well as its loud extraverts. Therefore consider asking the introverted member of staff to come into work at least once a week, on the team meeting day. Give some thought to how you can best encourage them to participate when they are present in the office, to ensure that their voice is heard.

Agreeableness

People who are high on agreeableness are friendly, warm and gregarious. They also hate conflict. These employees will be delighted to return to the office to see all their friends and colleagues again. And because they hate conflict, they're unlikely to argue with you when you ask them to turn up at the office.

In contrast, those employees who are low on agreeableness – in other words, disagreeable employees – are likely to give you a hard time when you ask them to return to the office.

The starting point when dealing with this group of people is to remind yourself that people who are low on agreeableness don't mean to be hostile or antagonistic when they confront you or argue with you. It just feels that way. From their perspective, they are simply being honest and straightforward and expressing how they feel. In their eyes, they aren't arguing but debating.

If you try to view resistance from them as debate or negotiation, you'll find your request to get them back to the office to be a lot less stressful than if you frame it as an argument or battle. Like in any debate or negotiation, make sure that you have some solid reasons why it's necessary for the person to return to the office – 'because I say so' just won't cut it with people like this. Then firmly and assertively negotiate for what you want. Be respectful and listen carefully to the other person's reasons and give them time and space to think. You will find that the person will respond well to this approach and respect you for your straightforward manner.

Neuroticism

People who are low on neuroticism are emotionally stable, resilient and resourceful individuals who will probably be more than happy to return to the office.

Of all the employees, the individuals who will experience most difficulty in returning to the office are those who are high on neuroticism.

These people are prone to experience high levels of negative emotion – anxiety, apprehension and depression. They respond very poorly to external stress and are likely to feel very safe and secure working from home, but experience the office as mildly threatening and certainly anxiety provoking. Their anxieties are genuine, and you will need to offer them more support in coming back to work than any other of the groups of people I covered in the preceding sections.

The approach with high-neuroticism employees should be similar to the approach for employees who are low on openness. You should consider a gradual, predictable, phased return to the office, perhaps over months rather than weeks. If you are their line manager, you should be prepared to offer them a great deal of time and support while they are in the office. Take a look at Chapter 7 on mental well-being and the hybrid organisation for more detailed advice on how to minimise the stress for high-neuroticism employees in the hybrid team.

Attachment style and the hybrid organisation

Have you ever worked with someone who was needy and maybe a bit clingy? Although they were competent, they seemed to need constant reassurance and support? Or maybe you've worked with someone whom you felt was aloof and standoffish and who would never ask for help no matter what? There is another aspect of personality that will affect your attitude to hybrid working, and that is attachment style.

I introduced attachment theory in Chapter 2. To summarise, attachment theory is a psychological framework that describes how we form emotional bonds and relationships with other people, places and organisations. According to attachment theory, we develop an attachment style based on our experiences with primary caregivers, usually our parents. This attachment style is deeply ingrained and influences our behaviour and relationships throughout our life (Mikulincer & Shaver, 2017).

There are four main attachment styles. These styles describe and explain how we relate to others. A person's dominant attachment style will have a significant impact on their interactions in the workplace.

The four attachment styles are as follows:

- **Secure:** People with a secure attachment style are comfortable with intimacy and are able to seek support from others when needed. At the same time, they have firm boundaries and are able to stand up for themselves. They have positive views of themselves and others. They find it easy to form healthy and fulfilling relationships. Eric Berne, the founder of Transactional Analysis, summed this up as

'I'm okay, you're okay' (Berne, 1964). At work, employees with secure attachment styles tend to, as you might expect, have strong communication skills and positive attitudes and are able to form healthy and productive relationships with others. They collaborate effectively and seek help and support from colleagues when needed. If we described this attachment style in big five personality model language, the person with a secure attachment style would be high on extraversion, low on neuroticism and average on the other three factors. They are unlikely to object to returning to the office.

- **Anxious-preoccupied:** Those with an anxious-preoccupied attachment style are insecure and overly preoccupied with their relationships. They feel a need for constant reassurance and validation from others. They have negative views of themselves but positive views of others, and struggle with trust and abandonment issues. In Berne's words, 'I'm not okay, you're okay.' When at work, people with an anxious-preoccupied attachment style will often struggle with trust and may have difficulty delegating tasks or seeking help from others. They tend to take criticism or feedback personally, which can lead to defensiveness or conflict in the workplace. In big five terms, this person will be high on extraversion and high on neuroticism. They need to be with other people to feel validated but also feel anxious with others. This employee will be anxious to get back to the office, but will be very needy and need much reassurance and emotional support.
- **Dismissive-avoidant:** People with a dismissive-avoidant attachment style distance themselves from others and avoid close relationships. They may have positive views of themselves but negative views of others, and may struggle with vulnerability and emotional expression. In Berne's terms, they believe, 'I'm okay, you're not okay.' Employees with this attachment style struggle with teamwork and collaboration, because they prefer to work independently, coming across as aloof and sometimes a bit arrogant. They often have difficulty communicating their needs and ideas effectively to others. They are also more prone to conflict or misunderstandings because of their avoidance of emotional expression and vulnerability. These folk are the low-extraversion and low-agreeableness employees. They are likely to resist returning to the office, and argue their case that they should work from home in a clumsy and overly direct manner. If the person is performing well working at home, then you might want to consider allowing them to work from home as much as possible.
- **Fearful-avoidant:** Those with a fearful-avoidant attachment style have negative views of themselves and others (I'm not okay, you're

not okay), and may avoid close relationships due to fear of rejection or abandonment. They struggle with intimacy and experience a lot of difficulty trusting others. Employees with fearful-avoidant attachment styles struggle with both trust and vulnerability, which can make it difficult to form strong relationships with colleagues and managers. They have a tendency to avoid conflict and find being assertive to be very stressful. This can lead to big problems with communication and productivity in the workplace. In big five language, this person would be high on agreeableness and high on neuroticism. Again, there is a good case to be made for letting these employees work from home as much as possible.

Some advice for encouraging people back to the office

As well as all the individual personality factors I have described so far in this chapter, some people have practical reasons for preferring to work from home. These could include having children or other dependent people to look after or facing a long, unpleasant commute. Others know that they are more productive working from home, and so returning to the office for its own sake just doesn't make any sense.

Zooming out from the personality issues we have just explored, there are some straightforward, common sense actions you can take that will encourage almost anyone, regardless of their personality, to return to the office part time.

Start by reminding yourself that this isn't a black-and-white issue for most people. There are upsides and downsides for everyone when it comes to returning to the office. Some people may find it reassuring to 'get back to normal' and return to their routine and see their colleagues, while others may not be ready.

The first step is to do your best to find out how people in the organisation feel about returning to work. The best way is to ask them face to face or at least over Zoom.

Having said this, you probably shouldn't assume that your employees will speak up if they are anxious about returning, as they may be afraid of appearing weak or not living up to expectations. It is your responsibility to create a safe environment where employees can express their concerns.

Another good option is to conduct anonymous surveys to gather information about how employees feel about returning to work. If you do a survey, give a lot of thought to the responses and apply some creative thinking to how you might address their concerns. For example, if several people mention the stresses of a long commute, consider staggered start and finish times.

When employees share their concerns, make sure you allow for people to have mixed and complex feelings. Do not pressure them to hide their negative feelings or dismiss their concerns. Do your best to acknowledge and open up the emotional ambivalence. The more people are able to talk about their mixed feelings, the less likely they are to act them out. This will create a culture where people can adapt and change more easily. This will be especially true of employees experiencing anxiety about coming back.

Finally, remember that people are different. A 'return to the office' policy or hybrid-working strategy has to walk the line between being simple and clear yet having enough flexibility to take account of the variation in employee personality.

Questions to reflect on

1. What are the practical problems that might be obstacles to people returning to the office?
2. What could you do to minimise these problems?
3. How does your personality affect your attitude to hybrid working?
4. What are your feelings about returning to the office, and how might they influence your behaviour towards others?
5. How can you use the big five model to better understand any reluctance to returning to the office in people you work with?

Key points

- Most people feel ambivalent about returning to the office.
- People's attitude to returning to the office is largely determined by their personality.
- Our personality is made up of five factors: openness, conscientiousness, extraversion, agreeableness and neuroticism.
- Those people who are low on extraversion (quiet, introverted people) and/or high on neuroticism (people prone to anxiety) are likely to struggle to return to the office.
- Attachment style will also affect a person's attitude and behaviour around hybrid working.
- There are four main attachment styles: secure, anxious-preoccupied, dismissive-avoidant and fearful-avoidant.

Note

1 This self-assessment has been adapted from: Soto, C. J. & John, O. P. (2017). 'Short and Extra-short Forms of the Big Five Inventory–2: The BFI-2-S and BFI-2-XS'. *Journal of Research in Personality*, 68, 69–81.

References

Aksoy, C. G., Barrero, J. M., Bloom, N., Davis, S. J., Dolls, M. & Zarate, P. (2022). 'Working from Home around the World'. *SocArXiv*. https://doi.org/10.31235/osf.io/q4dyg.

Bannister, D. (1966). 'Psychology as an Exercise in Paradox'. *Bulletin of the British Psychological Society*, 19, 23–6.

Berne, E. (1964). *Games People Play: The Psychology of Human Relationships*. London: Penguin.

McCrae R. R. & Costa, P. T. (2006). *Personality in Adulthood: A Five Factor Therory Perspective* (2nd ed.). Guilford Press.

Mikulincer, M. & Shaver, P. R. (2017). *Attachment in Adulthood, Second Edition: Structure, Dynamics, and Change* (2nd ed.). New York: Guilford Press.

Robinson, J. (2022). 'British Workers Lead the World in REFUSING to Return to the Office'. *Daily Mail*, 16 May. https://www.dailymail.co.uk/news/article-10820493/British-workers-lead-world-REFUSING-return-office.html.

Soto, C. J., Kronauer, A. & Liang, J. K. (2015). 'Five-Factor Model of Personality'. In *The Encyclopedia of Adulthood and Aging* (pp. 1–5). Hoboken NJ: John Wiley & Sons, Inc.

4 Communicating in the Hybrid Organisation

Michael Drayton

Effective communication is critical for any high-performing organisation. However, hybrid working creates significant barriers to effective communication. This chapter explores the communication challenges of hybrid working and provides practical solutions to improve online and in-person interactions.

The *Titanic*: Lessons for communication in complex systems

The *Titanic* was the greatest ship of its time. It was the Edwardian equivalent of the Airbus 380, designed to transport a large number of passengers quickly and safely across the Atlantic. Like the Airbus, the majority of *Titanic* passengers travelled in economy, with a select few in the ship's equivalent of business and first class. The *Titanic* was as cutting-edge for its time as the A380, with the latest and most advanced technology of the early twentieth century. The ship had a sophisticated navigation system as well as an advanced communication system that allowed it to communicate with other ships and shore stations via wireless telegraphy. This system was state-of-the-art at the time and was considered a major technological achievement.

The *Titanic* was also the safest ship of its time, with features like watertight compartments and large, robust lifeboats that we now take for granted but were considered optional – desirable but not essential – in Edwardian shipbuilding. It was the safest ship ever built.

On April 14, 1912, tragedy struck. The *Titanic* collided with an iceberg and began to sink rapidly, taking over 1,500 people with it. This had the same profound impact on the Edwardian world as a fully laden A380 coming down the middle of the Atlantic would have on ours.

The question is, how could such a tragedy have occurred given the *Titanic*'s cutting-edge technology, safety features and overall build quality?

The *Titanic* sank because of human psychological failings rather than technological failings, and the main psychological failing was communication.

DOI: 10.4324/9781003387602-4

First, there was poor communication between the *Titanic* and other ships in the area. The *Titanic*'s wireless operators were preoccupied with transmitting and receiving passenger messages, which distracted them from the increasing amount of radio chatter about icebergs and warnings from nearby ships. If they had been aware of these warnings and passed them to the bridge, who knows, the ship might have been able to avoid the iceberg altogether.

Second, there was a lack of communication between the ship's officers and the crew. The officers were mostly English-speaking, while the crew was made up of many different nationalities, including French, Italian and Scandinavian. The language barrier made it difficult for the officers to give clear instructions to the crew, and for the crew to understand the officers' orders.

Furthermore, one of the most critical communication breakdowns that occurred during the *Titanic*'s sinking was the crew's failure to convey the full extent of the damage to the officers on the bridge after the ship collided with the iceberg. Rather than providing an accurate assessment of the situation, they downplayed the severity of the damage and assured the officers that the ship had only sustained surface-level damage and would remain afloat. It is understandable. The *Titanic* was constantly marketed as the world's only virtually unsinkable ship, and many crew members likely believed that the ship could withstand the impact without major damage.

The *Titanic* shows how communication breakdowns, not just technology failures, can lead to catastrophe. Like the *Titanic*, modern hybrid organisations rely heavily on technology yet can underestimate human factors like communication. Just as the *Titanic* sank despite advanced systems, major failures can still happen in today's complex organisations when communication breaks down.

The story of the *Titanic* and the modern hybrid organisation

All of the elements in the story of the sinking of the *Titanic* can be abstracted out and seen every day in any large organisation. This is particularly true when it comes to communication breakdowns. The *Titanic* and the events surrounding it serve as a metaphor for the modern hybrid organisation.

Like the *Titanic*, modern hybrid organisations are technologically complex. There is frequently an overreliance on technology to manage systems (resulting in a decrease in developing robust human systems) and a belief that technology will save us. Because everyone had the brief that the *Titanic* was unsinkable, they underestimated the risk. The *Titanic* was unsinkable . . . until it sank. *Too Big to Fail* is a book by journalist Andrew Ross Sorkin about the collapse of the Wall Street bank Lehman Brothers (Sorkin, 2010). Of course, Lehman Brothers (and Barings Bank) were too large to fail, just as the *Titanic* was too large to sink.

The radio operators on the *Titanic* were overwhelmed by day-to-day tasks, just as we are often overwhelmed by day-to-day tasks at work and struggle to see the bigger picture. We have a tendency to overlook what is important.

Language and culture were barriers to effective communication on the *Titanic*. The majority of the officers spoke English and belonged to a specific culture and social class. Many of the crew members spoke different languages and came from different cultures. Most large organisations today are made up of multicultural and frequently cross-national teams.

What are the communication challenges in hybrid working?

All high-performing organisations and teams have effective structures to support communication. The structures, however, changed almost overnight. Employees used to talk to each other face to face before the pandemic and lockdown. Teams would meet face to face. Much of the communication, creative conversations and those that added the most value occurred in casual settings, such as the staff restaurant or around the metaphorical 'water cooler'.

There are some things that you just cannot replicate in an online virtual communication system, no matter how sophisticated the technology. Comparing the experiences of joy, misery and friendship, as well as the petty squabbles that occur in any regular workplace, to the usually arid and transactional meetings that occur on Zoom is a bit like comparing the actual experience of being on the *Titanic* with a computer game about the *Titanic*.

A well-functioning workplace is like a well-tended garden. It is a place where friendships can blossom. Of course, weeds can grow as well, and you must be careful to remove them before they take over. The real-world office is the soil in which a strong organisational culture can grow and become stronger. The millions of bits of information brought in from outside by the organization's employees feed the organization's creativity. The millions of tiny interactions and 'collisions' (more on these later) between the people in the organisation feed the organisation. Paradoxically, the organisation also converts the 'manure' of conflict into food for growth.

If we stay with this metaphor of the organisation as a garden, the journalist Julia Hobsbawm, in her book *The Nowhere Office* (Hobsbawm, 2022), compares office communication to birdsong – the communal exchanges of ideas and emotions over millions of overlapping interactions in a day. It's hard to replicate such a complex environmental system in an online virtual world. It's bound to be a pale imitation of the real thing.

In her book, Hobsbawm quotes Kevin Ellis of PricewaterhouseCoopers (PwC), who describes real face-to-face office interactions like this: 'When I'm in the office I can probably speak to five people in an hour. Just wandering around their desks. There is a kind of birdsong of the office. Everyone's saying good morning. How are you doing today?' A different executive talked about the creativity that is found in these serendipitous encounters: 'Creative conversations happen in the corridors. It's someone perching on the desk saying, "Oh, you have to read this or that,"' (Hobsbawm, 2022).

During and following the pandemic lockdown, communication shifted online. Like most things to do with hybrid working, this has had many advantages as well as disadvantages. People enjoy not having to commute but moan about back-to-back Zoom meetings, lack of personal contact and support, and even less time to actually get the real work done.

How hybrid working affects communication

Let's start with a story.

Once upon a time, there was a happy village where people chatted over garden fences, in the queue at the post office and in the village coffee shop. Often, if one of the villagers had a problem, one of the other villagers would be able to help them. The villagers knew each other well and had a strong sense of belonging to their happy village. They were proud of their little village and everything it stood for. Life was good, and everyone was happy.

One day, a storyteller arrived in the village and told tales of a far-away land where people talked using boxes and invisible magic called 'the internet'. The villagers were fascinated, and they couldn't wait to try this new way of communicating.

They set up their own boxes and began to talk to their friends. They didn't even need to leave their little cottages. At first, it was exciting. They could buy bread from the baker's and stamps from the post office and these would be delivered to their door. The village postman, Jeff Bezmore, set up a village store and delivery service called Hundred Acre Woods and promised to deliver anything by the next day. All was good.

However, as time passed, the villagers began to realise that their previously strong community was beginning to break down. They found that communicating through the boxes was different from their old face-to-face chats. Without body language, facial expressions and tone of voice, it was harder to express their emotions and what they really wanted to say. Misunderstandings began to pile up, and the villagers started to feel lonely and disconnected. They missed the simple pleasures of chatting with their friends and neighbours. They missed the sound of laughter and the warmth of a hug. They missed chatting in the queue at the post office and having coffee together. They began to feel like they no longer belonged in the happy village and some moved away, looking for a nicer happy village . . .

This is an analogy for the reality of hybrid working in most organisations. As more and more people work remotely, it can be difficult to maintain the same level of connection, collaboration and creativity that comes with in-person interactions. The lack of face-to-face communication can easily lead to misunderstandings and a breakdown of the company culture.

While it has its benefits, hybrid working also poses serious long-term challenges to building a strong organisational identity and culture. The physical separation of employees can make it hard to maintain a consistent company culture and foster a sense of identity within the organisation. People miss the 'chats in the post office queue' and having coffee in the 'happy village coffee shop'. And some even move away to a nicer 'happy village' or different company because they feel they don't belong in or are even part of your 'happy village' organisation anymore.

Communication is at the heart of the problem. Or, more accurately, the often sterile transactional style of virtual communication. To stay connected, we now rely, more often than not, on virtual communication tools like video calls, instant messaging and email. While these tools are beneficial in many ways, they are not the same as face-to-face conversations that foster creativity and a sense of belonging. When you are not in the same physical space as your colleagues, it is easy to miss nonverbal cues or tone, which can lead to a variety of misunderstandings and communication breakdowns with the potential to cause confusion and, in some cases, hurt, which can harm the overall team dynamic.

Employees find it more difficult to identify with and feel a sense of belonging to an organisation when they work in a hybrid setting. When employees work remotely, they can easily become disconnected from the company culture and feel as if they are not part of a team. They get into a contractor mindset rather than a group member mindset. This can result in decreased motivation and engagement, affecting productivity.

Interpersonal 'collisions' and hybrid organisations

In Chapter 2, I touched on the story of Tony Hsieh, the former CEO of Zappos. Hsieh was a phenomenally successful entrepreneur. He grew up in San Francisco, the child of Taiwanese immigrants. His father was an engineer and his mother was a social worker, and Tony either inherited or picked up from his parents a combination of problem-solving skills and emotional empathy that would shape his approach to business. Hsieh was adept at coming up with imaginative solutions to hard problems, creating strong bonds and cultivating a sense of belonging, which he used to transform Zappos. He championed the concept of an online store driven by a radical customer-centric approach. For example, Zappos pioneered an unconditional return policy (nothing special now, but unheard of at the time). Innovative ideas such as this made Tony Hsieh an important mover and shaker in the booming online retail market. Hsieh was second only to the likes of Amazon's Jeff Bezos. The title of Hsieh's 2010 book encapsulates his philosophy: *Delivering Happiness: A Path to Profits, Passion and Purpose* (Hsieh, 2010); its theme is the interaction between happiness and business success.

Zappos had, without doubt, an unconventional corporate culture, especially in the US of the late 2000s. Central to Tony Hsieh's philosophy and strategy was his emphasis on the idea of 'collisions' – unplanned, serendipitous encounters that spark creativity and innovation. He believed that promoting an environment where employees could interact and connect with one another would generate novel ideas and solutions.

This approach was one of the major factors in Zappos' success. It fostered and grew an organic exchange of ideas and cross-pollination between different smart people, teams and departments. It was a petri dish for rapidly and effectively developing strains of cognitive diversity. And it paid off big time. Hsieh amassed a personal fortune estimated, conservatively, at $700 million. Zappos was very profitable and at the same time was consistently recognised as one of *Fortune's* 'Best Places to Work'. That's quite an achievement.

To facilitate these productive collisions, Hsieh designed the Zappos physical office space in such a way that employees would have lots of opportunities to encounter one another, in shared common areas or through the use of strategically placed coffee machines. By engineering these chance encounters – these 'collisions' – Hsieh effectively stimulated creative conversations and collaboration, resulting in a dynamic and innovative work culture and environment.

Hsieh encouraged employees to embrace their individuality, diversity of culture and ideas, and to express themselves authentically. He was a pioneer in establishing a culture of psychological safety. Zappos became synonymous with a work culture that valued risk-taking, authentic, honest communication and failure as a learning opportunity. Hsieh's ideas were subsequently developed by Amy Edmondson, from Harvard Business School, who popularised the concept of psychological safety in the workplace (Edmondson, 2019). Edmondson's research showed that psychologically safe environments lead to higher employee engagement, innovation and overall organisational success.

Hsieh's approach extended beyond the walls of Zappos. He spent about $350 million to revitalise the seedy, rundown downtown Las Vegas that was Zappos' (and, indeed, Tony Hsieh's) home. His vision and funding transformed the neighbourhood into a thriving centre for arts, culture and technology. Through the Downtown Project, Hsieh created an urban environment where collisions could occur naturally and where people from different industries and backgrounds could collaborate and spark off one another.

Zappos' culture and its built environment that encouraged these 'collisions' yielded spectacular benefits. The company had an impressively low employee turnover rate, a testament to Zappos' nurturing and supportive environment.

These informal social interactions – chats while perched on a desk, chats over coffee, running into people from different departments: 'collisions' – are crucial in the life of an organisation and its individual employees.

Hybrid working has been great for most businesses and employees. But it has its risks and downsides. People don't talk as much. There are fewer, if any, serendipitous 'collisions' resulting in creative ideas. People tend to feel less attached to the organisation and find it easy to move on. A 'happy village' organisation is great for employees and for performance and profit. The key to holding on to your 'villagers' seems to be increasing the opportunities for social (rather than virtual) interactions and 'collisions'. This is a strong argument for bringing your staff together physically rather than virtually as often as you can.

Changing social norms

The shift to online communication has disrupted social norms at work. Leaders have become more remote (you never actually see them) and, paradoxically, more accessible to employees ('Email me at any time'). Boundaries have become fuzzy. A meeting with the boss now takes you into their home, and neither of you wears business attire ('Was the FD really wearing a Pink Floyd T-shirt?').

At board meetings, executives would frequently indicate their position in the dominance hierarchy by where they sat – the closer you were to the CEO, the higher up the pecking order you were! This is a lot more difficult to achieve in a Zoom meeting.

Clear social norms foster a sense of cohesion in which people understand their place in the dominance (social) hierarchy, how to behave at work and what the boundaries are in their specific workplace (what is acceptable and what isn't).

Many social norms have been abandoned, creating a void that will inevitably be filled by new social norms. Some of these will be helpful, others not.

The importance of communication for organisational culture

Before we proceed, let's spend a moment reflecting on what organisational culture is. The famous organisational psychologist and business guru Edgar Schein gave a good description:

> Organisational culture is a set of fundamental assumptions developed, discovered, or invented by a specific group as they learn to manage external adaptation and internal integration challenges. These assumptions have proven effective enough to be deemed valid and are subsequently taught to new members as the proper way to perceive, think, and feel regarding those issues.
> (Schein, 1984)

He went on to describe three levels within organisational culture:

- **Observable artefacts:** These are the visible elements encountered by individuals when they first join or interact with an organisation, such as dress code, language formality and spatial organisation. For example, a prestigious law firm's office would have a different appearance than an advertising agency's workspace. To comprehend these artefacts, it's essential to examine the organisation's values.
- **Espoused values:** The values of the organisation can be found in mission statements and other documents, and they reflect the founders' and leaders' beliefs about the organization's ideal state. These values reflect what members of the organisation say but do not always reflect what they do. There is frequently a large gap between espoused values and the reality of organisational behaviour. Actual behaviour is frequently shaped by members' fundamental subjective assumptions. Organisational culture, like an iceberg, has visible and invisible components, with the latter being more difficult to discern.

An example of this gap between a mission statement and actual behaviour is the Enron scandal (Elkind & McLean, 2004). Enron was an American energy company that went bankrupt in 2001 after committing massive accounting fraud. Enron's mission statement included the following values: 'Respect, Integrity, Communication and Excellence'. However, Enron's actual behaviour was far from

these professed values. The company was involved in one of the largest corporate fraud cases in history. They engaged in numerous fraudulent practises in order to conceal their financial problems and maintain the appearance of financial success.
- **Basic subjective assumptions:** These are the beliefs held by members of the organisation. They develop when particular behaviours prove effective in solving short-term problems and thus become habitual and embedded in the culture. These behaviours (which work) often contradict the espoused values of an organisation. In such cases, the assumptions almost always win – because at one level, they solve the problem (Schein, 1990).

For example, how many start-up tech companies have 'innovation' as an espoused core value? Every one, I'd guess. In the early days, the company rewards employees who come up with creative and original ideas that help the business grow. However, as the company expands, it starts to prioritise stability and growth over innovation. Management begins to avoid risks and prefer proven solutions, even though they still claim that innovation is a core value. Employees notice this shift and start to conform to the new focus on stability. They may still espouse the value of innovation, but their day-to-day actions lean towards maintaining the status quo. These new, unspoken assumptions – that stability and avoiding risks are what really matter – become embedded in the organisation's culture.

Think of the organisation as being like an elephant ridden by a mahout. The mahout represents the espoused values. The mahout sits atop the elephant, guiding it and making decisions about where to go. This guidance represents the organisation's stated values and beliefs, the things that are openly discussed and promoted within the company. However, the elephant itself represents the underlying, basic subjective assumptions of the organisation. These assumptions are the true driving force behind the elephant's movements, just as they are the true driving force behind the organisation's actions. The elephant is powerful and has its own instincts and behaviours that have developed over time, much like the unspoken beliefs and habits within the organisation. Even though the mahout (espoused values) may try to direct the elephant to turn right (towards innovation and creativity), if the elephant (basic subjective assumptions) wants to go left (towards stability and risk-avoidance), the elephant and mahout will go left. In the end, the elephant's instincts and behaviours will have a more significant impact on the path it takes than the mahout's directions. The organisation, like the elephant, ultimately follows the direction set by its deeply ingrained assumptions and habits, even if they sometimes contradict the espoused values.

Communication is the conduit through which organisational culture is nurtured. Not just the 'official' espoused communications from the leadership such as mission statements and the like, but the thousands of daily interactions that take place in the workplace, the hundreds of individual behaviours that are being constantly shaped by the culture in the organisation.

The frequency and quality of communication shapes not only social norms and cohesion and business culture but also the degree of trust, collaboration and innovation among employees. This was the essential lesson of Tony Hsieh and Zappos.

It's like a spider's web, where each strand represents a line of communication connecting individuals within the organisation. The web's resilience lies in the strength and interconnectivity of its strands, much like an organisation's success depends on the quality and frequency of communication among its members. As employees share their ideas, challenges and solutions, the web grows stronger, more complex and more capable of withstanding external pressures.

What is the optimal way to communicate online?

The evidence for the importance of good communication in any organisation, particularly a hybrid organisation, is overwhelming. Now, let's move on and get down to brass tacks. What practical things can you do to improve communication in your organisation? First, you need to consider how to improve online communication.

Many people like the convenience of working from home, but this naturally involves Zoom[1] meetings. These meetings can be mentally and physically exhausting, particularly when they are back to back, which can be common, especially for senior people. Staring at a screen for long periods of time is also draining and can cause sore eyes, headaches and an aching back. Technical problems, such as poor bandwidth and connection issues, can add to the stress and frustration. When people have their cameras turned off it's even harder to figure out what's going on, and whether people are engaged.

Is this the most efficient way of getting things done and adding value to the business? The research literature suggests not.

'Bursty communication' and remote team performance

Recent research (Riedl & Woolley, 2020) shows that it might not be virtual communication as such that is the problem, but rather how the communication is organised.

We discussed earlier in the chapter the importance of 'collisions' and 'water cooler conversations' in team formation and creativity. I express my strong doubts as to whether virtual communication can truly replicate the creativity and innovation that occur as a result of those serendipitous watercooler collisions back at the office.

Some companies, such as Apple and Google, appear to share my concerns. These businesses have begun to discourage remote work. The belief is that only mandatory office attendance can recreate the watercooler magic thought to be required for breakthroughs.

But what if I'm wrong and this push to revert to full-time office-based work is misguided? What if innovation has less to do with virtual communication and more to do with how such virtual team communication is structured? Riedl and Woolley suggest this may be the case.

According to their findings, constant communication and availability do not optimise remote team performance as previously thought. Instead, a 'bursty' communication rhythm is preferable, with short bursts of intense interaction followed by longer periods of deep focus.

This study looked at 260 software developers from 50 countries who worked in remote teams. Some teams received cash incentives, similar to on-site perks at tech firms, while others did not. Surprisingly, the incentives had no effect on the quality of the work. What made a difference was teams adopting a bursty communication style.

Rapid back-and-forth exchanges allowed quick sharing of ideas and unblocking of issues. Yet prolonged periods of silence enabled teams to concentrate and execute on tasks without distraction. The bursty teams significantly outperformed those with elongated, disjointed virtual communications.

It seems the watercooler itself is not the key ingredient for innovation, but rather the rhythms and focus it permits. With purposeful virtual communication norms, the convenience of remote work does not mean sacrificing creativity.

So, how can organisations enable bursty communication? Instant messaging apps and other synchronous tools make it easy to ask and answer questions quickly within set time limits, without being interrupted all the time. Videoconferencing is good for more complicated conversations, and asynchronous platforms like wikis and documents let people see each other without being interrupted.

In essence, combining focused individual work with targeted, intense team interactions can virtually recreate collaborative dynamism. With the right digital rhythms, the innovation thought to necessitate office watercoolers can flourish remotely.

Communication in diverse, cross-cultural teams

Many online teams, particularly senior leadership teams, comprise members from different countries, often different continents. The members of the team have grown up in different cultures with different social norms and ways of communicating. One factor that is often ignored when talking about communication in remote teams is how this diversity affects communication. Imagine a team made up of members from Germany, the US and Japan (an actual team with whom I had the pleasure of working during lockdown). How does that diversity of culture affect the performance of the team?

In their paper 'Creating Value with Diverse Teams in Global Management', Joe DiStefano and Martha Maznevski, from the International Institute for Management Development (IMD) in Lausanne, Switzerland, discuss the challenges faced by global teams and provide some great ideas on how to overcome them (DiStefano & Maznevski, 2000).

The authors emphasise the tremendous value to be had from collaborating with people from different cultural and geographic backgrounds. They suggest that diverse teams can bring together different ideas, pools of knowledge and approaches to work, making the most of the power of cognitive diversity. However, the authors explain, the reality is that cross-cultural teams are often terrible and frequently underperform when compared with homogenous teams. In practice, global teams often fail to deliver the expected value due to conflicts and/or inaction.

The authors identify three types of cross-cultural teams:

- **Creators** are high-performing teams that fully exploit diversity to create new ideas and solutions. They are able to identify and proactively use the individual strengths of each team member to create something new that would not have been possible without their diverse perspectives. Creators are able to manage conflicts effectively and encourage open communication among team members.
- **Equalisers** are teams that manage diversity well but do not necessarily create new value. Equaliser teams tend to deny any difference and assert that, 'We are all the same, we are all equal.' While this is true ethically and morally, in terms of skills and ability it isn't true. They tend to agree on a set of norms for everyone without much anguish, often using the norms of the majority or dominant group. Equaliser teams may be successful in managing diversity, in a way that minimises conflict, but they fail to reap the benefits of the diversity to create something new.
- **Destroyers** are teams that struggle with diversity and often fail to achieve their goals. Destroyer teams tend to dismiss or ridicule each other's norms, leading members on the receiving end to withdraw from the interaction. Destroyer teams are generally paralysed into inaction or worse due to conflicts arising from cultural differences. They spend most of their time arguing about their differences rather than creating value.

DiStefano and Maznevski suggest that organisations should strive to develop creator teams by leveraging diversity effectively. This can be achieved by following the Map, Bridge, Integrate principles they describe in the paper. These principles guide team interactions and help team members make the most of their differences to create new value. They are designed to help diverse, cross-cultural teams become creators by effectively managing diversity. Here's how the principles work in action:

- **Mapping** involves describing the differences among team members in objective, measurable ways. This means identifying the strengths and weaknesses of each team member and understanding how these differences can be used to create something new. By mapping their differences, team members can gain a better understanding of each other's perspectives and identify areas where they can complement each other.
- **Bridging** involves communicating in ways that explicitly take differences into account. This means acknowledging cultural differences and finding ways to bridge them through open communication, active listening and empathy. By bridging cultural differences, team members can build trust and create a more inclusive environment where everyone feels valued. The team can identify how cultural differences may impact communication and work-style preferences. For example, a team member from the United States may prefer direct communication, while a team member from Japan may prefer a more indirect communication style. By understanding these cultural differences, the team can adjust their communication style to ensure that everyone feels heard and understood.
- **Integrate (Integrating)** involves creating team-level ideas by carefully monitoring participation patterns, resolving disagreements and creating new perspectives. This means encouraging all team members to contribute equally while also managing conflicts effectively. By integrating diverse perspectives into the decision-making process, teams can create something new that would not have been possible without their diverse perspectives.

The Map, Bridge, Integrate principles are not a one-off event but rather an ongoing process that requires hard work and commitment from all team members.

DiStefano and Maznevski's paper has significant implications for hybrid teams.

I began this chapter by writing about the importance of effective communication in high-performance teams. When team members are in different time zones or have different cultural backgrounds, hybrid teams face unique challenges. The BRIDGE principle emphasises the importance of communicating in ways that explicitly take these cultural differences into account, as well as spending time bridging them through active listening, open dialogue and empathy.

Another implication of the paper for hybrid teams is the importance of integrating diversity, primarily through active participation pattern management. It can be difficult to ensure that all team members have an equal opportunity to participate in hybrid teams due to practical issues such as time zone differences and the awkwardness of Zoom or Teams calls in aspects such as not seeing body language and facial expressions that clearly. However, hybrid teams can effectively use diversity and create new value by actively managing participation patterns and ensuring that all team members have an equal voice. Quiet, shy people, for example (or people from a culture that values deference) should be gently encouraged to speak, while the loud extroverts should be gently encouraged to make space for the quieter members of the team.

Google implemented this value of diversity and giving everyone on the team a voice in their Project Aristotle research. Project Aristotle was the codename for Google's investigation into why some teams performed better than others. The Project Aristotle researchers discovered, like Amy Edmondson, that psychological safety was by far the most important factor driving success. Charles Duhigg described this phenomenon in the *New York Times*:

> Individuals on teams with higher psychological safety are less likely to leave Google, they're more likely to harness the power of diverse ideas from their teammates, they bring in more revenue, and they're rated as effective twice as often by executives.
>
> (Duhigg, 2016)

Creating a culture of psychological safety is difficult and messy and is beyond the scope of this book. However, in his book on cognitive diversity, *Rebel Ideas*, Matthew Syed describes two easy-to-implement techniques that help to introduce psychological safety in an organisation.

Although not specific to hybrid teams, these techniques can easily be adapted to help build 'creator' diverse teams.

Brainwriting

Brainwriting is a way of actively managing participation and generating creative ideas. It's different from its older sibling brainstorming, because instead of presenting your ideas verbally, out loud, I would ask you to write them down on cards and then post them on a wall for the rest of the group to vote on.

This works well for two reasons. First, everyone gets a chance to contribute (equal contribution is one of the key factors in psychological safety) no matter how shy they might be. The organisation gains access to the thinking of everyone in the team, not just one or two more extroverted, confident people.

The second advantage of brainwriting is that status and authority are detached from the ideas. The golden rule of brainwriting is that nobody may identify themselves on their idea card – no matter how subtly they might do this. Nobody can use a job title, hints or distinctive handwriting to identify themselves (block capitals only, please). This is important because by doing this you separate the idea from the status of the person who came up with it. People vote on the quality of the proposal, rather than the seniority of the person who suggested it. In *Rebel Ideas*, Matthew Syed writes:

> When brainwriting is put head to head with brainstorming, it generates twice the volume of ideas, and also produces higher quality ideas when rated by independent assessors. The reason is simple. Brainwriting liberates diversity from the constraints of dominance dynamic.
>
> (Syed, 2019)

Questions to reflect on

- How would you rate your organization's communication effectiveness and efficiency? Give your organisation a grade from 0 (poor) to 5 (great).
- What made you give that grade? Identify three factors.
- What three things could you do to improve communication?
- What opportunities are there in your organisation for 'collisions' (informal social interactions)? How much 'birdsong' is there in your organisation?
- Is your organisation over-reliant on technology for communication? If so, in what way?
- How do your typical online meetings feel? Give this a grade from 0 (draining/exhausting) to 5 (inspiring).
- How might the idea of 'bursty communication' work in your organisation?
- Do people in your organisation have enough time for deep work?
- In your organisation, do you prioritise getting the work done or attending online meetings?

- How could you use the Map, Bridge, Integrate principles to improve performance in your organisation?

Key points

- Communication is one of the most important factors in a high-performance organisation.
- Hybrid working presents an enormous obstacle to good-enough organisational communication.
- Collisions (unplanned spontaneous social interactions) are vital in building a high-performance, psychologically safe and innovative culture.
- Zoom meetings can be improved by using them to communicate in short, intense bursts of communication rather than long, drawn-out traditional meetings.
- It is much harder to get the most out of cognitive diversity in hybrid organisations. To maximise the performance of diverse, cross-cultural teams, it is critical to explicitly acknowledge the diversity, make an effort to adapt to different communication styles and manage the team so that individual talents are maximised.

Note

1 I'm using the term Zoom as shorthand for generic teleconferencing.

References

DiStefano, J. J. & Maznevski, M. L. (2000). 'Creating Value with Diverse Teams in Global Management'. *Organizational Dynamics*, 29 (1), 45–63.
Duhigg, C. (2016). 'What Google Learned from Its Quest to Build the Perfect Team'. *The New York Times Magazine*, 26.
Edmondson, A. C. (2019). *The Fearless Organization: Creating Psychological Safety in the Workplace for Learning, Innovation, and Growth*. New York: Wiley.
Elkind, P. & McLean, B. (2004). *The Smartest Guys in the Room: The Amazing Rise and Scandalous Fall of Enron*. London: Penguin.
Hobsbawm, J. (2022). *The Nowhere Office: Reinventing Work and the Workplace of the Future*. London: Hachette UK.
Hsieh, T. (2010). *Delivering Happiness: A Path to Profits, Passion and Purpose*. New York: Grand Central Publishing.
Newport, C. (2016). *Deep Work: Rules for Focused Success in a Distracted World* (1st ed.). London: Piatkus.
Riedl, C. & Woolley, A. W. (2020). 'Successful Remote Teams Communicate in Bursts'. *Harvard Business Review*, 28 October. https://hbr.org/2020/10/successful-remote-teams-communicate-in-bursts.

Schein, E. H. (1984). 'Coming to a New Awareness of Organizational Culture'. *MIT Sloan Management Review*, Winter. https://sloanreview.mit.edu/article/coming-to-a-new-awareness-of-organizational-culture.

Schein, E. H. (1990). 'Organizational Culture'. *American Psychologist*, 45 (2), 109–119.

Sorkin, A. R. (2010). *Too Big to Fail: Inside the Battle to Save Wall Street* (1st ed.). London: Penguin.

Syed, M. (2019). *Rebel Ideas: The Power of Diverse Thinking*. London: John Murray.

5 Evolving Workplaces and Hybrid Organisations

Michael Drayton

We all have a tendency to see only what's in front of us. We arrive at the office and get on with whatever we are doing. We make the unthinking assumption that things have always been like this and will be the same forever. We come into the office every day and just get on with things without giving a second thought to how things used to be or what things might be like in the future.

The pandemic and lockdown put an end to that. If you'd have said to the average leader on New Year's Day 2020 that in three months' time most, maybe all, of their office-based employees would have to work from home, and furthermore, they would have to make that transition in weeks, not months or years, they would have looked at you as if you were insane and laughed. They may have humoured you and said that such a change would be impossible to implement. Yet, it happened. Unimaginable change was implemented in days for some and weeks for others. And amazingly, it all seemed to work out pretty well.

Some of us enjoyed the change and the freedom that working from home brought us. Others hated it and missed the predictability, routine and camaraderie of office life. I think it's safe to say that most people felt unsettled and uncertain of what the future would hold for them. And that was on top of the fear and uncertainty of how the COVID-19 pandemic would turn out.

In the first part of this chapter, I will describe how the office workplace has evolved and changed, often dramatically so, over the years. The office has always been a dynamic place, transforming itself and evolving to accommodate new economic demands, new technology, changing social norms and, of course, the changing needs of the workforce. If you were to compare an office in 1960 with an office in 2020, they would be completely different. In the 1960 office, you would see actual separate offices with doors rather than the open-plan design of the 2020 office. Computers have replaced the typewriter and the typing pool. People in the 1960 office were far more formal in their dress, manners and speech.

However, one thing *hasn't* changed over the years. If you take away all the desks, technology and fashion, you are left with people –

DOI: 10.4324/9781003387602-5

a group of human beings coming together to make something. The form of the office and the form of work change; for example, technology keeps evolving. But the essence remains the same – human beings with their aspirations, fears and a need for relationships. The ability of leaders to understand and develop this aspect of the hybrid workplace will be the focus of the rest of the chapter.

And it's this human factor that working from home disrupts. It gets in the way of people forming attachments, and it's these attachments that form a net that provides support for employees and the context that adds value to the organisation. People bump into each other ('collide'), help each other solve problems, and come up with new, innovative ideas. They form into a group that identifies with the organisation. It's hard to have these informal and often spontaneous interactions over a Zoom call.

Another big difference between the old 'nine-to-five' office work and hybrid work is that hybrid working has a significant impact on home and work life. Along with the interpersonal challenges associated with leading a hybrid organisation, there are more practical challenges, such as how best to manage the workflow and task allocation when some people are in the office and others are at home.

In leadership, there's nothing new under the sun, because leaders and their organisations have been through similar dramatic changes in the past. For example, look at the massive changes in organisational life brought about by the development and introduction of the personal computer. The disruption to old ways of working was dramatic in the 1980s. Computers revolutionised every aspect of work, arguably as much as hybrid working has. You could also say the same about the invention of the typewriter at the end of the nineteenth century.

Like the River Thames flowing through the City of London, the office environment is always in motion, adapting and changing to suit the landscape and in turn modifying that landscape. Back in 1943, Winston Churchill said, 'We shape our buildings and they shape us.' We have been pushed into hybrid working and hybrid working is dramatically shaping every aspect of organisational life.

The history of the office: *Mad Men*, Bürolandschaft and the gig economy

Our workspaces have undergone remarkable transformations over the decades, from the glitzy offices of 1960s Madison Avenue to the innovative layouts inspired by German 'Bürolandschaft'. These shifts, influenced by cultural, technological and social changes, have shaped the very essence of the office. We will trace the path that led us to modern office designs and the rise of remote work as we delve deeper into this investigation. Join us in understanding the intricacies and driving forces behind these evolutions.

Mad Men: Office life in mid-1960s Manhattan

A smoky haze fills the boardroom of Sterling Cooper. Don Draper leans back in his chair and stretches before taking a sip of whisky from his crystal highball tumbler. He is dressed in a tailored navy-blue Brooks Brothers suit, a crisp white shirt, and a narrow, black knitted tie. Don is the embodiment of the Madison Avenue advertising executive – the ad man. At the far end of the room, silver-haired Roger Sterling, one of the agency's partners, takes a long drag on his cigarette before downing his own glass of whisky in one. He refills his glass from the bottle on the drinks trolley in the boardroom and proposes a toast. 'Don, you did it again, buddy,' he says, in celebration of Don's successful pitch to Pan Am. The door is open and the clacking of the latest IBM Selectric typewriters can be heard coming from the large Sterling Cooper typing pool. Don is exhausted and he wanders back to his corner office, with its picture windows overlooking the skyscrapers of Manhattan. He loosens his tie and lies down on the sofa in his office for a nap.

This is a made-up scene based on the popular American TV series *Mad Men*. The show is set in the 1960s and follows the lives of advertising executives, particularly Don Draper and others who work for the fictional advertising agency Sterling Cooper, situated on New York's Madison Avenue (hence, 'Mad' Men). The programme is a brilliant and evocative depiction of office life in 1960s America. It provides a lens into the past, showing us how US corporate culture, social norms and interpersonal dynamics have changed over time.

The strangeness of *Mad Men* is one of the reasons it is so fascinating and entertaining. It seems almost unbelievable that such a place ever existed. Its glamour and fashions, as well as the heavy drinking and smoking at work and misogyny, appear exotic and appealing as well as repulsive. Of course, for Don Draper and his colleagues, it is just normal – that is how things were in the 1960s. If we put Don in a time machine and transported him to the year 2001 and the world of Ricky Gervais's *The Office*, he would probably find it equally strange and would need a stiff drink.

If we go deeper than the entertainment value of *Mad Men*, what does it tell us about the evolution of the office workplace?

One of the fun aspects of *Mad Men* is admiring the cool 1960s fashion. Formal office attire played a big role in the 1960s. Men were expected to wear suits and ties, while women wore dresses and skirts. Today's office dress codes have become a lot more relaxed. You could turn up today for your job as a civil servant not in a bowler hat and carrying a furled brolly but wearing a Def Leppard hoodie and Levi 501 jeans.

The clothes in *Mad Men* are also a symbol of the rigid hierarchical structure of 1960s office life. There was a clear delineation of responsibilities and authority. Today, most organisations have adopted a far flatter organisational structure and work at promoting collaboration and open communication.

One of the less pleasant aspects of 1960s working life as depicted in *Mad Men* is the appalling way that women are treated at Sterling Cooper. *Mad Men* shows vividly the rigid and stereotypical gender roles of the 1960s. In the programme, women are shown in mainly admin and secretarial roles, while the male characters do the interesting, glamorous stuff. The female characters are routinely sexually harassed and expected to accept this without complaint. This is shocking in the light of changing social attitudes (for instance, the #MeToo movement) and legal protection against harassment and discrimination.

Finally, the office technology in *Mad Men* is fascinating. Don Draper lived in a world of rolodexes, typewriters and fax machines. They didn't have mobile phones, but phones that were tethered by a line and operated via a dial not a screen. It would be inconceivable for an office to function without computers, email and smartphones.

Superficially, Sterling Cooper looks like a fun place to work, and the clothes are nice. But would you really want to work in that smoky atmosphere and the culture of misogyny of the 1960s? Probably not.

Bürolandschaft and the birth of the open-plan office

Towards the end of the 1960s, Don Draper would have likely witnessed the move towards open-plan offices. A move that no doubt would have horrified him.

The idea of open-plan offices originated in Germany in the years following the end of the Second World War (Kaufmann-Buhler, 2021). The aim was to foster a more collaborative and egalitarian workplace environment as a reaction against the authoritarianism of the Third Reich. By removing physical barriers (such as individual offices) in the office, the Bürolandschaft model (which translates as 'office environment') aimed to promote teamwork, creativity and innovation by encouraging face-to-face communication, not unlike Tony Hsieh's idea of encouraging 'collisions', mentioned in Chapter 4. Like many new ideas, Bürolandschaft was born from good intentions and had its positives and negatives. It did indeed encourage collaboration; but this was 1950s Germany and the prevailing culture was still rather rigid and hierarchical, with many feeling that too much collaboration and creativity was a distraction from getting things done. Consequently, Bürolandschaft itself began to evolve and change.

Like so many aspects of organisational life, a compromise emerged. This took the form of keeping the open-plan office, but adding cubicles. This was the idea of the designer Robert Propst, whose 'Action Office' concept (Propst, 1966) was an attempt to retain the advantages of the open-plan office while minimising noise and distraction. Cubicle offices, a bit like high-rise tower blocks, were an idea that looked good on paper but didn't work that well in practice. Cubicles soon became synonymous with the anonymity and dehumanisation of work – they became the battery hen cage for office workers. Understandably, the cubicle office gradually fell out of favour and most organisations drifted back to the open-plan model.

The big idea about open-plan offices was that they encourage communication and collaboration; however, anecdotal accounts suggest that in fact the opposite is true – that open-plan offices actually get in the way of collaboration. Researchers Bernstein and Waber (2019) used some hi-tech gear to look deeper into the relationship between open-plan offices and the social dynamics of communication and collaboration. They used cutting-edge wearable devices and data-collection tools to track both physical and digital interactions at the main offices of two top-tier Fortune 500 companies.

The study was structured to compare communication patterns before and after the transition from cubicles to an open office environment. The researchers chose workplaces that represented different industries, and carried out their observations once employees had adapted to their new environment. The results were striking as well as counterintuitive. Rather than enabling face-to-face interactions, the data clearly showed that following the transition to open-plan offices, face-to-face interactions decreased by about 70 per cent. In contrast, electronic interactions such as email and messaging increased in order to compensate for this decline in personal communication.

This is really interesting and confirms the personal experience I had years ago. I was working with an engineering company, and I noticed that people, mainly engineers, who were based in a big open-plan office seemed to prefer sending an email to a colleague who was perhaps ten yards away to actually wandering over to their desk and speaking to them.

How can you explain this? The researchers discussed the work of an eighteenth-century philosopher, Denis Diderot, as a possible explanation for the strange and counterintuitive phenomenon. Diderot was discussing theatre and came up with the concept of the fourth wall. He suggested that performers should imagine an invisible barrier separating them from the audience during a theatrical performance. This would allow them to focus solely on their role and block out distractions. In a similar way, people in open-plan offices create a metaphorical fourth wall, which their colleagues respect. If someone is deeply engrossed in their work, others avoid interrupting them. If someone attempts to start a conversation and receives an annoyed look from a colleague, they are less likely to do it again. In open-plan offices, these fourth-wall norms quickly spread among employees.

The office and the gig economy

The evolution of the office took a whole new turn in the early 2000s with the emergence and then explosive rise of the gig economy. This is where people take on short-term tasks or 'gigs' rather than traditional, long-term roles. They found work through apps like Uber, Airbnb or TaskRabbit, enjoying the flexibility to choose when and where they work. This approach offers a sense of freedom, but it doesn't come without its drawbacks. Unlike regular employment, gig workers often miss out on benefits like sick pay and paid holidays. There's less job security. It's a blend of flexibility and unpredictability.

Despite the uncertainty of the gig economy, some employees began to reject the tyranny of the office nine-to-five. Technology, particularly rapidly expanding internet and cloud technology, has made it relatively easy to carry out many jobs from anywhere without the need for a formal office. Tim Ferriss's (2011) best-selling book *The 4-Hour Work Week: Escape the 9–5, Live Anywhere, and Join the New Rich* expressed this new attitude and approach to work. Ferris became a millennial celebrity by claiming that anyone with a laptop and an internet connection could travel the world while earning a good living.

People suddenly realised they could freelance and work from home, a coffee shop or one of the shared office spaces that sprouted up to meet the needs of this growing tribe of gig economy freelancers. Coworking spaces like WeWork and Regus grew in popularity because they allowed people to work in a friendly environment with fast internet and other people to chat with, and if they needed a private meeting room, they could book one by the hour. For a few years, I worked out of a coworking space in London, which was fantastic. For a very reasonable membership fee, it provided me with a quiet place to work and meet people in central London, as well as good-quality coffee on tap. This is another example of how the workplace adapts to changing demands and reflects the changing nature of work.

The office as a symbol

The psychoanalyst Carl Jung wrote that symbols are a foundational component of the human psyche (Jung, 1956). By 'symbol', he meant something that stands for or represents something else. For example, a flag is a symbol for a country. When we see the Union Jack, we immediately think about Great Britain, its values, culture and history.

Jung believed that our brains use symbols to make sense of things and to communicate ideas or feelings. We don't just use symbols for personal understanding, but also to share ideas with others. Symbols are how we transmit personal and collective meaning.

Let's take an example. Think of the symbol of a heart. For most of us, a heart symbol usually represents love. When you draw a heart symbol on a card for your friend, your friend understands it as an expression of your love or friendship. It has a personal as well as a collective meaning. Most people associate a heart with love, hence the idea of a collective meaning. For instance, every year on Valentine's Day, heart symbols are seen everywhere, from cards to decorations, symbolising a universal, or collective, expression of love.

Symbols like these play an important role in helping us understand and express our individual and shared feelings or ideas about work and our workplace.

The office exists in two places. There's the external real-world office – the bricks and mortar of the building, the tables and computers and so on. There is also the office that exists inside our heads – the symbolic office; the office plus the meanings and emotions that we attach to the office. The office exists as a tangible external reality and also as an intangible internal psychological symbol of something else.

For some the office symbolises stability, for others a prison. For many it symbolises a kind of family and a place to belong. For some it's a place to make relationships and find support and reassurance of one's worth. For some lucky people it's a symbol of meaning, purpose and creativity. In short, the office means different things to different people.

Life within the office is also rich with symbolism. I remember years ago I had a friend who was a civil servant. She told me she had been promoted and had to temporarily move out of her office while the estates department replaced her perfectly good grey cord carpet because people of her recently acquired grade were entitled to plusher navy-blue carpet.

It isn't only the practicalities that trigger anxiety about hybrid working, it's also the emotional consequences of disrupting the deep-seated symbolic meanings that are attached to the office workplace – attached to the practicalities. By recognising and understanding the symbolic associations we can better address the psychological and emotional needs of the workforce during the upheaval of the transition to the hybrid organisation.

Most times we don't perceive reality (particularly other people) as it really is. We project on to reality meanings derived partly from our own past experiences and partly from the culture in which we grew up and now live. For example, if you are a manager, you may find that one of your direct reports behaves towards you in a very deferential and respectful manner – as if you are the font of all wisdom. At the same time, a different employee seems to react to you in a slightly sullen and hostile manner – like you are about to tell them off at any moment.

What's interesting is that these different reactions are independent of your actual behaviour. It's like each employee sees you as being a completely different person, and both perceptions are different to how you see yourself. You have been transformed into a symbol by these two employees – probably a symbol that represents authority. Maybe the first person had good experiences of authority figures as they grew up. For them, authority symbolises kindness and support. The second employee may have experienced a punitive and unfair authority figure who would wield their authority capriciously. For them, authority symbolises unfairness and unpredictability. Unfortunately, you, as the figure that symbolises authority in the organisation, attract these projections. You have become a symbol of authority.

When I trained as a clinical psychologist, a wise supervisor said something I've always remembered. He urged caution whenever a patient asks, 'Do you believe in God?' When I asked why, he said, 'Because you don't know if the God they are asking about is a kind, loving and forgiving God, or a harsh, vengeful and punishing God.' The office can be a bit like that: for some it's a nice place, for others a prison.

Symbols, according to Jung, serve as a link between our rational conscious mind and our often irrational unconscious mind. For example, our unconscious feelings about the nature of work, or what our work symbolises, will usually manifest themselves in very practical and observable ways.

When I worked in the National Health Service (NHS), it struck me that certain hospital departments, although important, were associated with (were symbols of) unpleasant feelings such as fear and shame – for example, the mortuary or the sexually transmitted diseases clinic. Interestingly, these departments were usually tucked away at the back of the hospital, well out of sight. They became symbols of the emotions associated with their functions – fear and shame. Just as we often tend to push such feelings to the back of our mind, the hospital pushes the departments that symbolise them to the back of the hospital. In short, a mortuary has a real-world rational existence as well as a much deeper unconscious symbolic existence.

According to Jung, symbols help us access these deeper layers of our psyche, to reveal patterns and meanings that would otherwise remain hidden. Thinking about the symbolic nature of organisations will help you understand why one of your employees responds to you as if you are a critical tyrant (when you are not) and why your compliance department is located in a different building two miles from the corporate HQ.

The symbolic meaning of hybrid working

There is a practical external reality to the hybrid organisation as well as a deeper symbolic meaning. For example, 'working from home' is a symbol of freedom, autonomy and trust for Jane; but for Jacob, it symbolises exclusion, abandonment and loneliness. The same experience but different meanings. And of course it is the meaning and associated feeling that will drive behaviour. It will determine the level of engagement, performance and creativity.

What this means to the busy leader is that when you are considering the move to permanent hybrid working, you will need to give thought to both the practicalities and the deeper symbolic meaning of those practicalities if you want to get the most from your employees. Your new structure has to symbolise autonomy and freedom at one end of the continuum, and belonging and security at the other. This isn't as difficult or complex as it might sound (it is difficult and complex, but not impossibly so).

Hybrid working is more than just a logistical rearrangement; it's a paradigm shift in organizational culture and values. Recognising the symbolic underpinnings of such a working model is critical. While logistics such as furniture, IT infrastructure and protocols are important, the workforce's mindset and emotional perceptions are the foundation of this transformation. The delicate balance between autonomy and belongingness will determine whether or not this transition is successful. For many leaders, the challenge is not only reorganising the physical workspace, but also addressing and nurturing their employees' psychological spaces. Before diving into the tangible aspects of change, it's essential to first understand and address the intangible, deeply personal interpretations of what the hybrid workplace symbolises for each individual. Only by aligning the external environment with internal expectations can a smooth and effective transition to a hybrid working model be achieved.

Making the change

Essentially, your task is to transform the external tangible office organisation and workflow in a manner that takes into account your employees' internal, psychological and symbolic representation of the office. As well as changing the office furniture, IT systems and workflow, you have to change your employees' mindset.

Let's consider an example. Imagine you have an employee named Sophie. For her, working from home has been great. She is a very conscientious person, meaning she works hard and is very organised. Consequently, she gets things done and still finds time to prepare a nice healthy lunch every day and manage a three-kilometre run around her local park on most days. She also puts the two hours a day she has saved on commuting to good use by pursuing her hobby of forex trading (which she learnt during lockdown and brings in a tidy second income).

For Sophie, working from home symbolises freedom and autonomy. For Sophie, having to return to the office for two days a week symbolises bureaucratic stupidity; just doing something for the sake of it, rather than with any real purpose or good reason. When she is having a bad day, it also symbolises bullying (Sophie was bullied as a child); the raw exercise of malicious power. In fact, Sophie has become, of late, a very active, articulate and at times forceful opponent of your gentle campaign to get people back into the office on Tuesdays and Wednesdays. Sophie has been informally elected as the representative of this resistance to change. She has evolved into what one of your older colleagues dismissively describes as 'our own little barrack room lawyer'. For you, although you would not dream of saying this publicly, she has become a right pain in the neck. You have discussed the issues with Sophie and explained the reasons for getting everyone back to the office for a couple of days a week. You've told her all about Tony Hsieh and 'collisions', but she just rolls her eyes and says things like, 'Did you read that in the *Harvard Business Review*?' You find Sophie to be hard work.

But wait a minute! Before you dismiss Sophie completely, perhaps you could learn something from her. Perhaps there is some truth to what she is saying. Perhaps the obstacles she is erecting contain the germ of a solution. Maybe if you listened to her carefully . . . That is what you decide to do. You sit down with Sophie, resolving to keep your mouth shut and pay close attention to what she says. The meeting goes exceptionally well: Sophie feels heard and respected, and you learn a lot.

After the meeting, you sit down quietly to review the bullet-point notes you made during your conversation with Sophie. These are the headlines:

- *'What's the point of traipsing into the office to do stuff that can be done equally well at home?'*
- *'I don't get as much done in the office because of the constant interruptions.'*
- *'Coming into the office is bad for my health because I don't get as much time to exercise or prepare a healthy lunch.'*

Your notes go on to say that once Sophie had vented her complaints, she went on to talk about what she missed about coming into the office:

- *'I miss the people. I miss having the opportunity to talk over ideas that I'm unsure about – just the informal chats.'*
- *'I miss the social side of work – having lunch with my friends. I can sometimes feel a bit lonely at home.'*
- *'I miss the energy of work – just the buzz of the office.'*

What can you learn from Sophie's ideas that you could apply to make the return to the office on Tuesdays and Wednesdays a bit easier for her, but also for the whole team?

When you began to dig a little deeper and listened hard, you discovered that Sophie actually had two contradictory symbols of the office. The first one, which you already knew about, was the office representing the opposite of freedom. However, as she carried on speaking, and thinking, a new symbol began to emerge: that of the office as a friendly place, a forum for the exchange of ideas and a place that alleviates loneliness.

Furthermore, Sophie's argument that coming into the office to do work that can be done just as easily at home makes a lot of sense. This also ties in with her idea that some tasks are actually harder to perform in the office because the office can be a big source of interruptions.

Now, how can your 'return to the office' plan take into account the symbolic representations of the office that you've identified? Here are two simple ideas:

- Collaborate with team members to divide up work tasks into two broad groups: those that need focus and concentration, and those that need discussion and brainstorming. The tasks that benefit from quiet can be done at home, and the tasks that need social energy can be saved for the office.
- If one of the secondary (but nonetheless important) tasks of getting people back to the office is encouraging 'collisions', exchanging information and building a sense of belonging and social capital, then actively work to maximise this. Organise and pay for office lunches. Put good coffee machines at strategic places, where people gather in the office. Organise an afternoon walking group to further encourage communication as well as keeping the energy levels up.

These are just a couple of ideas based on a conversation with one person (Sophie). Although they are simple ideas, they embody a different philosophy and a different way of thinking about the structure and function of the office.

This new way of thinking about how you will use the office to improve performance involves understanding and changing the symbols associated with the office as well as changing the furniture. It involves changing the office inside people's heads as well as the office in reality.

Work tasks, psychological energy and the enabling environment

What type of environment will either help or hinder your employees' ability to perform tasks? In a hybrid model, the impact of the work environment on task execution becomes even more pronounced. Each location, the office or home, comes with its own set of advantages and disadvantages.

Let's take market research as an example. The quiet and controlled environment of home is an ideal setting for deep data analysis and report writing. On the other hand, when the same team needs to discuss their findings and strategise, an office setting will be more beneficial. The collaborative energy of an office space encourages livelier and more dynamic discussions and brainstorming. This energy is a lot harder to achieve remotely.

Similarly, while designing a new marketing campaign, initial brainstorming sessions will probably benefit from the direct interaction and creative energy that an office environment provides. But the actual creation and implementation of the campaign elements could be done more effectively at home, where the individual team members can focus without interruption.

How can you determine, in a systematic way, which tasks are aided or hampered by working from home or in the office? The steps below will assist you in creating a hybrid task-allocation table that you can modify and use as a template for your organisation.

Step 1: Identifying tasks

- The first step involves creating a comprehensive list of all the tasks that need to be performed within the organisation. This list should cover routine tasks, project-specific assignments and strategic responsibilities. By identifying these tasks, the organisation ensures that it has a clear understanding of the various activities required to compete effectively in the marketplace. For example, in a software development company, tasks could include coding, testing, documentation and project management.
- To illustrate this step, let's consider a fictional company called TechSolutions. The senior leadership team (SLT) at TechSolutions

decide to implement the hybrid working task-allocation system. They begin by conducting a thorough analysis of their operations and compiling a list of all the tasks that are integral to the organisation's success. This includes tasks such as software development, customer support, marketing campaigns, financial management and product research.

Step 2: Understanding required skills

- Once the tasks have been identified, the next step is to determine the specific skills and competencies needed to perform each task successfully.
- Continuing with our example, the SLT at TechSolutions proceed to analyse the skill requirements for each task on their list. They recognise that software development tasks require expertise in programming languages, problem-solving abilities and an understanding of software architecture. These kinds of tasks need focus and concentration and are usually carried out alone. On the other hand, marketing campaigns require skills in market research, copywriting and social media management. Doing these tasks effectively requires brainstorming and lots of discussion. By clearly outlining the skills required for each task, TechSolutions can identify the core tasks that keep the business successful and the core tasks that will have to be allocated to either office or home.

Step 3: Matching task to environment

- The final step in the hybrid-working task-allocation system is to match each task to the most suitable environment based on its nature and skill requirements. Certain tasks are clearly better suited for individual work, while others benefit from collaborative team-based approaches. The goal is to ensure that tasks are performed in an environment that maximises productivity and efficiency.

Returning to our example, TechSolutions evaluate each task on their list and consider the nature of the work involved. They determine that software development tasks generally require focused concentration and individual workspaces, because the distractions of an open-plan office hinder progress. Conversely, marketing campaigns may benefit from a more open and collaborative environment, encouraging conversations, creativity and idea-sharing among team members. By carefully considering the nature of each task and its skill requirements, TechSolutions determine the most suitable working environment for optimal task execution – office or home.

Table 5.1 Task allocation in the hybrid organisation.

Task	Required Skills	Best Environment	Rationale
Comprehensive market research	Research methodologies, analytical thinking, data interpretation, written communication	Remote for analysis and report writing; office for discussion of insights	The controlled environment at home is ideal for deep analysis and concentrated writing, while the office encourages better discussion and collaboration for insights.
Developing a new marketing campaign	Creativity, understanding of consumer behaviour, expertise in various marketing channels, collaboration	Office for brainstorming and initial planning; remote for campaign execution	The direct interaction and creative energy in the office are ideal for brainstorming, while remote work allows for focused execution without interruption.
Financial reporting	Detail-oriented, proficiency in financial software, strong numerical skills, data analysis, written communication	Remote	Financial reporting requires a high level of concentration and attention to detail, which can be effectively achieved in a quiet home environment.
Project management	Leadership, problem-solving, communication, collaboration, time management	Both	Remote work allows for individual tasks to be carried out efficiently, while office work enables better coordination and relationship-building in the team.
Customer service	Interpersonal skills, problem-solving, patience, product knowledge, communication	Office	Direct interaction with team members can aid in problem-solving and enable quicker response times. The office environment also provides immediate support if needed.

Questions to reflect on

- How has the culture of my organisation changed and evolved since the onset of the pandemic and the implementation of lockdown? Are these changes enhancing the effectiveness and cohesion of the team, or are they creating challenges that I need to address?
- What does hybrid working symbolise for me? How might this affect my leadership style?
- How can I recognise and integrate the symbolic nature of work in task allocation to foster a deeper sense of purpose and engagement among team members in a hybrid work setting?
- How can I best distribute tasks to maximise productivity, taking into consideration the varying attributes/strengths/weaknesses of the home and office workspace?
- How can I adapt my leadership style and task-delegation methods to foster a sense of trust and autonomy in my team, supporting their work in both home and office environments?
- How can I encourage open communication and collaboration in my team, ensuring that tasks are well understood and effectively executed regardless of where team members are located?

Key points

- Offices have dramatically transformed from separate rooms in the 1960s to open-plan designs in recent decades, influenced by technological progress, societal changes and workforce needs. However, the essence of human collaboration and interaction remains constant.
- The COVID-19 pandemic forced a shift to working from home and a hybrid work model. This triggered a re-evaluation of office effectiveness.
- Employees increasingly demand the ability to work from home, appreciating benefits such as reduced commuting time, increased flexibility and improved work–life balance.
- Hybrid organisations need to foster a culture of trust and autonomy, provide the necessary tools and resources, and encourage regular communication and collaboration among employees regardless of their work location.

References

Bernstein, E. & Waber, B. (2019). 'The Truth about Open Offices'. *Harvard Business Review*, 1 November. https://hbr.org/2019/11/the-truth-about-open-offices.

Ferriss, T. (2011). *The 4-Hour Work Week: Escape the 9–5, Live Anywhere and Join the New Rich*. New York: Random House.

Jung, C. G. (1956). *The Collected Works of C. G. Jung: Symbols of Transformation* (Volume 5) G. Adler, M. Fordham & S. H. Read (eds.); R. F. C. Hull, trans.; 1st ed. Abingdon: Routledge.

Kaufmann-Buhler, J. (2021). *Open Plan: A Design History of the American Office (Cultural Histories of Design)*. London: Bloomsbury Visual Arts.

Propst, R. L. (1966). 'The Action Office'. *Human Factors*, 8 (4), 299–306. https://doi.org/10.1177/001872086600800405.

6 Security in the Hybrid Organisation

Elsine van Os

The value of any organisation is contained in two key places: its data and its people. Most data is stored digitally as well as in people's heads. This data is very valuable to other people; to competitors, to organised crime and to others, like government agencies. Protecting valuable classified commercial data has become much more difficult now that many organisations are hybrid, with many employees now interacting with data from home. Statistics are concerning. Year on year, the number of insider-driven data exposure, loss, leak and theft events increases 32 per cent on average and the move to hybrid working is an important cause of this (Code 42, 2003).

Let us begin with an example. In January 2021, two employees working at the call centre of the Dutch Municipal Health Service (GGD) were arrested for selling personal data obtained from the GGD systems used for COVID-19 testing, including addresses, phone numbers, email addresses and citizen service numbers (NOS, 2021). The employees misused their authorised access to the GGD systems and extracted a large amount of personal data. The stolen data was then sold on various online platforms, including chat services like Telegram, Snapchat and Wickr.

Mourad, who was studying commercial economics at the time, described his actions as 'very stupid and naive', saying that he mainly wanted to earn some extra money by selling the personal data. Amin, on the other hand, had illegally looked up and shared data but did not sell it. Amin claimed that he did not think he was doing anything wrong and that they often looked up test results of friends and acquaintances. According to him, the GGD had never explicitly stated that he could not search for and share everyone's data. At the time of his arrest in January, Amin was still studying fiscal law at Erasmus University. He had previously been convicted in 2017 for a serious assault, for which he received a community service sentence.

The illegal trade of this sensitive information raised a wide range of concerns, among them concerns about privacy and the need to protect personal data, especially considering the presence of medical information in the compromised systems. It also raised significant questions about how well employers know their employees and the level of

DOI: 10.4324/9781003387602-6

scrutiny they have on them. It highlighted the importance of trust, proper background checks (what did the GGD actually know about Mourad and Amin?) and monitoring systems to ensure the integrity and security of sensitive data. It also raised concerns about the accountability of organisations, including the government, in protecting citizens' confidential information.

It was an exceptional time and context during COVID-19. The GGD had to hire many new team members who had to work remotely. The situation came with unique challenges. However, the challenges of remote work in our hybrid work environment are here to stay and the number of incidents is growing. This incident at the GGD was not an isolated event; rather, it serves as a prominent illustration among many organisations grappling with a new type of threat: ensuring data protection and effectively addressing employee misconduct. As such, it is evident that this incident is not the first of its kind, and nor will it be the last.

To answer the question of how organisations manage security risks we need to dive into history and understand how organisations have managed this in the past. This will be the starting point of this chapter. Thereafter, we will look at the theory behind 'insider risk management', which is the key to managing employee risk in the hybrid organisation. We will review how individuals 'derail' from organisations, using the Critical Pathway to Insider Risk Model. And finally, I will give pointers for insider risk management in general and within the hybrid organisation in particular, using the employee life-cycle framework.

A brief history of organisational security

Security challenges in the workplace have significantly changed over time. Originally, organisations tried to defend themselves from external physical threats like trespassing, vandalism and serious acts like terrorism. This external focus on threats remained with the rise of digitisation but changed from physical to cyber security. Organisations asked themselves how to keep unauthorised individuals from digitally entering the 'property' or in this case the IT infrastructure.

Since the 1990s we have seen a strong rise in attention to cyber security, and understandably so. The rise of the digitisation of information and processes brought new risks and challenges to protect the organisation and its information and processes. For example, it became easier to extract a whole library on a USB stick instead of walking out of an office building with boxes of documentation. The more we became dependent upon IT, the more vulnerable we were as well.

We were fully focused on the big bad outer world, further exacerbated by 9/11, which was seen by the American government as an intelligence failure. The government and intelligence agencies were criticised for their inability to detect and prevent the plot despite warning signs and intelligence reports. Intelligence gaps, failures in information sharing and analysis, and a lack of coordination between various agencies contributed to the failure to prevent the attacks. As a consequence, the government increased its reliance on private contractors to supplement intelligence operations. This expansion aimed to bring in additional expertise and resources to improve intelligence gathering and analysis. Furthermore, there were efforts to enhance data sharing and collaboration among different intelligence agencies and departments. The digital internal gateway was born. A large community was connected on sensitive intelligence manners in order to do their jobs, creating potential new risks.

The story of Chelsea Manning

In 2010, former US Army analyst Bradley, later Chelsea, Manning passed a vast trove of classified military and diplomatic documents to WikiLeaks (United States Army, 2007). This major leak included documents about the wars in Iraq and Afghanistan, and it drew attention worldwide. Some praised her as a whistle-blower, but others criticised her as a threat to national security. Manning was arrested, court-martialled and convicted on multiple charges, including violations of the Espionage Act. She was sentenced to 35 years in prison but had her sentence commuted by President Barack Obama in 2017.

Manning's actions led to lots of discussion about how to protect secret information and make security better in the military and intelligence agencies. In 2011, Obama issued an order, Executive Order 13587, to improve the security of government networks to prevent future leaks. This aimed to allow safe sharing of secret information and improve cybersecurity.

In 2012, a policy was introduced to manage the risks from insiders, setting clear standards. The National Insider Threat Task Force was formed to develop this programme. This marked the start of efforts to handle risks from insiders. The Manning leaks showed how important it is to protect our data, systems and the people who use them, and the impacts such leaks can have on our operations, values, safety, security and reputation. The fact that data can be easily stolen and shared online is frightening. Imagine if your personal emails or chats were leaked for everyone to see.

Insider threat in organisations

In the years after 2012, there was a growth in tension with regards to insider threat in the workplace. The issue of 'bring your own device' (BYOD) emerged with the increasing popularity and prevalence of smartphones and personal mobile devices in the workplace. Employees started using their personal laptops, smartphones and tablets for work-related tasks, blurring the line between personal and professional device usage. The advent of advanced mobile technology coupled with the growing demand for flexibility and productivity prompted organisations to adopt BYOD policies. However, this also brought concerns regarding data security, privacy and the potential for unauthorised access or data breaches.

The use of social media in the same timeframe contributed to further blurring of those lines between professional and personal aspects of individuals' lives. With the widespread adoption of social media platforms such as Facebook, Twitter, LinkedIn and Instagram, people increasingly integrated their personal and professional identities online. This created new challenges for organisations:

- Employees could inadvertently or intentionally share sensitive information about their organisation or job responsibilities on social media platforms.
- Employees who felt disgruntled or had negative sentiments towards their organisation could use social media to vent their frustrations or make damaging statements that harmed the organisation's reputation.
- Employees could misuse social media platforms to transmit sensitive information outside the organisation. This could include sharing classified documents, customer data or intellectual property through direct messaging, file uploads or other means.
- Social media platforms could serve as a vector for distributing malware, which could be used to compromise an organisation's systems or gain unauthorised access. Insiders with access to internal networks could unknowingly or purposefully spread malware through social media interactions in what is often called social engineering attacks. These are attacks by external actors aimed at tricking individuals, often through social media interactions, into actions that benefit attackers or provide them with sensitive data (Salahdine & Kaabouch, 2019). Social engineering has become one of the biggest challenges associated with the use of social media.

The COVID-19 pandemic accelerated existing challenges further blurring the lines between work and personal life. As a result, concerns about the insider threat grew substantially. Here are some of the key factors that contributed to this evolving landscape:

- The physical separation of employees in remote work settings raised concerns over weaker security measures in the home network

on the one hand and reduced direct oversight of employees on the other, potentially emboldening employees to engage in malicious activities with a lower risk of detection.
- Employees were assessed to be more distracted working from home, making them more error prone and capable of unintentionally causing insider incidents (Tessian Research, 2022).
- Remote work posed challenges in monitoring and detecting insider threats, such as unauthorised data exfiltration or misuse of privileges.
- Due to the pandemic, companies hiring staff to work remotely were constrained in terms of being able to get to know their employees. Think back to the GGD incident and the hiring push they had under the new (crisis) circumstances. Who did they actually employ? How much did they know about their own staff? How much *can* you get to know staff in a remote setting?

Research conducted by the Ponemon Institute in 2022 shows a rising trend in the number of security incidents experienced by companies annually. It found that 67 per cent of companies are facing between 21 and 40 or even more incidents each year. This is an increase from previous years: in 2020, 60 per cent of companies reported the same range of incidents, and in 2018, the figure was 53 per cent (Ponemon, 2022). Another study found that 75 per cent of insider-threat criminal prosecutions were the result of remote workers (Dtex, 2022). Against the background of all the developments in recent years, this is understandable, but it's also a very complex subject for organisations to tackle, as demonstrated in the case of Nick Sharp.

The story of Nick Sharp and Ubiquiti

Nick Sharp, a senior software engineer and 'Cloud Lead' at Ubiquiti, an American tech company offering IT products and solutions for remote work, had privileged access to the company's servers from 2018 to 2021 (United States Attorney's Office, 2023; United States District Court, Southern District of New York, n.d.). In December 2020, while interviewing for another job, Nick misused his access to download a significant amount of Ubiquiti's confidential data. He then altered the company's computer systems, changing log retention policies and manipulating file names to shift the blame onto his co-workers.

In January 2021, while working with a team to repair the damage he had caused, Nick sent a ransom note to Ubiquiti. He posed as an anonymous attacker who had illegally accessed the company's networks, demanding 50 Bitcoin (around $1.9 million) for the return of the stolen data and to disclose a system vulnerability. When Ubiquiti declined to pay, Nick leaked some of the stolen files.

In March 2021, the FBI searched Nick's home and confiscated electronic devices, including the laptop he used for data theft. Shortly after, he began spreading false stories about the incident and Ubiquiti's response, claiming to be an anonymous company whistle-blower. He asserted that an unknown individual had hacked the company, gaining administrator access. This misinformation led to Ubiquiti's stocks plunging and a loss of over $4 billion in market value.

As the FBI investigation intensified, Nick attempted to deflect suspicion by falsely implicating his co-workers. He even suggested that his home IP address had been planted to incriminate him. In court, he portrayed himself as a security-minded individual and denied his previous claims of the cyberattack being a security drill. Ultimately, Nick was sentenced to six years in prison and ordered to pay $1.6 million in restitution to Ubiquiti for the damages his actions caused (United States Attorney's Office, 2023).

Were you able to understand the complexity of Nick's story? He created numerous problems within the company, yet his position of trust allowed him to assist in fixing the damage he himself had instigated!

What signs did his co-workers miss about his behaviour? Ubiquiti recruited new employees with the promise of flexible work hours and the opportunity to work from home. Could this have played a role? In any case, the story of Nick Sharp highlights the era we're living in, where elevated access levels and insufficient oversight of employees and systems can lead to massive organisational damage.

What is an insider threat?

'Insider threat' is a broad term, covering a variety of intents and impacts on an organisation. An insider is anyone who has authorised access to an organisation's data, systems, facilities and/or assets. They could be an employee, for example, or a contractor or business partner.

Dtex Systems eloquently describes the distinction between insider risk and insider threat:

> Anyone who has access to sensitive information is an insider risk. Humans are imperfect and make mistakes. Even the most conscientious worker could accidentally email data to the wrong recipient, misplace their computer or have company data stolen from their car. Risk does not imply malicious intent. That is reserved for insider threats – those employees, vendors or partners who plan and execute actions to steal or release data or sabotage corporate systems.
> (Dtex, 2022)

Types of insider threats

There are three distinct types of insider threats: the unintentional, the intentional and the rule breaker. Each category has significant differences in terms of behaviour and impact on an organisation.

The unintentional insider

The unintentional insider threat refers to current or former employees, contractors or business partners who possess or had authorised access to an organisation's network, system, data and other valuable assets that require protection. These individuals inadvertently compromise the confidentiality, integrity or availability of data and systems due to accidents or negligence, without any malicious intent. We all are unintentional insider threats; we should be under no illusions about the fact that we make mistakes. We are all vulnerable to clicking on a phishing email and thereby letting external attackers into our systems, or accidentally sending an email to the wrong email address and disclosing sensitive data to a third party. I mentioned earlier the COVID-specific challenges of the quick move to remote work and the risks this has posed. Especially these accidental or 'unintentional' insider acts have increased since that time.

The intentional insider

The intentional insider threat is the same category of person who has or had authorised access; however, they intentionally surpass or misuse their access in ways that negatively impact the organisation's information confidentiality, integrity or availability.

The coerced insider

Intentional insiders can be self-motivated or coerced. Nick Sharp can be seen as a self-motivated insider. He was a disgruntled employee who sought to conduct a data theft by himself without any outside pressure or help. In some cases, as the demands and risks escalate, what started as self-motivation for insiders who support external actors may transform into coercion, reaching a point of no return. Some intentional insiders, though, were never self-motivated; they were coerced into their actions.

Insiders can be coerced into providing support to various external actors, like organised crime groups or state actors. These actors can exploit and exert pressure on individuals within an organisation to facilitate illicit activities. Insiders may become vulnerable to coercion due to factors such as financial difficulties, personal vulnerabilities, criminal threats or the exploitation of personal relationships.

Advantage can be taken of pre-existing relationships or personal connections in order to manipulate insiders. Actors may leverage family or social ties to coerce compliance with their illicit activities. This form of coercion creates an atmosphere of fear and intimidation, discouraging individuals from reporting or disclosing their involvement in criminal operations.

The logistics sector, for example, which has gone through a big digitisation push, has become a harder target for criminal groups. They now need more insider support to ensure their illicit business continuity. By coercing these insiders, criminals can gain unauthorised access to sensitive cargo data, manipulate supply-chain operations or even orchestrate illicit activities such as smuggling or theft. In 2021 the National Crime Agency (NCA) of the UK alerted furloughed port and airport workers to this very threat and the heightened risk of exploitation by organised crime groups amid the ongoing COVID crisis. The warning specifically highlighted the vulnerability of staff with in-depth knowledge of border controls and processes, emphasising the need for caution as global travel restrictions continued to ease (National Crime Agency, 2021).

The infiltrator

Another type of intentional insider is the infiltrator, who purposefully joins the organisation with the intention of causing harm. Individuals or even groups can infiltrate and establish a presence within an organisation. They may intentionally target roles that provide direct access to their objectives – oftentimes sensitive information. Posing as legitimate employees, they exploit their positions to facilitate their illegitimate activities.

Infiltrators are a rare find. They generally stay below the 'radar'; they're professional liars (they're good at what they do); and it's often hard to uncover whether they entered an organisation with nefarious purposes or whether this evolved over time within the job. They can be the most damaging. Think of an employee who job-hopped from tech company to tech company to steal data for a state actor until it was uncovered by the authorities in this Western country.

The rule breaker

The rule breaker does not harbour an intentional desire to harm the organisation. In fact, they may want to help, not cause harm. However, their behaviour or lack of action inadvertently puts the organisation at risk. For instance, consider an employee who is prohibited from taking work home, yet transfers work files onto a USB stick to continue working on their personal computer at home just to meet a deadline in time, and in doing so they put the security of the organisation's assets at risk. Such an incident actually occurred to an employee at Europol who took confidential work files home on an unprotected hard drive and connected it to the internet by mistake, exposing the files externally (Zeiher, 2016).

Types of insider acts

The harm individuals can bring to an organisation can be categorised into several types of insider acts:

- *Data theft*, the main subject of attention in the hybrid organisation, involves insiders exploiting their access to steal or misuse data, intellectual property or other valuable information from the organisation.
- *Sabotage* involves deliberate actions aimed at undermining or incapacitating an organisation through obstruction or destruction, often using technology.
- *Unauthorised disclosures or media leaks* occur when classified or confidential information is communicated or transferred to unauthorised recipients, potentially causing harm or creating exposure.
- *Workplace violence* refers to intentional physical or psychological violence or threats of violence against individuals or groups within the organisation.
- *Fraud and corruption* involve deceptive acts carried out to gain unlawful benefits, with fraudsters manipulating data for personal gain.
- *Insider trading* involves individuals with non-public information about a company trading its stock or securities, for personal gain.

These insider acts pose significant risks to organisations and can result in financial losses, damage to reputation and compromised security.

The latter three categories of workplace violence, fraud and corruption and insider trading are the traditional categories of concern. The first three categories are primarily data driven and therefore, for reasons mentioned earlier, they are key concerns in this timeframe. But these categories of insider acts are the ultimate outcomes.

More importantly, who are the people who commit these insider acts? You are probably interested in what motivates them, but there's so much more to it than motivation. The best model to use to understand individual transgressions or derailment is the Critical Pathway to Insider Risk from Shaw and Sellers.

The Critical Pathway to Insider Risk

When notorious double agent Robert Hanssen was arrested by his colleagues from the FBI after 20 years of espionage, he said, 'What took you so long?' (Vise, 2002). To answer this (rhetorical) question we need to take a close look at the process a person goes through before and while committing an insider act.

In 2015 clinical psychologist Eric Shaw and former counterintelligence analyst Laura Sellers made a significant contribution to the understanding of insider risks. They examined hundreds of subjects convicted of a range of insider acts, as well as those who were simply removed from their organisations rather than arrested. Based on these cases, Shaw and Sellers developed the Critical Pathway to Insider Risk (Shaw & Sellers, 2015). The Critical Pathway provides a structured explanatory model to help leadership and coworkers in the workplace better identify whether and when an employee is at higher risk of deviating from the norm and heading towards committing an insider act. The following figure shows the risk factors associated with going down the pathway towards the commitment of an insider act.

A caveat before I explain the model: It is important to note that these pathway components provide a risk profile, but there are mitigating factors throughout the pathway which can help individuals to stay on the path and never commit an insider act. In addition, this research is all retrospective, based on successfully prosecuted cases. This can bias the outcomes of the study towards the more severe cases. It is also not a predictive model, as it was impossible to identify how many people with identifiable risk factors did NOT go down the

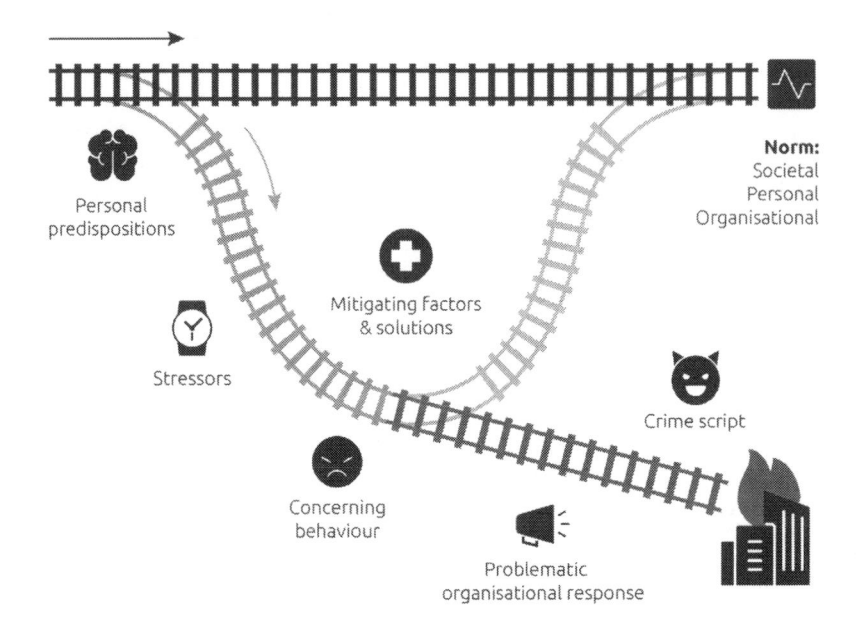

Figure 6.1 Critical Pathway to Insider Risk (adapted by Signpost Six from Shaw & Sellers, 2015).

pathway to committing insider acts. In fact, it is estimated that only one in a thousand people with concerning behaviours actually commit an insider act.

A few general conclusions can be drawn from the Shaw and Sellers research. Insider acts always have a history and a temporal progression rather than being a sudden action in the moment. Insider incidents always arise from the interaction between a person and their environment. Deviation from the norm occurs through a combination of personal characteristics or vulnerabilities and various stressors that a person experiences. This leads to concerning behaviours by the individual. When an organisation fails to respond adequately or provides a problematic response, the insider will progress further towards the insider act through contemplation, preparation and execution of their action. This latter stage is referred to as the crime script and it's the final stage before an insider act is committed.

The following sections will explore the pathway steps, both theoretically and in the context of the hybrid organisation.

Personal predispositions

The first step of the Critical Pathway involves personal predispositions. These were first researched by Band and colleagues in 2006, with a focus on cases of espionage and sabotage. 'Personal predispositions' refers to individual characteristics that can contribute to the risk of engaging in behaviours related to insider acts, as well as the nature, continuation and escalation of these actions (Band et al., 2006). These predispositions are often linked to maladaptive reactions to stress factors leading to conflicts and rule violations, chronic dissatisfaction, strong responses to organisational sanctions, concealment of rule violations and a tendency to escalate conflicts in the workplace. Personal predispositions explain why some insiders carry out malicious acts while co-workers who are exposed to the same conditions do not act maliciously. Specific characteristics can be indicative of personal predispositions, like serious mental health disorders, including alcohol and drug addiction; challenges in the social skills spectrum and decision-making bias; a history of rule violations; and social network risks.

Social network risks are increasingly gaining attention; these are the risks that disgruntled or calculating employees within the organisation or individuals or organisations outside the organisation might facilitate or solicit employee participation in insider acts. Think of employees mistakenly clicking on these phishing emails mentioned earlier, for example. In a more globalised world and an even more global workforce where remote working has become the norm, people and societies become more interconnected and exposed to different cultures, ideologies and perspectives. Their sense of identity and loyalty can become more complex, increasing the opportunities for divided loyalties to emerge and potentially contributing to insider acts like espionage.

According to research, ideological motivations to engage in espionage have become a growing factor. At the same time, advancements in communication technologies have made it easier for foreign intelligence agencies to identify and target individuals with divided loyalties. As Dr Drayton stated in Chapter 2: 'People form attachments not only to other people and groups, but also to places and things.' If the workplace and your desk are at home, then the organisation you work for is at both a physical and *mental* distance, and so can your loyalty be.

In addition to personal predispositions and behaviours, *organisational* predispositions and behaviours, such as excessive trust of employees, a reluctance to 'blow the whistle' on co-workers and inconsistent enforcement of organisation policies, can also influence an organisation's exposure to insider acts, predominantly because the organisation lacks oversight and provides too much access (and opportunity) to misuse and abuse that access without any consequences. Arguably, Nick Sharp had too much access with little oversight at Ubiquiti.

Stressors

The second step on the Critical Pathway is stressors. All of us have stress in our lives, but in the case of insiders, significant personal, professional and financial events appear to trigger their underlying personal predispositions, leading to an increased risk of insider acts. Apprehended spies interviewed for the Project Slammer study in the 1980s mentioned that stressors were the first and foremost triggers for them to go down the pathway to espionage (CIA, 1990).

Adapting to the hybrid work environment can have positive effects in some cases, but it's not without its challenges and stress factors, either. Earlier in this chapter, I discussed the blurring of boundaries between work and life, but also think of general adjustment and adaptation for people who find such changes hard to deal with, and consider challenges in communication, collaboration, IT setup at home and so on. Tessian research on the psychology of human error found that distraction, stress and fatigue influence people's ability to consistently make good cybersecurity decisions, increasing the unintentional insider threat (Tessian Research, 2022).

Although the world has recovered from the worst of the pandemic, the State of the Global Workplace 2023 Report from Gallup states that employee stress remains at a record-high level. The 'Common Sense Guide to Mitigating Insider Threats' provides an overview of the most common stressors based on a collection of incident data since 2001, as shown in Table 6.1 (Carnegie Mellon University SEI, 2022).

Table 6.1 Top five stressors observed across insider threat incidents.

Stressor	Number of Incidents
Termination	375
Resignation	245
Internal position change	55
Organisation merger and acquisition activity	43
Emerging financial problems	33

Organisational change processes are ongoing in large organisations as they adapt to external factors such as the hybrid work environment, and these can have a significant impact on insider risk. Our environment and workplace are in a constant state of stress and change now probably more than ever, as demonstrated by deteriorating mental health statistics for young people even after the pandemic (Bouma, 2023). Research by the UK's Centre for Research and Evidence on Security Threats into counterproductive work behaviour and insider acts found that change is a continuous experience that affects an organisation's structure, processes and social systems, triggering emotional and cognitive responses in individuals (Searle & Rice, 2018). Negative employee experiences during organisational change can contribute to insider threats, as changes in roles, relationships and resources can alter employees' psychological attachment. Organisational change can have several negative impacts:

- The work environment becoming less predictable can lead to employees diverting their attention in order to understand and adapt to the changes.
- Inadequate communication during change can result in misunderstandings and rumours.
- Leadership changes that often accompany organisational change can affect expected behaviours from both leaders and employees.
- Some individuals may perceive the change process or its outcome as unfair, particularly those who have lost power and influence.

Concerning behaviours

The next step on the Critical Pathway – concerning behaviours – is the most important for you as a colleague, supervisor or management, because it may be the most visible sign of insider risk: the tip of the iceberg. In nearly all instances, individuals who engage in more serious misconduct typically breach minor rules beforehand. Consequently, they often draw the attention of management due to their violations of policies, practices, rules, acceptable interpersonal behaviours and even laws. Consider behaviours such as substance abuse, interpersonal conflicts, aggressive or violent actions, unauthorized expenditures on company accounts, fluctuating moods, subpar job performance, absenteeism or tardiness, sexual harassment, dishonesty regarding qualifications, dress code infractions and inadequate personal hygiene. This makes it so important to report concerning behaviours, in order to be able to connect the dots.

Keep in mind that the Critical Pathway to Insider Risk was designed to be an anomaly-based framework that is highly sensitive to outliers, and it has its drawbacks as it tends to overlook individuals who do not exhibit extreme behaviour or clear signs of escalating risk. Consequently, there is a possibility of failing to detect those who may be silently advancing towards an insider attack (Lenzenweger & Shaw, 2022).

Since the pandemic and the move to the hybrid organisation, several challenges with understanding concerning behaviours have emerged. In the past, working late at night at our computers was the exception; nowadays we are scheduling our own time and we're working more flexibly. Working and downloading data off-hours might have been an indicator of suspicious behaviour in the past, but nowadays employees may have different schedules, work from various locations or have flexible working hours. This makes it harder to pinpoint specific off-hours when someone might be engaging in unauthorised activities.

The reporting of concerning behaviours has changed as well. Since the pandemic and the rise of remote working, co-workers observe less misconduct in the workplace and are less inclined to report on it (Gartner, 2022), especially Gen Z (Ethisphere, 2023). Reporting was already an issue before the pandemic. According to Gartner in 2019, nearly 60 per cent of all misconduct observed in the workplace was never reported (Gartner, 2019). Reporting is essential to foster an ethical culture in the workplace and prevent an individual going further down the Critical Pathway. It helps leadership with taking the right measures as early as possible and therefore the reporting challenge needs to be addressed.

Problematic organisational response

Organisations frequently react to worrisome behaviours in ways that amplify, rather than mitigate, the insider risk. Keeping in mind the research question, 'What actions do colleagues, supervisors or management take that make matters worse?' Here are several ways in which organisations can inadvertently exacerbate the situation:

- They often remain unaware of an individual's dissatisfaction, personal tendencies, sources of stress or troubling behaviours. The

necessary information simply isn't being gathered or integrated in any way.
- Upon recognizing a troubling behaviour or a potential sign of insider risk, they neglect to conduct a more thorough investigation.
- They start to investigate a concerning behaviour but fail to consider the possibility of insider risk. They might look at it from an employee health point of view or think of it as a general Human Resources matter, but fail to consider the potential damage that can be done to the organisation. Both perspectives need to be taken into account.
- They take sudden and swift actions against employees for concerning behaviours, including sanctions, suspensions and even terminations, without understanding the potential implications for insider risk. As shown in Table 6.1, abrupt termination can greatly increase insider risk if there's no plan to mitigate the risk.
- They consciously keep in place employees with concerning behaviours. Organisations can be faced with what they see as dilemmas. They can't lose the expertise the particular individual brings. This might have been the case with Cameron Ortis.

The Cameron Ortis case shows how badly things can go wrong if an organisation doesn't respond properly to concerning behaviours (Ling, 2021). Ortis was a senior intelligence officer with the Royal Canadian Mounted Police (RCMP). He was accused of stealing and selling police information, including to an as-yet-unnamed foreign group. An independent review ordered by the RCMP found that there was a failure from the leaders at every level in dealing with earlier complaints about Ortis (Cooper & Bell, 2020). Despite complaints starting in January 2017, the RCMP didn't take the right action until an external party, the FBI, identified him as part of an organised crime network years later. Ortis was seen by leaders as being good at his job and handling internal processes.

This case shows what can happen when co-workers notice concerning behaviours but there are no effective systems in place to deal with it. It also shows the tricky balance for leaders in keeping highly skilled workers while also making sure everyone is treated equally, no matter what behaviour they display. If the RCMP leaders had dealt with the issue properly, they might have avoided more damage. Plus, it would have had less of an impact on the work culture and other staff. At his subsequent trial, the jury found Ortis guilty of four counts of breaching Canada's official secrets law, one count of breaching trust and one count of misusing a computer system. As I write this, he is awaiting sentencing but prosecutors are pushing for a twenty-eight-year sentence, the maximum allowed under Canadian law.

Crime script

An insider act seldom occurs without planning and preparations. The insider crime script, at the end of the Critical Pathway, refers to preparations, planning, rehearsals and security efforts by the subject committing or about to commit an insider act. These activities may be associated with surveillance or research in preparation for the insider act, getting cooperation from others, acquiring the resources or skills needed, rehearsal and testing, and deception or other forms of operational security to avoid discovery. Many activities in this phase are online, in systems. Table 6.2 shows the top-five data exfiltration methods given in the 'Common Sense Guide to Mitigating Insider Threats' (Carnegie Mellon University SEI, 2022).

If no additional (IT) security measures are taken for employees working remotely, this type of work setting poses unique and additional challenges. Four out of five security managers in organisations believe hybrid work is increasing the need for data security and training thereof (Code 42, 2003). However, it is good to remind ourselves that measures at this stage are relatively late in the Critical Pathway. Behavioural indicators precede technical indicators, and as the expert community states, if you want to get 'left of boom', you'll need to gain visibility on these behavioural indicators first (Greitzer et al., 2016).

Mitigating factors

Mitigating factors like resources, social support, positive experiences in another domain, 'simply' leaving the job, taking away the opportunity to conduct an insider act and a network of supportive family and friends have the potential to redirect an employee away from conducting an insider act. This remains the same whether you work in a hybrid work environment or not. However, one can argue that there are less of these mitigating factors available in a hybrid work

Table 6.2 Top five data-exfiltration methods observed across insider threat incidents.

Data Exfiltration Method	Number of Incidents
Email	141
Removable media	90
Paper	80
Web	61
Verbal	42

environment. For example, personal predispositions such as a history of previous violations or social network risks can be offset by social support, but social support in the professional environment is harder to come by when working remotely. Also, the hybrid work environment comes with additional challenges; think of the increased lack of reporting of concerning behaviours and as we know reporting is necessary for leadership to take action early. Overall, in a hybrid work environment mitigating factors can be more limited as social check in's and support at work is less self-evident.

What the Critical Pathway demonstrates is that insider risk is primarily a human process. We can use technology for detection, but it is even more important to link the appropriate mitigating measures to human behaviour. Understanding that there is a pathway means understanding that there are options for prevention, detection and early response. The Critical Pathway shows that there is a pattern with cumulative risk factors, but also that there is a role for both leadership and co-workers to recognise and adequately act on these risk factors early on. The next section looks at the steps organisations can take to mitigate the risk.

Insider risk management in the hybrid organisation

There are numerous strategies for managing insider risks. Guidelines applicable to the private sector are available from the US Government and from the National Protective Security Authority in the UK, among others. Many Western governments are also working on similar guidelines and resources. The pandemic has provided many lessons in managing insider risks. My approach focuses on employee life-cycle management, considering primarily the individuals who have legitimate access to the organisation, whether they are employees, contractors or others. This approach aligns well with the Critical Pathway.

Begin with some self-reflection

Any organisation will always need to self-reflect first. That is the starting point. You need to understand where you are in order to understand where to go. Gain this visibility by conducting an insider risk assessment. You need to ask yourself (as an organisation) the following questions:

1. **What types of threats are a concern to my organisation?** Think of the types of insider acts earlier listed: data theft, sabotage, unauthorised disclosures, violence, fraud and corruption, and insider trading. Which one is a priority to you and why?

2. **What makes my organisation vulnerable to these threats?** Here you can think of organisational change processes at play (and therefore stressors) or severe competition in the market. In other words, what in your DNA can make you vulnerable as an organisation?
3. **What are we already doing about this?** And perhaps more importantly, what are we not doing yet and should be doing about it?

The results of this assessment will raise new questions like:

1. What is our risk appetite?
2. What's acceptable and what is not?
3. What countermeasures should we focus on as a business?
4. What is the road map towards closing those gaps?

Such an assessment is not a one-off exercise. The threat landscape keeps changing, which impacts the challenges ahead. The move to remote working brought new threats to organisations which need to be accounted for. Let's now have a good look at the countermeasures an organisation should have in place as a minimum.

The life-cycle model

Organisations need to manage risks at the employee, contractor and third-party level throughout the Critical Pathway to Insider Risk. For ease I will refer to employees, but remember that an insider is anyone with trusted access to the organisation's assets, systems and resources.

The Life-cycle Management Model is a method you can use to visualise the different steps of your employee engagement while fulfilling the organisational need for products, services and labour. Employee Life-cycle Management is a holistic approach which incorporates roles and responsibilities for everyone in the organisation and especially HR, ethics and compliance, line management, data owners, procurement, IT and security. A holistic approach is essential to prevent siloed or fragmented risk management. Traditionally, the separate steps of the cycle are responsibilities assigned to different departments, which means that measures and information flows are not coordinated, and indicators for insider incidents may be missed because they occur in separate silos. A well-managed life-cycle will result in a productive organisation that is more resilient against insider risks.

The iterative model has five distinct phases (see Figure 6.2), based on the understanding that the insider risk consists of what people bring into the organisation, their interaction with the organisation itself and the period during which the relationship is either terminated or renewed.

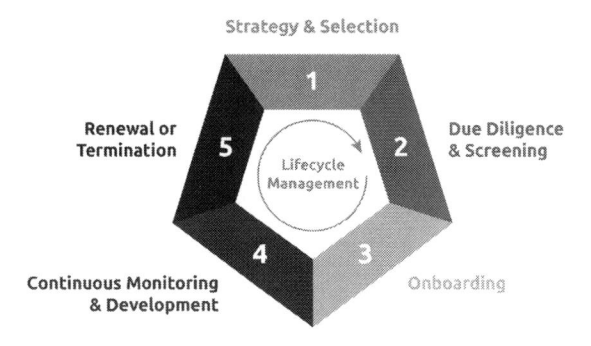

Figure 6.2 Employee life-cycle management.
Source: Signpost Six.

Phase 1: Strategy and selection: adjusting to a new type of workforce

The sourcing strategy in the business life-cycle begins with determining the business needs and developing an appropriate approach. However, unrealistic representation of requirements can result in unsatisfactory sourcing and increased insider risk. For instance, procuring IT services with substandard compatibility may lead to risky workarounds. Similarly, hiring individuals who don't match their intended roles can result in job dissatisfaction and stress, posing a risk to insider security. Sourcing decisions involve considering in-house capabilities, hiring new staff or outsourcing to third parties.

Unfortunately, many departments involved in the sourcing process often overlook insider risk. Clear requirements are crucial for accurate risk assessments which determine the level of due diligence and screening needed to identify and mitigate insider risks. Avoid recruitment practices such as offering bounties for employee referrals. They can be effective but carry inherent insider risk due to biases stemming from personal connections. Be attentive to diversity in the workplace as hiring extensively from a single social network can introduce biases, groupthink and competition for loyalty among employees.

The current phase in the market can be called a 'war for talent'. In many sectors, there is a limited pool of individuals with the necessary skills, experience and qualifications, and this is expected to grow over the years. As organisations strive to fill critical positions with top performers, they find themselves in direct competition with other companies vying for the same talent. This poses an immediate dilemma for insider risk management. It's hard to find the right talent, and therefore the measures you take to find them can supersede insider risk concerns. It's an employees' market with high demands which sometimes aren't in the best interests of the organisation they work for. For example, remote working demands from new hires can have an impact on workplace connection and loyalty, which in turn is a mitigating factor for insider risk.

Phase 2: Due diligence and screening: staying up to date with a changing threat landscape

During the due diligence and screening phase of the life-cycle management model, it is important to view these processes as tools rather than standalone objectives. Not all roles and third parties require extensive screening, and subjecting all new hires to the same level of screening can lead to unnecessary costs and delays. The key is to establish a risk-based approach that determines the appropriate level of scrutiny based on the organisation's risk appetite. This ensures that due diligence and screening are proportionate to the risks involved, consistent, fair and efficient.

The conclusions drawn from the screening should be based on predetermined indicators identified during the risk assessment and integrated into the strategy, rather than relying on random search results. The screening outcomes provide valuable information that will enable hiring managers to make informed decisions, detect individuals with harmful intentions, identify those vulnerable to external influences and ultimately prevent the hiring of potentially risky individuals.

A globalised and remote workforce poses screening challenges. It is more difficult to verify identity and credentials due to limited in-person interactions and to access reliable information about candidates' employment history, references and criminal records, while at the same time ensuring data protection and privacy compliance and navigating international screening complexities. Sometimes these challenges can't be overcome, but some of the consequences of these challenges (the organisation not knowing its employees and the employees not knowing or understanding the organisation) could be addressed in the next phase: onboarding.

Phase 3: Onboarding: how to connect and build a shared identity when working remotely

The onboarding phase in the life-cycle management model involves several important aspects. Administratively, it begins with signing contracts and non-disclosure agreements that outline terms, responsibilities and consequences for failing security and compliance requirements. These legally binding agreements hold harmful insiders accountable. Once administrative tasks and security training are completed, privileged access rights can be granted. However, many organisations, especially smaller ones, have limited resources for comprehensive onboarding programmes, often relying on a 'sink or swim' approach or shadowing existing employees.

It is crucial to use the onboarding process as an opportunity to discuss expectations and responsibilities, and foster loyalty and engagement by immersing new hires in the company culture. Clear and accessible policies and guidelines should be consistently communicated throughout the employee life-cycle to ensure understanding and compliance, as misconceptions can increase insider risk.

In a remote work environment, the organisation should emphasise developing a strong onboarding process that includes training on remote work practices, security protocols and the organisation's culture and values, in addition to clarifying the available support structures if employees require professional and mental support. This cannot be a one-off 'exercise'. It needs to be repeated during employment to retain awareness.

Phase 4: Monitoring and development: a balanced approach between supportive mechanisms and visibility on risk

The fourth phase in the life-cycle management model is monitoring and development. Most employees carry some level of risk during employment and therefore it's key that an employer gains visibility and acts on the employees' concerning behaviours. It is much harder to do this in a hybrid work environment as explained before. In order to maintain a clear understanding of employee conduct and effectively address any issues, the organisation should prioritise three key domains:

- **Fostering a supportive work environment:** With the increasing concerns about workplace stressors in the back of our minds, this is the most important area of focus in this phase. Organisations implement various measures to create a supportive work environment, foster employee engagement and satisfaction, reduce stressors and manage risk. These include providing a variety of support programmes, promoting work–life balance and offering well-being budgets. By providing these positive incentives, organisations demonstrate their commitment to the well-being and success of their employees, fostering a sense of loyalty and reducing the likelihood of insider risk.
- **Creating an IT-secure remote-work setting:** Switching to remote-working conditions presents various IT challenges for organisations. These challenges include ensuring reliable internet connectivity,

segmenting sensitive data to limit access to need-to-know, facilitating seamless collaboration and communication, providing remote access and support, managing data privacy, ensuring scalability and performance, and enhancing employee IT literacy. Addressing these challenges is very important to prevent unintentional insider risks or mistakes being made, and it requires careful planning, investment in technology infrastructure, cybersecurity measures, and ongoing support and training for employees.

- **Collecting and connecting the dots:** Organisations need to have visibility on employees' concerning behaviours in interpersonal relationships as well as understanding behaviours in the IT systems (think of the crime script in the Critical Pathway to Insider Risk). Effective monitoring systems need to be in place to protect the organisation and its assets. These systems allow for the identification and prevention of potential risks. By proactively monitoring for any anomalies or concerning behaviours, organisations can swiftly address issues, mitigate risks and maintain a culture of transparency and trust. Think of one of your employees suddenly uploading sensitive documents to the cloud when they do not ordinarily do so. You would like to see this behaviour and double-check the intent behind it, or investigate if the situation warrants it.

Managing insider risk requires striking a delicate balance between treating employees fairly and ethically while at the same time maintaining visibility regarding potential insider risk. Privacy is an important theme. How much visibility do you gain on risk using intrusive technological measures at the expense of the privacy of an employee?

Phase 5: Renewal or termination – employee and data retention

The last phase in the life-cycle management model is renewal and termination. Employees can see a renewal of arrangements for three reasons:

- **Promotion:** Most of the time promotion is a joyous event and an excellent opportunity for the employee. But in some cases, people get promoted for the wrong reasons. It does happen that individuals get promoted to 'promote away' someone with concerning behaviours, and this impacts staff morale and moves the problem elsewhere. This avoidance can be problematic in the long term.
- **Demotion:** There is a risk of significant disgruntlement when an employee gets demoted. Line management has to be especially alert when there are indicators like this and assess the risks based on the possible damage an insider can do. This will determine the need for and type of mitigating measures.

- **Horizontal movement:** In this situation the employee might need to be re-screened. Depending on the organisation and whether the employee switched between different departments or branches and levels or types of access, the same onboarding principles used with new hires should be followed. Although the employee is remaining in the same organisation, differences may be significant, and engagement might need to be renewed or strengthened.

The final option in this phase that needs a special mention is termination. This is a very vulnerable phase. Research has shown that intentional insiders often conduct insider acts within 90 days of their termination (Carnegie Mellon University SEI, 2022). After the pandemic, with employees leaving their jobs en masse (known as 'the great resignation'), organisations were particularly concerned about the loss of their intellectual property and competitiveness in the market (Cramp, 2022) and this isn't over yet. In Gallup's 2023 'State of the Global Workplace Report', more than half of employees globally expressed some level of intent to leave their job. With so many employees potentially departing, there is a very high risk to organisations of losing data as well as valuable employees and their expertise.

Ideally, an organisation will focus on employee retention and prevention of termination, but sometimes it is actually better that an employee parts ways with the organisation. Once the process of an impending exit has been set in motion, a formal off-boarding procedure must be started. The interaction between the organisation and an employee could have soured. The off-boarded individual has knowledge of and access to your operations, assets and vulnerabilities. The confidentiality, integrity and availability of critical assets may be compromised, posing a significant insider risk in this phase of the cycle. The off-boarding procedure should include the following:

- **Risk-based controls:** As soon as there is awareness of a termination in the organisation, risk-based controls should be put in place to prevent and detect insider acts, like limiting access or monitoring behaviour. With limited to no risk, a staff member can continue to work until his or her final day. At the other end of the spectrum, in high-risk situations, an employee can be asked to leave the premises immediately, revoking all physical and digital access. As with all mitigating measures, they have to be proportionate to the risk. Unnecessary actions taken may generate or enhance negative sentiments and disgruntlement.
- Before departure, an exit interview should take place. This is a data point to get feedback about the organisation and the state of mind of the employee, and it helps the employee leave on the best terms possible for both parties.

Learning from experience

Reflecting on the full employee life-cycle with the Critical Pathway to Insider Risk in mind and during the extra-challenging time of hybrid working, it should be clear that there is no one quick fix, and no organisation is exempt from employee risk. It is also a mindset, especially for management in organisations.

Matthew Bunn and Scott Sagan's publication, *A Worst Practices Guide to Insider Threats: Lessons from Past Mistakes*, highlights several key points regarding insider threats and organisational vulnerabilities (Bunn & Sagan, 2014). Companies make the following assumptions:

- *Assumption 1: Serious insider problems are a case of NIMO (Not In My Organisation)*. Most organisations trust their employees, perhaps too much, and this can lead them to believe incidents are not intentional. Employee motivations and beliefs can change due to circumstances.
- *Assumption 2: Background checks will solve the insider problem.* Background checks are static and reflect a point-in-time profile of a person. People who enter the organisation may be 'cleared' only to later reveal themselves as an insider. A more continuous method of due diligence may be warranted.
- *Assumption 3: Red flags will be read correctly.* Sometimes HR records go to different destinations when a person transfers units, as was the case for Nidal Malik Hasan, who is currently on death row after a mass shooting on a US military base. People may ignore red flags for political reasons. Individual and group interests may not align with organisational objectives. Having an organisational structure and policies to manage red-flag events (knowing what to do when concerns are flagged) when they occur strengthens the security culture and the integrity of the organisation.
- *Assumption 4: Insider conspiracies are impossible.* Conspiracies do indeed happen, and they are most often related to organised crime or espionage. They are more difficult to detect, but according to RAND if they account for approximately 10 per cent of the insider acts which is still significant, and it's important to consider this especially during investigations (Bunn & Sagan, 2014).
- *Assumption 5: We can rely on single protection measures.* Relying solely on a single protective measure is not an effective deterrent. We know risk can evolve over time. If you, for example, just focus on the entry phase of an employee at the organisation, you miss these evolving risks. You'll have to manage risks throughout the employee life cycle.
- *Assumption 6: Organisational culture and employee disgruntlement don't matter.* Organisations may be more concerned about external

threats or focus on technical detection measures not realising that organisational culture and employee disgruntlement are essential components of managing insider risk as they influence employee behaviour, provide early warning indicators and offer opportunities for preventive actions that can mitigate the potential for harm.
- *Assumption 7: Insiders don't know about security measures and how to work around them.* Once in place, systems become static, and insiders, especially privileged insiders, know how to defeat them. Robert Hanssen, a senior FBI analyst convicted in 2001 of 15 counts of espionage, had ways of accessing all the information he needed, avoided lie detectors and controlled his contact with outsiders. Who will watch the watcher?
- *Assumption 8: Security rules are followed.* Competing motivations are inevitable with security programmes. Every security procedure that must be followed detracts from productivity, and productivity can be heavily incentivised. Make sure employees both accomplish the mission and support security.

Questions to reflect on

1. What types of insider threats are a concern to my organisation?
2. What makes my organisation vulnerable to these threats?
3. How do I manage security within my organisation?
4. Do I consider insider risks within my organisation?
5. How is my organisation tackling this?
6. What type of new or extra precautions has my organisation taken to manage insider risk with the move to a more hybrid workplace?
7. Do I have a person taking responsibility for these risks and a governance structure in place to oversee rising insider risk concerns or actual incidents unfolding?
8. What do I do to keep up to date with a changing external environment that potentially impacts risks within the workplace?
9. How do I ensure a good balance between employee well-being and support, and risk detection and consequence management?

Key points

- Insider risk evolves gradually over time, often in response to change. The current work environment, with its hybrid structure, is undergoing significant changes, making the current period and the foreseeable future particularly susceptible to vulnerabilities.
- The hybrid organisation poses additional and new challenges that need to be managed striking a balance between care for the person, the system in which the person works and the risk the person can pose to the organisation and ultimately themselves.

- The Critical Pathway to Insider Risk Model shows that employee/environment interaction is where organisational risk factors play a key role.
- Be aware insider acts can happen in and undermine your organisation in both public and private sectors by employees, contractors and anyone with trusted access and raise this awareness within your organisation.
- Start with a risk assessment before embarking on a programme. This will provide you with focus and direction.
- Professionally assess the threat, and then act on your assessment. It's damaging to know the threat and not act adequately upon it.
- Take a dynamic approach. Risk assessment and management is an ongoing, live and dynamic process rather than one that is static or a snapshot in time.
- Employee life-cycle management is cyclical and there are unique risks and mitigating measures in each phase.
- Job satisfaction and organisational support are two sides of the same coin and play a large role in preventing insider risk.
- A balance needs to be struck between safeguarding the relationship with the employee and protecting the organisation's critical assets.

References

Band, S. R., Cappelli, D. M., Fischer, L. F., Moore, A. P., Shaw E. D. & Trzeciak, R. F. (2006). 'Comparing Insider IT Sabotage and Espionage: A Model-based Analysis'. *Carnegie-Mellon University*, SEI/CERT Coordination Center. https://insights.sei.cmu.edu/documents/776/2006_005_001_14798.pdf.

Bouma, K. (2023). 'Mentale gezondheid van meisjes gaat achteruit: bijna de helft piekert, is snel angstig en vaak ongelukkig'. *De Volkskrant*, 28 June. https://www.volkskrant.nl/nieuws-achtergrond/mentale-gezondheid-van-meisjes-gaat-achteruit-bijna-de-helft-piekert-is-snel-angstig-en-vaak-ongelukkig~ba96b8d8.

Bunn, M. & Sagan, S. D. (2014). *A Worst Practices Guide to Insider Threats: Lessons from Past Mistakes*. Cambridge, MA: American Academy of Arts and Sciences.

Carnegie Mellon University (2022). 'Common Sense Guide to Mitigating Insider Threats', 7th Edition. *Software Engineering Institute*. https://resources.sei.cmu.edu/asset_files/WhitePaper/2022_019_001_886876.pdf.

Center for Development of Security Excellence (CDSE) (2022). 'Insider Threat Program for Industry: Job Aid'. https://www.cdse.edu/Portals/124/Documents/jobaids/insider/insider-threat-job-aid-for-industry.pdf.

CIA (1990). 'Project Slammer Interim Report', 12 April. Redacted and declassified version https://www.cia.gov/readingroom/docs/DOC_0000218679.pdf.

Code 42 (2003). 'Annual Data Exposure Report 2023'. https://www.code42.com/resources/reports/2023-data-exposure.

Cooper, S. & Bell, S. (2020). 'Confidential Report Reveals Untold Story of Cameron Ortis, RCMP's Troubled National Intelligence Centre'. Global News, 17 November. https://globalnews.ca/news/7460679/cameron-ortis-macneil-report.

Cramp, N. (2022). 'The Great Resignation: Mitigating the Risk of Data Loss'. *VentureBeat*, 7 April. https://venturebeat.com/datadecisionmakers/the-great-resignation-mitigating-the-risk-of-data-loss.

Dtex (2022). 'Insider Risk Report: Psycho-Social Behaviors, Remote Work & the Rise of the Super Malicious Insider'. https://www2.dtexsystems.com/2022-insider-risk-report.

Ethisphere (2023). 'Ethical Culture Report 2023'. https://ethisphere.widen.net/s/rgmldwrwxc/ethisphere-2023-ethical-culture-report-jan2023.

Gallup (2023). 'State of the Global Workplace: 2023 Report'. https://www.gallup.com/workplace/349484/state-of-the-global-workplace.aspx.

Gartner (2019). 'Gartner Says Just 41 Percent of Workplace Misconduct Is Reported'. 12 March. https://www.gartner.com/en/newsroom/press-releases/2019-03-12-gartner-says-just-41-percent-of-workplace-misconduct-is-reported.

Gartner (2022). 'Gartner Says the Pandemic Has Reduced Compliance Reporting 30%'. 15 June. https://www.gartner.com/en/newsroom/press-releases/2022-06-15-gartner-says-the-pandemic-has-reduced-compliance-reporting-30-percent.

Greitzer, F. L, Imran, M., Purl, J., Axelrad, E. T., Leong, Y. M., Becker, D. E., Laskey, K. B. & Sticha, P. J. (2016). 'Developing an Ontology for Individual and Organizational Sociotechnical Indicators of Insider Threat Risk'. Eleventh International Conference on Semantic Technology for Intelligence, Defense, and Security (STIDS), Fairfax, VA, 19–27.

Herbig, K. L. (2017). The Expanding Spectrum of Espionage by Americans, 1947–2015'. *Perserec*, Technical Report 17–10, August. https://apps.dtic.mil/sti/pdfs/AD1040851.pdf.

Koo, R. (2022). 'Insider Risk Intelligence and Research Report'. *VentureBeat*, 28 April. https://venturebeat.com/2022/04/28/the-super-malicious-insider-and-the-rise-of-insider-threats.

Lenzenweger, M. F. & Shaw, E. D. (2022). 'The Critical Pathway to Insider Risk Model: Brief Overview and Future Directions'. *CITRAP*, 1(1), 2 August. https://citrap.scholasticahq.com/article/36186-the-critical-pathway-to-insider-risk-model-brief-overview-and-future-directions.

Ling, J. (2021). 'The Rise and Fall of a Double Agent'. *The Walrus*, 20 April. https://thewalrus.ca/the-rise-and-fall-of-a-double-agent.

National Counterintelligence and Security Center (n.d.). 'National Insider Threat Task Force (NITTF) Mission'. https://www.dni.gov/index.php/ncsc-how-we-work/ncsc-nittf.

National Crime Agency (2021). 'NCA Warns Furloughed Port and Airport Workers Could Be Exploited by Organised Criminal Groups'. 26 July. https://www.nationalcrimeagency.gov.uk/news/nca-warns-furloughed-port-and-airport-workers-could-be-exploited-by-organised-criminal-groups.

National Protective Security Authority (n.d.). 'Insider Risk'. https://www.npsa.gov.uk/insider-risk.

NOS (2021). *'Verdachten datadiefstal GGD: "Niet van bewust dat het heel ernstig was"'*. 4 May. https://nos.nl/artikel/2379364-verdachten-datadiefstal-ggd-niet-van-bewust-dat-het-heel-ernstig-was.

Ponemon (2022). 'Cost of Insider Threats Global Report'. https://protectera.com.au/wp-content/uploads/2022/03/The-Cost-of-Insider-Threats-2022-Global-Report.pdf.

Salahdine, F. & Kaabouch, N. (2019). 'Social Engineering Attacks: A Survey'. *Future Internet*, 11 (4), 89; 2 April. https://doi.org/10.3390/fi11040089.

Savage, C. 'Obama Commutes Bulk of Chelsea Manning's Sentence'. *New York Times* 17 January 2017. https://www.nytimes.com/2017/01/17/us/politics/obama-commutes-bulk-of-chelsea-mannings-sentence.html.

Savage, C. & Huetteman, E. 'Manning Sentenced to 35 Years for a Pivotal Leak of U.S. Files'. *New York Times* 22 August 2013. https://www.nytimes.com/2013/08/22/us/manning-sentenced-for-leaking-government-secrets.html.

Searle, R. & Rice, C. (2018). 'Managing Organisational Change'. *CREST Research*, 6 March. https://crestresearch.ac.uk/resources/cwb-full-report.

Shaw, E. D. & Sellers, L. (2015). 'Application of the Critical-path Method to Evaluate Insider Risks'. *Studies in Intelligence*, 59 (2), 41–8.

Tessian Research (2022). 'The Psychology of Human Error'. 2nd ed. https://www.tessian.com/research/the-psychology-of-human-error.

United States District Court, Southern District of New York (n.d.). 'Nickolas Sharp Indictment'. https://www.documentcloud.org/documents/21123826-nickolas-sharp-indictmentpdf.

United States Army (2007). 'Bradley Manning Charge Sheet'. 2 October. https://irp.fas.org/news/2010/07/manning070510.pdf.

United States Attorney's Office (2023). 'Former Employee of Technology Company Sentenced to Six Years in Prison for Stealing Confidential Data and Extorting Company for Ransom'. 10 May. https://www.justice.gov/usao-sdny/pr/former-employee-technology-company-sentenced-six-years-prison-stealing-confidential.

Vise, D. A. (2002). 'From Russia with Love'. *Washington Post*, 6 January. https://www.washingtonpost.com/archive/lifestyle/magazine/2002/01/06/from-russia-with-love/b28c2127-65e5-43f3-8a9a-0e75ab851cb3.

The White House (2011). 'Executive Order 13587: Structural Reforms to Improve the Security of Classified Networks and the Responsible Sharing and Safeguarding of Classified Information'. 7 October. https://obamawhitehouse.archives.gov/the-press-office/2011/10/07/executive-order-13587-structural-reforms-improve-security-classified-net.

The White House (2012). 'Presidential Memoaum – National Insider Threat Policy and Minimum Standards for Executive Branch Insider Threat Programs'. 21 November. https://obamawhitehouse.archives.gov/the-press-office/2012/11/21/presidential-memorandum-national-insider-threat-policy-and-minimum-stand.

Zeiher, C. (2016). 'Europol in 'Shocking' Data Leak'. *Euractiv*, 5 December. https://www.euractiv.com/section/justice-home-affairs/news/europol-in-shocking-data-leak.

7 Well-being, Burnout and Engagement in the Hybrid Workplace

Michael Drayton

The COVID-19 pandemic forced a rapid shift to remote and hybrid working models for many organisations. Employees began working from kitchen tables, spare bedrooms and home offices. Video calls replaced in-person meetings, and 'WFH' (work from home) entered the lexicon.

For some, this transition was seamless. Freed from commuting and office distractions, they experienced greater productivity and better work-life balance. But for others, the isolation took a toll on mental health, communication suffered and engagement waned.

In this chapter, we'll explore how organisations and individuals can maximise well-being and engagement in a hybrid work environment. This entails honestly examining both the benefits and risks of hybrid arrangements to create psychologically healthy workplaces.

I take a systematic perspective on well-being in the hybrid organisation. The organisation and the manner in which the organisation organises the workflow bear the majority of the responsibility for a psychologically healthy work environment, rather than the individual employee. Work-related mental ill-health and burnout are caused by dysfunctional organisational systems rather than personal vulnerability or weakness (both play a role in the development of work-related mental ill-health, but the organisation plays the primary role). In this chapter, I examine well-being from a personal, organisational and systemic standpoint. One of the primary causes of poor mental health and burnout, for example, is a lack of purpose and meaning at work. I then propose some practical structures that organisations can implement to promote well-being, focusing on Aaron Antonovsky's research on the importance of coherence in building resilience in a healthy organisation.

We'll begin by looking at the pros and cons of hybrid work models. Then we'll discuss burnout as one significant mental health consequence, alongside broader well-being considerations. Next we'll provide practical strategies individuals and organisations can implement to foster resilience and meaning. We'll close by exploring leader self-care essentials.

By taking a holistic approach focused on the principles of comprehensibility, manageability and meaningfulness, employees and organisations can unlock hybrid work's full potential.

The hybrid work environment: A mixed blessing

First, let's acknowledge the indisputable advantages of hybrid working for many employees. Greater autonomy over one's schedule and not commuting to an office every day offers increased flexibility. This aligns with self-determination theory, which posits autonomy as a core psychological need (Ryan & Deci, 2000). Studies have linked perceived flexibility with higher job satisfaction, engagement and well-being (Gajendran & Harrison, 2007).

Eliminating lengthy commutes also conserves resources like time, energy and money for employees. The conservation of resources theory suggests this can help reduce stress (Hobfoll, 1989). Employees may regain several extra hours a week and no longer have to pay for transportation, parking and other daily work-related costs.

However, the story is more nuanced. The boundaries between work and personal life can become blurred in a hybrid setup (Felstead & Henseke, 2017). Without clearly defined work hours or a separate workplace, employees may feel constantly 'on call'. The inability to disconnect can dramatically increase after-hours work, creating an 'always-on' culture.

This hyper-extension of the workday jeopardizes any supposed benefits of flexibility. While employees enjoy working remotely, some simultaneously report growing overwhelmed by mounting work demands. The risk of burnout escalates without firm boundaries in a hybrid environment (Kossek & Lautsch, 2012).

Isolation also poses challenges in a distributed workplace. Technologies enable remote collaboration, but physical distance can stifle the spontaneous social interactions that build workplace bonds (Hinds & Cramton, 2014). This thwarts the fundamental human need for belonging (Baumeister & Leary, 1995). Loneliness and disconnection often result.

In summary, hybrid arrangements provide welcome flexibility but also disrupt work-life balance and relationships. Organisations must thoughtfully address these pitfalls through policies fostering boundaries, social ties and reasonable workloads. With proper implementation, the advantages can outweigh the risks. Next we'll explore burnout as one consequence of poorly managed hybrid models, before discussing broader well-being.

Tim's story

I was working as a clinical psychologist and one of my patients was a lawyer called Tim who was burnt out. Tim was a partner in a mid-tier city law firm who had been absent from work for the previous six months due to anxiety and depression. In our sessions I could occasionally see flashes of the jolly man he'd once been, and he struck me as being more of a Rumpole of the Bailey lawyer than a 'Sue, Grabbit & Run'[1] type lawyer. But this was his public persona, and beneath his mask of genial affability Tim was a deeply troubled man. His life outside work was a mess.

He was drinking three bottles of wine a night, and unsurprisingly, he slept badly. When he did sleep he would frequently wake in a panic following a nightmare. The nightmare was of him walking up the pathway that led to his office. He hardly left the house other than to wander down to Majestic Wine to stock up on booze.

We began therapy and Tim described his life. His story was unremarkable, with the exception of his work life. It was a living hell. He worked sixty hours most weeks, and he resented it.

Tim was not a 'Type A' personality who was obsessed with work. He felt compelled to work such long hours to keep up with his workload, which, oddly enough, he did not consider excessive. 'The problem is the constant interruptions at the office,' he explained. 'I will get started on something only to be called away to deal with something else. Then a client will call, and that's another half hour gone. At the end of the day, I still have to finish the task I'd started in the morning, so what do I do? I work late or take it home and finish it there.' This had been Tim's life for the past few years. That is, until the constant worry, the excessive booze and the sleepless nights caught up with him and he collapsed at work with chest pains.

Here he was: an overweight middle-aged man who was experiencing high levels of stress. Everyone, including Tim, assumed that he'd suffered a heart attack. An ambulance was called, and off he went, on blue lights, to the hospital. Following lots of tests, Tim found himself lying on a hospital trolley bed, wearing a gown that barely covered him, talking to a cardiologist. 'There's nothing wrong with you,' the cardiologist said. 'You've probably just had a panic attack.'

That was six months before I met Tim.

We began therapy by looking at Tim's personality. He had the typical personality pattern of those who succumb to burnout. He was highly conscientious and agreeable. This meant that he worked hard and was a warm and friendly person who valued his relationships and hated conflict. It also meant that his overwork was intrinsically driven. In other words, he didn't overwork because he had a tyrannical boss shouting at him. He overworked because he felt guilty if he didn't. The tyrannical boss was inside his head. His high level of agreeableness meant that he had a strong need to be liked and accepted by others. This made it very difficult for Tim to say 'no' to anything. Tim hated conflict. Which was odd, given his chosen occupation as a family lawyer. 'I'm actually okay – well, quite good in fact – at managing other people's conflicts, but not so good at managing my own conflicts,' he told me.

While I was treating Tim, I was reading a novel by Pat Barker called *Regeneration* (Barker, 2008). It's set during the First World War and tells the story of the relationship between the military psychiatrist W. H. R. Rivers and the war poet Siegfried Sassoon. Sassoon had been repatriated from the trenches of the Somme and sent to Craiglockhart Psychiatric Hospital to be treated for shell shock (what we would today call post-traumatic stress disorder). This is where he met Dr Rivers, who became his treating psychiatrist. Siegfried Sassoon was an enormously talented poet who had been deeply traumatised by his experiences in the trenches. One of his most famous poems, written in 1916, reads, 'The rank stench of those bodies haunts me still/and I remember things I'd best forget' (Sassoon, 2002). It was these 'rank stench' memories that Dr Rivers had to help Sassoon to cope with.

Before the war, Siegfried Sassoon was a bright, personable man with no history of mental illness. Then World War I turned his life upside down. He was sent to the trenches and was horrified by the conditions and trauma. In 1917, he wrote his famous 'A Soldier's Declaration', a protest against the war that was read out in Parliament and later published in *The Times* newspaper. He wrote: 'I am making this statement as an act of wilful defiance of military authority, because I believe that the War is being deliberately prolonged by those who have the power to end it' (Sassoon, 1917). This declaration, as well as Sassoon's sometimes manic, risk-taking behaviour in the trenches (he was known as 'mad Jack' by his fellow officers), landed him at Craiglockhart Psychiatric Hospital, where he met Dr Rivers.

Rivers admired and liked Sassoon. He recognised Sassoon as a sensitive and brave man. Sassoon had just received the Military Cross, and had also been afflicted by trench warfare.

As the conversations progressed, Rivers began to slowly realise his dilemma. His job was to 'cure' Sassoon – to make him well again; to restore him to how he was before he was sent to the trenches. But as soon as he had achieved this goal, Sassoon would be returned to the very environment that had caused his shell shock (his PTSD).

The parallels between Tim's situation and the one described in Pat Barker's novel were not lost on me.

Both men had, before 'work', been competent and well-adjusted people. Both Tim and Siegfried Sassoon were put into a highly stressful environment and both became ill as a result. W. H. R. Rivers' dilemma was also my dilemma. If Rivers restored Sassoon to health, he would be sent back to the trenches, the very environment that had caused his shell shock. If I were able to restore Tim to health, he would be sent back to the highly dysfunctional workplace that had caused his burnout.

I shared these thoughts with Tim. 'If I can get you better, I will give you three months back in the workplace before you are as bad as you were when we first met. The main problem is work, not you,' I told him. He agreed. Sassoon's shell shock was caused not by something within him but by an aversive and stressful environment. Tim's burnout was not caused by an intrinsic psychological problem or weakness; it was caused by a highly stressful work environment.

Tim suggested that I speak with the firm's partners in an effort to improve the situation. I did this, and the partners agreed that work could be organised more rationally and effectively. We implemented what, certainly to my mind, were fairly common-sense changes. These included firm start, break and finish times; periods of uninterrupted 'deep work' to allow the lawyers to get on with complex cases; and even a supervision group for lawyers doing family work to discuss and process the emotional impact of the work. The outcomes were not surprising (at least not to me). Stress and anxiety decreased, while productivity increased.

The main takeaway from this story is that stress and anxiety at work, which is common but can lead to a more serious condition – burnout (as it did with Tim), is caused by an interaction of extrinsic (the environment) and intrinsic (the person). But by far the most important factor is the environment.

The main takeaway from this story is that stress and anxiety at work, which is common but can lead to a more serious condition – burnout (as it did with Tim), is caused by an interaction of extrinsic (the environment) and intrinsic (the person). But by far the most important factor is the environment.

Burnout in the hybrid workplace

Before diving into solutions for the hybrid workplace, let's deepen our understanding of burnout. Whether you are a leader, a busy manager or an employee within an organisation, it's crucial to understand burnout for three key reasons:

- Understanding how and why burnout occurs can potentially prevent it from happening to you.
- If you are a manager and have a direct report at risk of burnout or already experiencing burnout, it's vital to understand the nature of the problem and how you can best assist them.
- As a leader in a hybrid organisation, understanding burnout will enable you to cultivate a corporate culture where burnout becomes a thing of the past. This, in turn, will lead to a highly engaged workforce, fostering high performance, creativity and overall employee well-being.

Once we grasp the complexity of the problem, we can begin to explore potential solutions.

What is burnout?

Take a moment to reflect on burnout. What mental image comes to mind? Do you envision a frazzled man or woman who is visibly agitated and struggling to cope? Perhaps you picture someone tirelessly rushing around, desperately trying to keep up, or a person sitting at a desk in front of a computer, looking utterly exhausted and defeated.

Burnout encompasses all these aspects and much more. Often when people think about burnout, they equate it with excessive workload. They may define burnout as sheer exhaustion resulting from an overwhelming amount of work. However, exhaustion is just one piece of the burnout puzzle. Other components include psychological and spiritual factors such as cynicism, hopelessness, helplessness and detachment – not only from work but also from life itself. These psychological, emotional and spiritual dimensions of burnout inflict far greater damage on individuals than physical exhaustion alone.

Writer Sam Keen eloquently described burnout as follows:

> Burnout is nature's way of telling you that you've been going through the motions; your soul has departed; you're a zombie, a member of the walking dead, a sleepwalker. False optimism is like administering stimulants to an exhausted nervous system.
>
> (Keen, 2010)

The term 'burnout' was first used in New York in the 1970s to describe how volunteers who worked with the city's population of drug addicts were emotionally affected by their work. The term was coined by the American psychologist Herbert Freudenberger, who helped to develop the free clinic movement in New York to support people suffering from addictions. Freudenberger, who devoted a large amount of time to these clinics, without pay, observed the gradual emotional exhaustion and declining motivation in some clinic volunteers, and termed this phenomenon 'burnout'. He defined it as 'a state of mental and physical exhaustion caused by one's professional life' (Freudenberger, 1975).

Jobs can be exhausting for lots of different reasons. Some people do jobs that are tedious, lack meaning and are badly paid. Others do very emotionally demanding jobs, working with people in pain (like the New York drug workers in Freudenberger's clinic). Some do jobs where the demands far outstrip the resources, and others work for employers who treat them badly. Whatever the situation, people can't simply absorb these stresses. They manifest in physical exhaustion, cynicism, detachment from the work and greatly reduced performance.

The organisational context of burnout

In 2018, the World Health Organization (WHO) recognised burnout as an official inclusion in the International Classification of Diseases (ICD-11), specifically under the category of 'Mental and Behavioral Disorders' (WHO, 2018). ICD-11 is a manual used by clinicians for diagnosing mental health conditions. It provides comprehensive descriptions of all mental illnesses, including lists of signs and symptoms that must be present for a particular diagnosis.

Burnout is classified as an occupational phenomenon rather than a mental illness in the ICD-11. The chapter on burnout is titled 'Factors Influencing Health Status or Contact with Health Services'. It emphasises that burnout only arises within the context of working for an organisation, distinguishing it from other mental health issues that can occur in any setting.

This distinction is significant because it indicates that employers and workplaces are necessary components for burnout to manifest. In other words, burnout is not solely an individual phenomenon confined to an individual's experience. Burnout is the consequence of a dysfunctional system.

A common mistake made by employers is attributing burnout exclusively to the individual and overlooking the circumstances within the organisational environment that contribute to burnout. The assumption often centres on the idea of a 'weak' individual who struggles to cope with work-related stressors. Consequently, the solutions derived from this misguided assumption tend to focus on the individual. While interventions such as antidepressant medication or psychological techniques like time-management training, mindfulness or cognitive behavioural therapy can be beneficial, they are ultimately individual-based solutions to a systemic problem. These approaches only address one aspect of the problem, neglecting the workplace environment that initially triggered burnout.

For every employee who succumbs to burnout and takes sick leave, numerous others teeter on the edge of exhaustion. Burnout serves as a symptom, indicating that something is amiss within the organisation – an underlying 'disease' that necessitates diagnosis and remedy. While it is crucial to assist individuals suffering from burnout, and I will discuss this later, the responsibility also lies with the organisation to address the root causes that led to burnout.

'A state of vital exhaustion'

The WHO (2018) describes burnout as 'a state of vital exhaustion'. This description is particularly poignant and evocative. The word 'vital' evokes images of energy, liveliness and absolute indispensability. 'Exhaustion' signifies extreme physical and mental weariness, depleting all reserves. These two words aptly encapsulate the experience of burnout. Individuals grappling with burnout feel utterly drained, their resources fully depleted. Simultaneously, they experience restlessness and heightened agitation, unable to switch off or relax. In my encounters with burnout sufferers, this combination of agitation and exhaustion has been a recurring theme.

ICD-11 further elaborates on burnout, defining it as a syndrome resulting from chronic workplace stress that has not been effectively managed. It is characterised by three dimensions:

1. Feelings of energy depletion or exhaustion
2. Increased mental distance, negativism or cynicism regarding one's job
3. Reduced professional efficacy.

It is important to note that burnout is specific to the workplace and should not be used to describe experiences in other areas of life (WHO, 2018).

Rather than approaching burnout as an individual 'illness', this definition places it squarely within the context of the workplace. As a result, the most effective approach to preventing burnout and assisting individuals experiencing burnout involves addressing the workplace environment as well as providing employees with support and guidance. A multi-level, systemic approach is required.

Burnout is a gradual process

Burnout represents the dramatic culmination of a long, arduous and distressing journey. There's no abrupt transition from being fine one moment to burnt out the next; it takes a significant amount of time to reach that stage. Although this may seem obvious, organisations and their support systems often react to burnout as an all-or-nothing phenomenon. Responses to burnout tend to be reactive rather than proactive. Organisations respond when the crisis unfolds, disregarding the numerous early warning signs. Most of us are aware when we are not coping well, and we often notice when our colleagues struggle too. However, it is common for us to turn a blind eye to these early warning signs of burnout and fail to take action. Numerous factors contribute to this tendency. To prevent burnout, individuals, managers and leaders – everyone within an organization – needs to adopt a proactive, compassionate, and systemic approach.

Now that we have explored the complexity of burnout, let's turn our attention to a work structure that has the potential to either exacerbate or alleviate this threat – the hybrid work model. As organisations across the globe adapt to a hybrid approach, it's important to examine how this model impacts employee well-being.

Maintaining personal well-being in a hybrid environment

As well as benefits, hybrid organisations bring a distinct set of challenges, including the potential for social isolation and the absence of structured work environments. These issues can produce feelings of alienation and lack of connection, leading to decreased productivity and in extreme cases, burnout.

Let's start by acknowledging the indisputable advantages of hybrid working to mental well-being. The hybrid work model offers an unparalleled degree of flexibility that empowers employees to design their own working schedule. A body of research (Gajendran & Harrison, 2007; Allen et al., 2015) has found that the perception of autonomy that comes from working from home (the researchers use the term 'telecommuting') can lead to higher job satisfaction, increased productivity and lower stress levels. The rationale behind this is grounded in self-determination theory (Ryan & Deci, 2000), which argues that autonomy is a fundamental human need and its fulfilment leads to improved motivation, job satisfaction and overall well-being.

Employees in a hybrid organisation can save money and time on commuting, potentially leading to better work-life balance (Jeffrey Hill et al., 2003). According to the conservation of resources theory (Hobfoll, 1989), conserving personal resources such as time and energy can reduce stress and improve overall life satisfaction. Bloom, Liang, Roberts and Ying (2015) discovered that embracing remote work results in a significant reduction in employee turnover while also saving significant commuting and workspace costs. Such financial advantages for both employees and organisations increase the appeal of a hybrid workplace.

At first glance, all of this appears to result in a win-win situation in which the employer saves money on office space maintenance and the employee is less stressed by work demands. Certainly, when we consider employee well-being while ignoring productivity benefits, social benefits and all of the attachment issues discussed in Chapter 2.

Simply from the standpoint of well-being, this sounds promising. However, as with most things in life, it is not so straightforward. Ignoring the potential pitfalls and risks associated with the hybrid work environment would be a mistake. One of the most serious risks, which is related to the attachment theory research discussed in Chapter 2, is the sense of isolation and alienation that many employees feel when working remotely.

According to research, social isolation at work can have a negative impact on mental health, job satisfaction and productivity (Golden et al., 2008). The need-to-belong theory proposed by Baumeister and Leary (1995) contends that humans have a fundamental need to form and maintain strong, stable interpersonal relationships. In a hybrid work model, a lack of regular social interaction can sabotage this essential need, leading to feelings of alienation and disconnection.

The lack of structure that's often a feature of a hybrid workplace can also pose challenges. Without the typical boundaries between work and home, employees may struggle to disconnect, leading to work–home interference, increased work hours and a heightened risk of burnout (Boswell & Olson-Buchanan, 2007; Golden & Veiga, 2005). The fuzzy boundaries in many hybrid workplaces are linked to burnout. Clear psychological and physical boundaries between work and non-work domains are crucial for ensuring work–life balance and preventing burnout (Kossek & Lautsch, 2012).

Felstead and Henseke (2017) critically examined the assumption that hybrid working is an unequivocal 'win-win' for both organisations and employees. They acknowledge that while it's true that the detachment of work from the office appears to be a growing trend that employees and to a lesser extent employers welcome, the complete picture is more nuanced. The study suggests that remote working can lead to higher organisational commitment, enhanced job satisfaction and improved job-related well-being. These benefits, however, come with their own set of complications. The dark underbelly of this hybrid revolution manifests itself in the form of overwhelming, poorly managed workloads and increasingly blurred lines between the employee's professional and personal life.

Employees who enjoy the freedom of working from home may at the same time find themselves becoming more and more overwhelmed by their work, with the boundaries between work and leisure time fading. The phenomenon of 'always being on', with an inability to switch off from work, is a tangible risk in the hybrid workplace. Consequently, the supposed freedom of a detached/hybrid workplace might inadvertently morph into a 24/7 commitment to work, jeopardising the very work–life balance it promised to enhance.

Thus, while it's important to celebrate the advantages of a hybrid work model, it's equally critical to acknowledge and address its potential pitfalls.

These pitfalls, however, are not insurmountable. Effective communication and supportive leadership can mitigate feelings of isolation

(Hinds & Cramton, 2014), while setting clear boundaries for work and personal life can prevent burnout (Sonnentag, 2012).

Implementing practical well-being frameworks, such as those proposed by Antonovsky (1987), and described below, can also play an important role in fostering resilience in a hybrid work environment.

While organisational factors play a major role in well-being, individuals also carry responsibility for caring for themselves in a hybrid organisation. Intentionally nurturing your physical, mental and social health enhances resilience.

Here are some steps you can take:

Create structure. Establish a clear boundary between work and personal time. Set standard work hours and stick to them. Take regular breaks for meals, exercise and rest. Compartmentalization provides order when the workplace and home blend together.
Minimise distractions. Schedule meaningful periods of uninterrupted, focused work ('deep work') each day. Turn off notifications, close extra browser tabs, use apps to block distracting websites. Allow deep concentration on complex tasks.
Stay connected. Don't isolate yourself. Proactively reach out to colleagues to chat or collaborate. Recreate casual social interactions that organically happen in shared workspaces. Feel comfortable asking for support when needed.
Look after yourself. Integrate stress management activities into your routine like meditation, journaling, exercise or hobbies. Listen to your mind and body's signals. Get outdoors, eat nutritious foods and don't neglect sleep.
Reflect on meaning. Clarify what makes your work meaningful. Engage in projects aligned with your values and strengths. Discuss role adjustments with your manager to enhance fit and purpose.

With self-discipline and self-awareness, you can take control of your well-being. But organisations must also establish supportive conditions, which we'll examine next.

Creating organizational environments for hybrid worker well-being

An organisation's policies, procedures, social norms and leadership practices constitute the broader ecosystem in which individual well-being flourishes or falters. While employees must proactively care for themselves, leaders carry significant responsibility for constructing a context where this becomes possible.

Here are some best practises organisations can embrace:

Encourage social connections. Don't let relationships atrophy in remote settings. Build camaraderie through small talk during meetings, virtual coffee breaks, team-building activities and non-work conversations.

Actively monitor workloads. Regularly assess workloads and adjust as needed to maintain a reasonable balance. Ensure employees feel comfortable voicing concerns about overwork.

Provide mental health support. Offer access to counselling, training on resilience practices and mental health days off. Combat the stigma around using these resources.

Clarify expectations. Frequently communicate desired work outcomes, policies on availability and performance metrics. Ambiguity breeds anxiety in times of change.

Check in regularly. Have empathetic, bilateral conversations about workflow challenges and successes. Solve issues collaboratively. Just asking 'How are you?' signals care.

Recognise achievements. From major milestones to small wins, acknowledge employees' accomplishments. Public and private praise fuels engagement and purpose.

Promote flexible schedules. Support modifications to start and end times that accommodate employees' needs and boost effectiveness. Trust employees to manage their time.

When organisations invest in employee well-being, it pays dividends in engagement, productivity and retention.

Aaron Antonovsky's sense of coherence theory

Following WWII, there was a flood of research into the trauma suffered by Holocaust survivors. However, in the 1970s, medical sociologist Aaron Antonovsky did something a little different. He was fascinated by the approximately 30 per cent of Holocaust survivors who went on to live normal, productive and reasonably happy lives. Antonovsky was curious about the psychological characteristics of these people who had survived the horrors of concentration camps, not only physically but also psychologically and emotionally.

He discovered that the survivors had a mindset that proved to be a powerful protective factor. Based on his research, he developed his 'sense of coherence' concept, which applies to individuals, groups and organisations (Antonovsky, 1987).

Three factors contribute to a sense of coherence:

- **Comprehensibility:** The belief that events in life are predictable and explicable
- **Manageability:** The belief that resources to cope are available
- **Meaningfulness:** The belief that challenges and difficulties are worth investment and engagement.

Drayton and Kuster (2022) argue that because of the upheaval resulting from COVID and lockdown, many organisations are, to use Kurt Lewin's term, 'unfrozen' (Lewin, 1947) – in other words, ripe for change. (I discuss Kurt Lewin's work on change in Chapter 1.)

Applying Antonovsky's SoC model in the hybrid organisation

The evidence discussed in this chapter strongly suggests that a sense of control over work, a sense that work is meaningful, clear job roles and responsibilities, and good communication all contribute to a good organisational culture. Furthermore, introducing the concept of coherence has the potential to strengthen the hybrid organisation. Here's how:

- **Comprehensibility:** Tell employees as much as possible about what to expect in the hybrid workplace. Be honest and transparent about plans and expectations. Being able to predict what might happen will greatly reduce employee anxiety.
- **Manageability:** Allow employees some control over their work arrangements and their job. If employees have a sense of personal agency, they will feel more confident because they are able to manage and impose order on events that have felt out of control.
- **Meaningfulness:** Make an effort to reconnect your employees with the meaning and purpose of their work. This sense of meaning is sometimes lost in the midst of a crisis.

These essential factors will minimise the anxiety associated with the changes resulting from hybrid working and provide a framework for organisations to create a strong culture of high performance and psychological safety.

While the organisation plays a crucial role in safeguarding employee well-being, individuals also carry responsibility for maintaining their own health. Let's now explore personal strategies that individual employees should embrace.

Employee engagement in the hybrid organisation

The advantages of having a sense of coherence for hybrid workers go beyond resilience and well-being. According to research, coherence has a positive impact on motivation and employee engagement (Steger & Dik, 2009).

Employee engagement reflects employees' level of connection and commitment to their roles and the organisation (Kahn, 1990). It includes genuine personal investment in work, rather than just formal job performance.

Maintaining engagement across distributed teams necessitates hybrid work that is personally meaningful, progressively challenging and psychologically safe. Employees and leaders must feel a sense of belonging and trust in their organisations.

Role crafting based on individual strengths, celebratory rituals that reinforce shared identity, and managers inviting two-way dialogue and acting on feedback are all strategies. More purposeful and consistent interpersonal connectivity is required in hybrid models.

Engagement occurs when hybrid work aligns with employees' self-concepts and values. Organisations play a critical role in actively shaping an ecosystem in which this match can occur.

What about the leader?

The last thing I want to talk about is how you, as a leader, can manage your own well-being when working remotely. Catherine Sandler at the Tavistock Institute has done some interesting work on how extreme stress affects leadership style (Sandler, 2012).

In Figure 7.1, the triangle on the left shows three common leadership styles. At the top, you have high-energy, charismatic leaders; on the bottom left, you have warm, inclusive, team-building leaders; and on

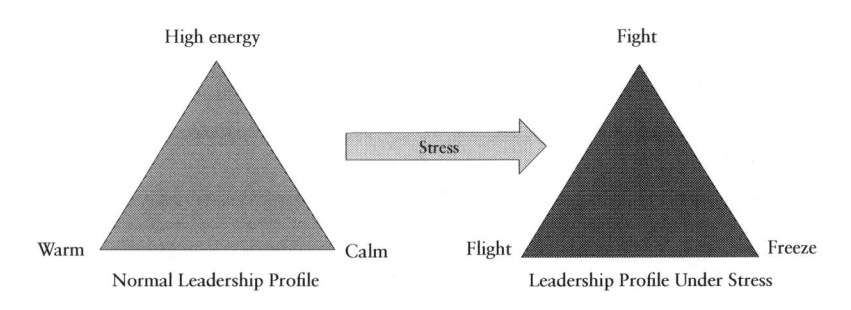

Figure 7.1 How stress affects leadership style.

the bottom right, you have level-headed and analytical leaders. Most people lie somewhere in between these extremes but will prefer one.

When leaders experience severe pressure, they get uneasy and their leadership style changes to that shown in the right-hand triangle. Charismatic leaders go into fight mode and end up being irritable and aggressive. Warm, inclusive leaders go into flight mode and disappear into the team, wanting to be everybody's friend, rather than the boss. Finally, calm, analytical leaders go into freeze mode, shutting their office door and finding it very difficult to decide what needs to be done. Again, these are extreme reactions I'm describing and most people will fall somewhere in between.

Take a few moments to think about where you might be on those triangles.

The biggest factor that protects people from burning out is the ability to switch off from work (Drayton, 2021). Successful people work very hard when they're at work, but when they finish, they can immediately switch their attention to things outside of work, such as family or hobbies. In contrast, a person on the road to burnout will cook a meal or try to get to sleep but will still be thinking about work. This is the biggest and most robust finding in the literature on avoiding burnout. So, have strict boundaries between work and your personal life and try to switch off when you finish.

Questions to reflect on

1. How can you implement more structure and boundaries in your daily routine to avoid burnout in the hybrid workplace? Consider setting work hours, taking regular breaks, and compartmentalising work and personal time.
2. What activities help you relax and unwind from work? Brainstorm new self-care practices like exercise, meditation or creative hobbies that you can incorporate into your routine.
3. Do you feel a sense of meaning and purpose in your current work? If not, what steps can you take to align your role more closely with your values and interests?
4. How connected do you feel to your coworkers these days? Make a list of potential ways to increase social interactions like virtual coffee chats, collaboration opportunities or team-building activities.
5. Have you noticed any early warning signs of burnout in yourself lately like exhaustion, cynicism or reduced effectiveness? If so, what resources or support could you use before it escalates further?

Key points

- Burnout is characterised by emotional exhaustion, cynicism and reduced professional efficacy resulting from workplace stress.
- The WHO recognises burnout as an occupational phenomenon, indicating it stems from organisational dysfunction rather than individual weaknesses.
- Burnout has become increasingly prevalent since the rise of hybrid work models prompted by the pandemic.
- Hybrid work provides advantages like flexibility and a good work–life balance, but can also lead to isolation, poor boundaries and burnout if not properly managed.
- Individuals should take responsibility for their well-being through practices like structured routines, social connections, physical activity, relaxation and seeking support when needed.
- Organisations play a critical role in fostering well-being by promoting meaning and purpose, social connections, mental health resources, reasonable workloads and regular check-ins.
- Antonovsky's sense of coherence theory highlights the importance of work feeling comprehensible, manageable and meaningful.
- Strategies based on Antonovsky's theory like clear communication, employee autonomy and role alignment with values can enhance organisational and individual resilience.
- The responsibility for well-being in hybrid models is shared between individuals proactively caring for their health and organisations creating supportive cultures.
- By working together, empowered individuals and caring leaders can maximise the potential of hybrid models for productive, engaged and psychologically healthy workplaces.

Note

1 Sue, Grabbit & Run is a fictional law firm frequently referenced in the satirical British magazine *Private Eye*. The name humorously alludes to an unethical legal approach, poking fun at hard-nosed, ambulance-chasing and opportunistic lawyers.

References

Allen, T. D., Golden, T. D. & Shockley, K. M. (2015). 'How Effective Is Telecommuting? Assessing the Status of Our Scientific Findings'. *Psychological Science in the Public Interest*, 16 (2), 40–68. https://doi.org/10.1177/1529100615593273.

Antonovsky, A. (1987). *Unravelling the Mystery of Health: How People Manage Stress and Stay Well*. San Francisco: Jossey-Bass.

Barker, P. (2008). *Regeneration*. Harmondsworth: Penguin Books.

Baumeister, R. F. & Leary, M. R. (1995). 'The Need to Belong: Desire for Interpersonal Attachments as a Fundamental Human Motivation'. *Psychological Bulletin*, 117 (3), 497–529. https://doi.org/10.1037/0033-2909.117.3.497.

Bloom, N., Liang, J., Roberts, J., & Ying, Z. J. (2015). 'Does Working From Home Work? Evidence From A Chinese Experiment'. *The Quarterly Journal of Economics*, 165–218.

Boswell, W. R. & Olson-Buchanan, J. B. (2007). 'The Use of Communication Technologies After Hours: The Role of Work Attitudes and Work-life Conflict'. *Journal of Management*, 33 (4), 592–610. https://doi.org/10.1177/0149206307302552.

Cooperrider, D. L. & Whitney, D. (2005). *Appreciative Inquiry: A Positive Revolution in Change*. New York: Berrett-Koehler Publishers.

Drayton, M. (2021). *Anti-burnout: How to Create a Psychologically Safe and High-performance Organisation*. Abingdon: Routledge.

Drayton, M. & Kuster, M. (2022). 'Healthy Organizations Post COVID 19 Need a Sense of Coherence'. *Occupational Medicine*, 72 (2), 109. https://doi.org/10.1093/occmed/kqab106.

Felstead, A. & Henseke, G. (2017). 'Assessing the Growth of Remote Working and Its Consequences for Effort, Well-being and Work-life Balance'. *New Technology Work and Employment*, 32 (3), 195–212.

Freudenberger, H. J. (1975). 'The Staff Burn-out Syndrome in Alternative Institutions'. *Psychotherapy: Theory, Research, and Practice*, 12, 73–82.

Gajendran, R. S. & Harrison, D. A. (2007). 'The Good, the Bad, and the Unknown about Telecommuting: Meta-analysis of Psychological Mediators and Individual Consequences'. *Journal of Applied Psychology*, 92 (6), 1524–41. https://doi.org/10.1037/0021-9010.92.6.1524.

Golden, T. D. & Veiga, J. F. (2005). 'The Impact of Extent of Telecommuting on Job Satisfaction: Resolving Inconsistent Findings'. *Journal of Management*, 31(2), 301–18. https://doi.org/10.1177/0149206304271768.

Golden, T. D., Veiga, J. F. & Dino, R. N. (2008). 'The Impact of Professional Isolation on Teleworker Job Performance and Turnover Intentions: Does Time Spent Teleworking, Interacting Face-to-face, or Having Access to Communication-enhancing Technology Matter?'. *Journal of Applied Psychology*, 93(6), 1412–21.

Hinds, P. J. & Cramton, C. D. (2014). 'Situated Coworker Familiarity: How Site Visits Transform Relationships among Distributed Workers'. *Organization Science*, 25(3), 794–814.

Hobfoll, S. E. (1989). 'Conservation of Resources: A New Attempt at Conceptualizing Stress'. *American Psychologist*, 44, 513–24. http://dx.doi.org/10.1037/0003-066X.44.3.513.

Jeffrey Hill, E., Ferris, M. & Märtinson, V. (2003). 'Does It Matter Where You Work? A Comparison of How Three Work Venues (Traditional Office, Virtual Office, and Home Office) Influence Aspects of Work and Personal/Family Life'. *Journal of Vocational Behavior*, 63(2), 220–41. https://doi.org/10.1016/S0001-8791(03)00042-3.

Kahneman, D. (2011). *Thinking, Fast and Slow*. Harmondsworth: Penguin Books, p. 499.

Keen, S. (2010). *Fire in the Belly: On Being a Man*. London: Bantam.

Kossek, E. E. & Lautsch, B. A. (2012). 'Work–family Boundary Management Styles in Organizations'. *Organizational Psychology Review*, 2, 152–71.

Larson, B. Z., Vroman, S. R. & Makarius, E. E. (2020). 'A Guide to Managing Your (Newly) Remote Workers'. *Harvard Business Review*, 18 March. https://hbr.org/2020/03/a-guide-to-managing-your-newly-remote-workers.

Lewin, K. (1947). *Field Theory in Social Science*. New York: Harper & Row.

Maslach, C. & Leiter, M. P. (2008). 'Early Predictors of Job Burnout and Engagement'. *Journal of Applied Psychology*, 93(3), 498.

Morikawa, M. (2020). *COVID-19, Teleworking, and Productivity*. Tokyo: Research Institute of Economy, Trade and Industry.

Newport, C. (2016). *Deep Work : Rules for Focused Success in a Distracted World*. London: Piatkus.

Riedl, C. & Woolley, A. W. (2017). 'Teams vs. Crowds: A Field Test of the Relative Contribution of Incentives, Member Ability, and Emergent Collaboration to Crowd-based Problem Solving Performance'. *Academy of Management Discoveries*, 3(4), 382–403.

Ryan, R. M. & Deci, E. L. (2000). 'Self-determination Theory and the Facilitation of Intrinsic Motivation, Social Development, and Well-being'. *American Psychologist*, 55(1), 68–78. https://doi.org/10.1037/0003-066X.55.1.68.

Sandler, C. (2012). 'The Emotional Profiles Triangle: Working with Leaders under Pressure'. *Strategic HR Review*, 11(2), 65–71.

Sassoon, S. (1917). 'A Soldier's Declaration'. http://ww1lit.nsms.ox.ac.uk/ww1lit/education/tutorials/intro/sassoon/declaration.

Sassoon, S. (2002). *Collected Poems* (Main edition). London: Faber & Faber.

Seligman, M. (2011). *Authentic Happiness: Using the New Positive Psychology to Realise Your Potential for Lasting Fulfilment*. London: Hachette UK.

Sonnentag, S. (2012). 'Psychological Detachment from Work during Leisure Time: The Benefits of Mentally Disengaging from Work'. *Current Directions in Psychological Science*, 21(2), 114–8. https://doi.org/10.1177/0963721411434979.

Sonnentag, S., Mojza, E. J., Binnewies, C. & Scholl, A. (2008). 'Being Engaged at Work and Detached at Home: A Week-level Study on Work Engagement, Psychological Detachment, and Affect'. *Work & Stress*, 22(3), 257–76.

World Health Organization (2018). *International Classification of Diseases for Mortality and Morbidity Statistics (11th Revision)*. Geneva: World Health Organization.

8 Leading the Hybrid Organisation
From Leader as Explorer to Leader as Healer

Michael Drayton

Leading any organisation is difficult, but leading a hybrid organisation is especially difficult. It is hard because you are in charge of an organisation that is changing. It is difficult to think of a more significant change in recent years than the transition from an office-based to a hybrid organisation. Any organisation that is undergoing significant change will experience a high level of anxiety among its employees.

Many employees will be worried about their future. They might be worried about whether they will be forced back into the office. Or if they hate working from home, they may question when they can get back to normality. Those who work from home may be concerned that they will be overlooked for promotions. Those in the office may be resentful because they suspect those working from home are skiving.

Most, if not all, employee anxiety boils down to concerns about status, certainty, autonomy, relatedness and fairness. In other words:

- 'Will this change affect my place in the pecking order?'
- 'What will happen to me?'
- 'Will I have any control or influence over what happens to me?'
- 'Will I still work with the people that I am used to?'
- 'Will I be treated fairly?'

I address these concerns in depth in this chapter. One of the most important tasks of a leader in a hybrid organisation is to contain and manage these anxieties and create systems that enable psychological safety.

This chapter explores the leadership themes of authority, motivation and conflict management and how these are different in the hybrid organisation. In my experience as a coach, leaders feel less certain about taking up their authority in a hybrid organisation (*'I don't feel confident telling people to come into the office'*). They struggle with knowing how to motivate hybrid teams and tend to avoid conflict, particularly relating to performance management.

For most leaders, managing all the ups and downs of hybrid working feels unsettling and unfamiliar. You understand the benefits

DOI: 10.4324/9781003387602-8

of working from home perfectly well and you understand and appreciate that many of your staff and colleagues prefer to work from home; but still you feel uneasy. There is *something important missing*.

Throughout this book, I have attempted to describe that 'important something'. It is the energy and . . . what is the word? Magic, perhaps? The synergy and gestalt produced by human collaboration. Gestalt is a psychological term that refers to the idea that the whole is greater than the sum of its parts. It suggests that when elements come together and are perceived as a whole, they take on different properties than if they were viewed separately (Kohler, 1992). Gestalt theory says that the way something is organised and structured determines how we experience it. The overall configuration has a greater impact than the individual pieces. A melody, for example, is more than just a collection of individual musical notes. When the notes come together in a meaningful way, they create something new – the melody emerges as a distinct experience. It is this gestalt that is often missing or greatly distorted in many hybrid organisations.

The gestalt is influenced by the face-to-face 'collisions' that happen in the office and the sense of a common task. How do you recreate this camaraderie when colleagues converge only in pixels? How can a sense of belonging, creativity and innovation survive without water cooler conversations? Does purpose still unite when the place we unite is virtual? Exploring this unmapped terrain requires pioneering leadership. In chapter one I wrote that the leadership style developed for a pre-pandemic organisation doesn't work quite so well in a post-pandemic hybrid organisation. As Marshall Goldsmith observed, 'What got you here won't get you there' (Goldsmith & Reiter, 2007).

Leading the hybrid organisation is like leading an expedition to explore as yet unknown territory. You have a basic map of the terrain and you know where you want to go, but it's a very low-resolution map and lots of parts of the map are just blank. It's like walking through a deep, dark forest at night. You're trying to stick to the pathways, but they're not clear because few people have been down that road before. You hear a twig snap and you don't know whether it's a small animal or a wolf. Is the essential employee who's hinting about leaving because you insist they work in the office three days a week serious about leaving or just trying to push you into letting them work from home when they want?

Leader as explorer: Leadership lessons from Ernest Shackleton

Staying with this metaphor of leading the hybrid organisation as an exploration, let's look at how a leader who was also a real-life explorer motivated his team, managed conflict and got to where they were going safely.

On 5 December 1914, Ernest Shackleton and his crew of 27 set sail to the South Pole on what he grandly called the Imperial Trans-Antarctic Expedition. Soon, their ship, the *Endurance*, encountered pack ice in Antarctica, and after 49 days at sea, they got stuck and became frozen into the pack ice, 'like an almond in the middle of a chocolate bar', as the ship's storekeeper, Thomas Orde-Lees, wrote in his diary. What unfolded over the next two years has since become a legendary tale of survival, resilience and, of course, leadership (Lansing, 1959).

Just for a moment, imagine what it must have been like for Shackleton leading that team. Living in the direst conditions: your vessel wrecked, provisions scarce and the frozen Antarctic winter closing in. This was Sir Ernest Shackleton's plight when ice entombed his ship. Yet he somehow kept his crew of 27 alive on ice floes for months until they reached Elephant Island. Shackleton and one of his crew then sailed a small lifeboat 800 miles across the world's roughest seas to find help. After that 16-day voyage to South Georgia Island, he trekked 32 miles across uncharted, glaciated mountains that had never before been climbed, to a whaling station to launch another ship to rescue the remainder of his crew, who had been marooned on Elephant Island for six months following Shackleton setting sail to get help. Miraculously, every crew member survived and made it home safely, due to Shackleton's extraordinary leadership (Morrell & Capparell, 2001).

Shackleton's leadership principles

In their book *Shackleton's Way: Leadership Lessons from the Great Antarctic Explorer*, Margot Morrell and Stephanie Capparell describe the principles that underpinned Ernest Shackleton's extraordinary leadership ability (Morrell & Capparell, 2001). These principles are universal and can be applied to any context, be it an Antarctic expedition or leading a hybrid organisation.

Although it might not seem like it at first glance, stranded on ice floes in the frigid Antarctic, Shackleton faced many of the same challenges leaders in today's complicated, hybrid business environment have to deal with: limited resources, complex team dynamics, uncertainty, and the need to adapt quickly to a rapidly changing volatile, uncertain, complex and ambiguous (VUCA) environment. Shackleton's creativity in solving hard problems combined with his enthusiasm and optimism carried his crew through the two-year ordeal, providing an inspirational model of leadership.

Leading by example

Shackleton demonstrated many leadership best practises. He consistently put his men's needs ahead of his own, taking on the most unpleasant tasks himself and never asking more of his men than he was willing to do. He was very visible, offering encouragement and pitching in wherever necessary. He remained calm in the face of crises, exuding a quiet confidence that helped steady his crew's nerves.

Shackleton proactively modelled the mindset he wanted his team to adopt. He embodied the attitude he wanted to see in the crew. Despite setbacks, he maintained a positive mindset and a 'can-do' attitude. Shackleton knew that his own behaviour set the tone, culture and mood of those he led, so he made it a point to act with courage and optimism at all times. For example, after the *Endurance* had sunk beneath the breaking-up ice, Dr Macklin, the ship's doctor, recalled, 'It must have been a moment of bitter disappointment to Shackleton, but as always with him, what had happened had happened . . . without emotion, melodrama or excitement he said, "ship and stores have gone, so now we'll go home"' (Morrell & Capparell, 2001).

In that one short and simple sentence, Shackleton conveyed to his team a goal and a vision. He redirected their attention away from the painful scene in front of them toward a positive outcome. And, most important of all, he communicated to them his own optimism.

Similarly, leaders in hybrid organisations must embody the mindset and values that they want their distributed teams to adopt. Like Shackleton, hybrid leaders should lead by example, remaining calm, confident and positive even when facing challenges like technology gaps or communication barriers. They should be highly visible, offering encouragement and support through regular video calls and team chats. They should also demonstrate the resilience required to persevere in the face of setbacks, conveying optimism and conviction that team goals can be met regardless of circumstances. Leaders can promote a unified culture and motivate remote employees to persevere in the face of adversity by modelling desired behaviours. Just as Shackleton redirected his crew towards a common goal after adversity, hybrid leaders must refocus their teams on vision and outcomes after inevitable hiccups in remote work. Leading by example is critical for bringing disparate workers together around common goals.

Adaptability

As circumstances changed, Shackleton adjusted his plans, always keeping his ultimate goals in sight. He was a proactive planner, hatching contingency plan after contingency plan in case his primary tactics failed. This flexible, forward-thinking approach enabled him to change plans quickly when needed.

When you lead a hybrid team, you have to be very flexible because things can change quickly when work is spread out. Like Shackleton, hybrid leaders need to be able to change plans when necessary while still keeping the end goal in mind. They should plan for potential challenges and have backup strategies ready. For example, leaders should have ways to get in touch with people if technology platforms go down. They should be able to deal with communication gaps by doing more check-ins. They should be ready to change deadlines or resources when production slows down. Leaders need to be flexible and plan for what could go wrong ahead of time so they can quickly change course when things change with remote work. Leaders of hybrid teams can deal with the uncertainty of distributed work by staying flexible, like Shackleton. When plans have to change, they can get their teams to work together on new ways to reach their goals. Adaptability enables progress despite disruption.

Communicating openly

Shackleton recognised the importance of frequent, open communication. He made sure to give his men an accurate picture of their situation, without sugar-coating the difficulties they faced. During stable times, he built personal connections with each man through casual one-on-one conversations. During crises, he communicated urgently to the whole crew, laying out the plan of action while asking for their full support.

Shackleton welcomed opinions and input from everyone, believing each person had valuable insights, although he made the final decisions. He also clearly communicated what he expected of his men in terms of contributions and mindset. By keeping everyone informed, aligning on goals and inviting participation, Shackleton secured the engagement of his team.

Crew member William Bakewell said, 'Shackleton had a nice way of getting into a conversation and he was very friendly and easy to talk to' (Morrell & Capparell, 2001). Bakewell noted that through these intimate one-on-one talks, Shackleton formed strong personal bonds with each man. These connections were the adhesive that held the team together. The crew knew that Shackleton truly cared about each of them as individuals. And this in turn made the men care deeply about Shackleton. They wanted to do their utmost for their leader who took such a humane interest in them. This interplay of mutual loyalty and regard is what the crew cited as the secret behind their 'remarkable unanimity' of spirit (Morrell & Capparell, 2001).

With hybrid teams, open communication across geographies is crucial. Leaders must if anything *over-communicate* context and strategy virtually. They should facilitate connections between remote team members and give everyone a voice through collaborative platforms. Finally, they should make a special effort to develop an individual and close relationship with those they lead.

Motivation and bolstering team morale

To maintain morale under less-than-ideal circumstances, Shackleton insisted on order and routine, devising activities and duties that gave each man a sense of purpose. He built camaraderie by encouraging collaboration and friendly competition. Mindful of how corrosive criticism can be to morale, he never criticised anyone publicly, focusing instead on fixing problems. He was generous with praise and helped his crew celebrate any small triumphs.

Shackleton also interspersed enjoyable activities into the routine, like games, contests, sing-alongs and amusement provided by the crew's talented banjo player. These were highlights that everyone looked forward to. By keeping his men occupied, productive, connected and entertained, Shackleton ensured that optimism prevailed.

With hybrid teams, leaders should promote social connections through remote coffee chats and virtual events. Remember that public recognition and praise across locations builds collective morale, and celebrating team wins keeps remote staff feeling motivated.

Cultivating optimism

Shackleton firmly believed in the power of optimism. He called it 'true moral courage' and demanded it from his men. He reframed difficulties as challenges to be met through teamwork and perseverance. Shackleton monitored his crew for pessimism, realising that negativity is contagious. He countered it immediately with humour or inspiration. Reginald James, who shared a tent with Shackleton, observed how he 'was constantly on the watch for any break in morale, or any discontent, so that he could deal with it at once.' Shackleton understood deeply the huge and immediate impact food had on morale. So he went to great lengths to vary the rations, try new recipes or issue some special treat to mark a birthday or other occasion. As James noted, Shackleton realised the profound power of even a small gesture or change of pace to lift spirits and combat dissatisfaction before it could spread (Morrell & Capparell, 2001).

By communicating possibilities instead of problems, keeping spirits up and leading by example, Shackleton nurtured a positive mindset that became self-reinforcing. This buoyant outlook carried the crew through unimaginable hardship, delivering them home safely against all odds.

A great way of reinforcing this optimism in a hybrid team is the 'What Went Well' exercise devised by Martin Seligman, founder of the positive psychology movement (Seligman, 2011). At the start of your next team meeting, set aside ten minutes and ask each member to talk about three things that went well over the previous week and why they went well. At first, you will probably find that people look at you blankly and say that they can't remember anything good happening. This is normal, because we tend to have a negativity bias: we focus on the things that have gone wrong, and when things go well, we forget and move on to the next problem, letting our successes fly away like ashes scattered in the wind. If this happens, ask your team to get their diaries out and look back at the previous week. When you do this you will be amazed at how many successes there have been and the immediate uplift in mood when people start sharing them. On the whole, people love talking about their successes and the good things that have happened – they just need a bit of encouragement and a framework within which to do it.

Shackleton's leadership principles in the hybrid organisation

In summary, here are some key ways a leader of a hybrid organisation can apply Shackleton's leadership principles:

- **Lead by example.** Be highly visible and accessible virtually. Take on difficult tasks yourself. Model the mindset and behaviours you want to see, especially maintaining optimism and confidence even in challenging times.
- **Communicate openly and often.** Over-communicate context, strategy and expectations across locations. Give regular virtual team updates. Seek input and have two-way dialogues. Build personal connections with one-on-ones.
- **Show flexibility.** Be ready to adjust plans and processes as circumstances evolve. Focus on goals while being open to new paths to get there. Empower your team to adapt as needed.
- **Motivate and lift morale.** Celebrate small wins. Recognise achievements publicly. Promote social connections virtually. Counter pessimism immediately. Keep spirits up with positivity and humour.
- **Embrace technology.** Use collaboration platforms to engage everyone in discussions and decision making. Create virtual spaces for informal connection. Leverage tools for remote team building.
- **Unite with vision.** Rally your hybrid team around shared goals and purpose. Remind everyone that though apart geographically, you are one team.

Shackleton applied adaptive leadership in uncertain conditions, and today's leaders can draw lessons from his approach when navigating uncertain hybrid environments.

Leading the anxious hybrid team

Just as Shackleton learned to motivate his crew in adversity, today's leaders face new challenges keeping hybrid teams engaged. A big obstacle to engagement is anxiety. Managing team anxiety is one of the key challenges for hybrid leaders.

Anxiety is a characteristic of many, if not all, hybrid teams. People are concerned about their position in the pecking order, whether working from home will jeopardise their chances of advancement, and what is going on in the office while they are away. People working at the office worry that they're missing out because other people are working from home. Managers worry that those working from home are skiving. People are concerned about whether their work is recognised because they receive little feedback and even less praise. People at home feel lonely and disconnected. People in the office also feel disconnected because half the team is here and the other half is somewhere else. All of these factors create a sense of underlying anxiety in the workplace.

Leading an anxious team has its own set of challenges. Neuroscience research shows that most types of stress at work can be linked to certain main ideas. David Rock, a neuroscientist, built his SCARF model on decades of research into the brain (Rock, 2008; Rock & Cox, 2012). The SCARF model outlines five domains that determine our reaction to change:

- **Status** – a sense of importance relative to others
- **Certainty** – being able to predict the future
- **Autonomy** – a sense of control over events
- **Relatedness** – feeling safe with others
- **Fairness** – fair exchanges between people.

When there is uncertainty in these areas, our threat response kicks in. Helping in these areas, on the other hand, sets off our reward response.

Understanding the threat and reward responses

The brain's threat response is activated by the amygdala, an almond-shaped set of neurons located deep in the temporal lobe. When the amygdala detects danger, it triggers the sympathetic nervous system, releasing stress hormones like cortisol and adrenaline (Rock, 2008). This in turn triggers the freeze, flight or fight response, which evolved to help us react quickly to threats. Here's what happens to us:

- **Body:** Our heart rate increases to pump more blood to the muscles. Blood pressure rises. Breathing speeds up to take in more oxygen.

Non-essential systems like digestion and immunity are suppressed so the body can divert energy to responding to the threat (Arnsten, 2015).
- **Mind:** The brain becomes hyper-alert, vigilant for further dangers. This hijacks cognitive bandwidth, making it harder to focus on creative tasks. The amygdala also impairs connections to the prefrontal cortex, the brain region responsible for rational thinking (LeDoux & Pine, 2016).

Brain imaging studies show that threats to the SCARF domains of status, certainty, autonomy, relatedness and fairness activate the same amygdala threat response. This releases cortisol and adrenaline, inhibits cognition and reduces prefrontal control (Eisenberger & Cole, 2012). However, when SCARF domains are supported, the brain's reward circuitry fires up, releasing dopamine and endorphins. These make us feel happy, motivated and productive (Rock, 2008). So, supporting SCARF domains activates the opposite neurochemicals compared to threat states.

By applying this knowledge to the challenges of hybrid working, leaders can adapt their behaviour and workplace systems to activate the brain's reward response instead of the threat response.

The SCARF domains in hybrid teams

So how does this apply to managing hybrid teams? Let's bring each domain to life through some stories about common situations in hybrid teams:

- **Status** (our sense of relative importance): Ana, a software engineer, has just led a big project, which she delivered successfully from her home office. But in the whole-team round-up video call, the CEO only praises the on-site team, completely ignoring Ana's contribution. She feels hurt and unmotivated and wonders if she should look for a different job. The CEO's behaviour has triggered a threat to her status (flight response).
- **Certainty** (being able to predict the future): When COVID hit, Will, a marketing manager, received barely any communication from leadership about changes to priorities or plans. Left in the dark, he felt deeply uncertain about the company's future direction. Stress hormones coursed through his body, and his threat response felt constantly 'on'. He found it hard to make decisions (freeze response).
- **Autonomy** (our feeling of control over events): Ayesha works remotely leading a customer support team. Her boss, Michelle, has started insisting on approving all of Ayesha's decisions before she

can take action. Micromanaged and unable to make choices, Ayesha feels her autonomy slipping away. She feels resentful, annoyed and unmotivated and worried about her future (fight response).
- **Relatedness** (the safety we feel with others): When the pandemic forced remote work, isolation quickly dampened spirits. Mohammed, a sales rep, used to enjoy chatting and exchanging banter with his colleagues at the office. Now working from home, he desperately misses those social bonds. His sense of relatedness has taken a nosedive. He feels lonely and disconnected and that he should find a job where he can interact with others. His threat response is triggered (flight response).
- **Fairness** (our sense of being treated equally): Sanjay's company has announced a new policy – only on-site employees will be eligible for promotion. Sanjay immediately perceives this policy as unfair, given that he works remotely in a different city but is just as deserving of advancement. His threat response is triggered and he feels angry and resentful (fight response).

As these stories illustrate, threats in the SCARF domains can activate our brain's threat response, leading to negative emotions like demotivation, uncertainty and isolation. But leaders who support SCARF can ignite the reward response. Here's how:

- **Make sure that remote employees have equal status to office-based employees.** Recognise achievements publicly across locations. Avoid 'out of sight, out of mind'.
- **Do your best to provide certainty.** Communicate about plans, expectations and changes openly and often. Align on goals.
- **Allow autonomy.** Enable remote staff to have control over their work methods and environment. Avoid micromanaging.
- **Build connections.** Facilitate social interactions and team building using on-site meetings as well as virtual ones. Have frequent informal check-ins.
- **Be very aware of perceived fairness/unfairness.** Avoid perceptions of bias or inequities in work or development opportunities across locations.

The SCARF framework provides a neuroscience-based model for leading hybrid teams successfully. When remote employees feel valued and united behind shared goals, the whole organisation benefits with engagement, innovation and results.

By striving to ensure that employees feel psychologically safe and valued, leaders reduce threat responses. A sense of connection and fairness increases engagement and morale. SCARF provides a model to understand how to bring together hybrid teams.

Taking up your authority

Taking on leadership authority is no small matter; it's about confidently stepping into the role, meeting the needs of your team and organisation, and fully recognising and embracing the duties it entails.

One problem I see a lot with senior leaders is that they have trouble or are even shy about using their authority. Why might this happen? There are a number of reasons:

- **Fear of failure:** This fear can be a major obstacle for leaders. It can arise from a deep-seated anxiety of making incorrect decisions or being incapable of delivering the anticipated results. It can create a barrier to taking risks, stymieing innovation and the ability to seize new opportunities. According to Coutu (2002), the ability to act in the face of fear and potential failure is a hallmark of resilient leaders, and overcoming fear of failure is a significant step in establishing effective leadership.
- **Imposter syndrome:** Defined by psychologists Clance and Imes (1978) as a persistent fear of being exposed as a 'fraud', this syndrome can be debilitating. Even when leaders have proven themselves competent and accomplished, they may still feel undeserving of their position and fear exposure. This self-doubt can lead to decreased confidence and hinder effective decision making.
- **The tendency to please people:** The desire to avoid conflict or maintain popularity can make it difficult for a leader to make hard decisions or assert authority, especially when difficult or unpopular measures are necessary (Goldsmith & Reiter, 2007).
- **Perfectionism:** The unrelenting pursuit of flawlessness and setting excessively high performance standards can create a paralysing fear of making mistakes (Hamachek, 1978). This can result in procrastination, decreased productivity and missed opportunities, as leaders get caught up in minutiae instead of focusing on broader strategic goals. One of the cornerstones of leadership is effective delegation. However, fear of delegation or the need to control all aspects of work can lead to an overbearing management style. As Morgenstern (2004) suggests, micromanagement can lead to a disempowered team and a stifling work environment. Leaders need to strike a balance between maintaining control and allowing team members to take on responsibilities and grow.
- **Self-limiting beliefs:** Beliefs like considering oneself too young, inexperienced or unqualified to lead can greatly impact the effectiveness of a leader. As per McKay and Fanning (2000), these internalised negative beliefs can limit a leader's potential and prevent them from fully asserting their authority.

- **Lack of confidence:** A leader who is unable to project the required self-assurance, speaking or acting tentatively, may struggle to earn respect and trust from their team.
- **Neglecting work–life balance:** In their pursuit of success, leaders often neglect health, relationships or self-care, leading to burnout and decreased productivity (Pfeffer, 2010). A leader's physical and mental well-being is paramount to their ability to lead effectively.
- **Impatience, or an excessive drive for immediate results:** This can hinder a leader's long-term strategic thinking (Eisenbeiss et al., 2008). A balanced perspective that values both short-term wins and long-term goals is crucial in leadership.

By acknowledging these obstacles and taking proactive measures to overcome them, leaders can foster the mindset, emotional intelligence and resilience needed to fully embrace their authority (Goleman, 1995). This understanding enables leaders to lead with confidence and decisiveness, hallmarks of effective leadership.

Fostering psychological safety in hybrid teams

To build the kind of team culture Shackleton did, you need to make sure everyone feels safe.

The term 'psychological safety' was popularised by Amy Edmondson, who defines psychological safety as 'a shared belief that the team is safe for interpersonal risk-taking' (Edmondson, 1999, 2018). In simpler terms, it's the assurance that one can speak up, contribute ideas, make mistakes and challenge the status quo without fear of retribution or ridicule. It forms the bedrock upon which productive, innovative and cohesive teams are built, regardless of whether they're in the same office or scattered across the globe.

In the realm of hybrid teams, psychological safety plays a dual role. Firstly, it facilitates open communication, which is critical in a setup where non-verbal cues are often missing and misunderstandings can arise. Secondly, it breeds trust and inclusivity, ensuring that remote members do not feel isolated or excluded. By encouraging each member to express their thoughts freely, leaders can bridge the geographical and digital divides, ensuring equal participation from all members.

Project Aristotle: Psychological safety in the corporate world

To see how psychological safety works, and adds value, in the real corporate world, let's take a look at Google's Project Aristotle. The project marked one of the most comprehensive investigations into understanding what distinguishes successful teams from less successful ones within

Google's rapidly growing workforce. Google sought to use its strong data-driven culture to unravel the recipe for perfect team synergy.

Project Aristotle was based on analysing more than 180 teams across Google, considering factors such as personality types, team structures, leadership styles and more. The assumption was that some concrete variables like optimal team size or the blend of personalities would emerge as determinants of high-performing teams.

Yet, the findings were surprising. The factors that one might assume would influence team performance – such as team size, tenure or the individual skills of team members – were not consistent across the most successful teams. Instead, the factor that stood out was, you've guessed it, psychological safety (Duhigg, 2016).

The Google researchers found that teams with a high degree of psychological safety consistently outperformed other teams. Members within these teams felt they could take risks, voice their opinions and be open about their mistakes without fearing embarrassment or reprisals from their peers or leaders. In essence, Project Aristotle reinforced Amy Edmondson's assertion that psychological safety is the cornerstone of effective team collaboration.

One of Google's top-performing teams, as discussed in Project Aristotle, wasn't composed of the company's star coders or most experienced managers. Instead, it was a diverse mix of individuals who, at first glance, seemed to have little in common. Yet, they were consistently achieving and often exceeding their targets.

The secret? Psychological safety was deeply ingrained in their operations. Meetings were a safe space where everyone felt comfortable sharing their ideas, no matter how unconventional. Team members openly admitted to their errors without fear of being punished or ridiculed. Everyone was heard, and everyone's contribution was valued. This culture of psychological safety empowered them to collaborate effectively, innovate constantly and deliver outstanding results.

Google's Project Aristotle underscores the power and potential of psychological safety in driving team performance in the corporate world. It validates that fostering an environment where team members feel safe to take interpersonal risks is not just an academic concept but a practical tool that drives real, measurable business results. This resonates profoundly in the context of hybrid teams, where the challenges of distance and digital communication can be effectively met by cultivating a culture of psychological safety.

How psychological safety can turn around a hybrid team

Here is a fictional story to illustrate psychological safety in a hybrid team. Amanda is the head of a global marketing team in a fast-paced tech company. When Amanda was promoted to lead the team, she found herself managing a hybrid team spanning four continents. Initially, team meetings were characterised by silence and nodding heads; ideas were scarce, and mistakes were hidden until they snowballed into crises.

Amanda recognised the stifled creativity and fear of mistake-making as symptoms of a lack of psychological safety. She knew that if she wanted her team to thrive, she needed to foster an environment where her team felt safe to take risks, voice their ideas and admit their mistakes without fear.

So, Amanda started by sharing her own errors in weekly meetings, demonstrating that it was okay to fail. She consistently encouraged her team members to speak up, and when they did, she listened and responded with gratitude. She also implemented regular one-on-one meetings with each member, allowing them the space to voice any concerns or share ideas that they might not be comfortable discussing in a group setting.

Over time, the culture within Amanda's team began to shift. Team members started engaging more openly during meetings, sharing innovative ideas and proactively admitting to and learning from their mistakes. The team began producing their best work, and the attrition rate fell dramatically. Amanda's efforts to cultivate psychological safety had turned a previously unremarkable group into a high-performing, collaborative team.

How to establish psychological safety in your hybrid team

Here are some practical steps you can follow to implement psychological safety within your hybrid team:

- **Establish an open communication culture.** Start by setting the tone for open communication. Encourage team members to speak up and share their ideas, concerns and mistakes. Regularly solicit their input and show appreciation when they participate.
- **Lead by example.** As a leader, demonstrate the behaviours you want to see. Share your own mistakes and how you learned from them, which shows that it's okay to make mistakes and promotes a learning culture.
- **Ensure equal participation.** Be vigilant to ensure that all voices are heard, not just those in the office. Actively involve remote members in discussions and decision-making processes.
- **Promote empathy and understanding.** Encourage team members to be empathetic and understanding, which helps build stronger, trust-based relationships within the team. This can be done

through team-building activities designed to foster mutual respect and appreciation.
- **Provide regular, constructive feedback.** Offer consistent feedback to your team members, praising their efforts and providing constructive criticism that can help them improve. Make it clear that feedback is part of the learning and growth process.
- **Create safe spaces.** Regular one-on-one meetings can provide team members with a safe space to express thoughts and concerns that they may not feel comfortable sharing in a group setting.

Also consider these two easy techniques that promote a culture of psychological safety, as described by Matthew Syed in his book on cognitive diversity, *Rebel Ideas* (Syed, 2019).

- **Brainwriting:** This is a way of generating creative ideas. It's different from its older sibling brainstorming because instead of presenting your ideas verbally, out loud, you write them down on cards and then post them on a wall for the rest of the group to vote on. This works well for two reasons:
  - Everyone gets a chance to contribute (equal contribution is one of the key factors in psychological safety) no matter how shy they might be. In this way the organisation gains access to the thinking of everyone in the team, not just one or two more extroverted, confident people.
  - Status and authority are detached from the ideas. The golden rule of brainwriting is that nobody may identify themselves on their idea card – no matter how subtly they might do this. Nobody can use job titles, hints or distinctive handwriting to identify themselves (block capitals only, please). This is important because by doing this you separate the idea from the status of the person who came up with it. People vote on the quality of the proposal, rather than the seniority of the person who suggested it.

Syed writes:

- When brainwriting is put head to head with brainstorming, it generates twice the volume of ideas, and also produces higher quality ideas when rated by independent assessors. The reason is simple. Brainwriting liberates diversity from the constraints of dominance dynamic. (Syed, 2019)
- **Amazon's Golden Silence:** For the past ten years, Amazon have started their meetings with thirty minutes of silence. During this time, people in the meeting read a six-page memo that summarises, in narrative form, the key agenda item. (It's important that this is written down properly and not summarised in bullet points, because

that way the people presenting the ideas have to really think about them.) The Golden Silence allows people to consider their views before learning the opinions of others. This time for reflection encourages and supports a diversity of thinking and real consideration of the strengths and weaknesses of the idea, and it reduces any risk that the strengths and weaknesses and diverse suggestions will either not be mentioned or be crushed by the dominance hierarchy that is typical in many corporate meetings.

Implementing these steps won't transform your team overnight. However, persistent efforts over time, like Amanda's, can create a psychologically safe environment that enables your hybrid team to thrive, irrespective of the geographical and digital divides.

The leader as healer

So far, we have used the metaphor of leader as explorer. Now let us look at a different metaphor: 'leader as healer'. I do not mean a physical healer; I mean someone who can help people deal with the stress and general emotional fallout that comes with switching to hybrid working. The organisational consultant Nicholas Janni developed the concept of 'leader as healer', which he articulates in his book *Leader as Healer* (Janni, 2021). Janni persuasively argues for a more holistic approach to leadership in today's complex business environment, urging leaders to prioritise healing and reconnection over control. Healing in this context does not refer to physical healing, but to the healing of disconnections within oneself, teams and organisations. The reality of hybrid working has somewhat fragmented these connections.

The crisis of disconnection

Organisations today face unprecedented challenges that demand fundamental shifts in leadership approaches. Hybrid working has disrupted traditional business models and ways of working. Hierarchical command structures are proving inadequate to navigate the complexity and pace of change.

Alongside these external pressures, there is a quieter crisis unfolding within many leaders and teams – one of profound disconnection. Janni suggests that in our focus on goals and results, we have normalised a way of operating that relies heavily on the thinking mind while excluding other aspects of our humanity.

This over-reliance on the cognitive rational mind has created an inner fragmentation. Our sense of self has become lifted out of our bodies as we live in our heads, consumed by the chatter of thoughts. We relate to each other predominantly through concepts, ideas and agendas without truly seeing, hearing or feeling one another's humanity.

Trust and psychological safety suffer as a result. Organisations become siloed and political, with leaders relying on control versus inspiration to drive results. At an individual level, people feel isolated, exhausted and lacking meaning or purpose. We long for connection, yet often organisations lack the structures and capacity for real presence.

These fissures existed before but have been exacerbated by the pandemic's disruptions. For two years, many worked in isolation, deprived of human contact. Now as organisations transition to hybrid working, leaders face divided and disengaged employees. The problem runs deeper than logistics – there is a far more profound psychological and emotional problem that needs to be addressed.

Janni argues that one of the factors contributing to this problem is that in most aspects of organisational life, our cognitive-thinking rational self has become overdeveloped while our emotional, intuitive, spiritual selves have atrophied. Mainstream leadership models prize the executor archetype, which focuses solely on driving outcomes through incentives and adherence to procedure. This transactional approach treats people like expendable cogs rather than human beings.

But the volatility and complexity of hybrid working overwhelm such mechanistic systems. Imposing order through brute force or carrots and sticks is doomed to fail. Compliance can be coerced temporarily, but creativity, passion and commitment cannot.

Thus leaders today face a crisis of the heart and soul across institutions. To meet this crisis, Janni proposes a new leadership paradigm: that of leaders as healers, who minister to the psychological and spiritual brokenness that has crept into modern organisations.

From leader as explorer to leader as healer

What does it mean to be a leader as a healer? At its heart is a shift from a self-centred to a systemic perspective. Healthy people see leadership not as a job or a title, but as a sacred duty to look out for everyone's well-being.

This begins with one's own inner work of identifying fears, our shadow self and emotional blockages. The Swiss psychologist Carl Jung had an idea he called 'the shadow' (Jung 1989). This is the part of a person's mind that contains things about themselves they don't want to admit to. The shadow is made up of qualities, feelings or desires that a person tries to ignore or keep hidden because they don't match the person's idea of who they are. For example, someone who sees themselves as nice may have a shadow that contains angry or selfish parts of themselves that they try to suppress. Jung thought everybody has a shadow in their unconscious mind. He believed that ignoring the shadow just makes it stronger. Jung thought accepting the shadow was important for having a balanced personality. Facing the parts of oneself found in the shadow could lead to wholeness, according to Jung.

Leaders must first commit to their own healing journey before they can hold space for others. Self-awareness and presence are prerequisites for effectively leading a hybrid organisation.

Healers lead through inspiration rather than coercion. Instead of using fear and pressure, they appeal to the higher aspects of human nature. Leaders should take a moment to try to see people as whole human beings, with psychological, emotional and spiritual sides.

Cultivating healing in the hybrid organisation

How do leaders cultivate healing in hybrid teams and organisations?

- **Create emotional safety.** Make space for feelings to be acknowledged, particularly difficult ones like fear, sadness and frustration. Meet discomfort with empathy and remind people they are not alone. Share your own vulnerability.
- **Encourage inclusion.** Every voice is important. Draw out introverted and quiet members. Listen deeply without judgement to expand your understanding.
- **Make clear the shared goal.** Guide people in discovering how their unique abilities can contribute to meaningful outcomes. Demonstrate how your personal goals and the needs of the organisation are compatible.
- **Encourage difficult conversations.** Bring to the surface hidden tensions, power dynamics and unspoken rules that inhibit collaboration. Address conflicts skilfully without blame. Lead with emotional maturity.
- **Include reflection.** Include time for telling stories, learning lessons and expressing gratitude. Nonverbal practises such as mindfulness can be used to supplement rational approaches.
- **Encourage genuine communication.** Model straightforward but compassionate communication. Build relationships across teams to dismantle silos. Call out dehumanising or manipulative behaviour.
- **Keep everything together.** Think about your choices through the lens of shared humanity and interconnectedness. Remind people that their work contributes to a better world.
- **Model healthy leadership.** Demonstrate self-care, vulnerability, integrity and purpose-driven guiding principles.

The path ahead

The volatile, uncertain, complex and ambiguous landscape of the hybrid organisation requires leaders who are adept at inner work and fostering collective healing. Change will be constant, and uncertainty will be normal. Stressful events that were once seemed exceptional will become more commonplace. In this environment, rational and logical analysis are insufficient. Leaders must be present and able to hold space for the emotional process of their teams. Leaders must shift their focus away from profit and shareholder value and towards meaning and purpose.

What would it look like in your organisation to approach leadership from a healing perspective? How could you apply some of these principles in your current role? Our world reflects the brokenness that exists within us. Each of us has a role to play in moving from fragmentation to wholeness, beginning within ourselves and spreading outwards across families, teams and society.

One thing is certain: traditional leadership models are reaching their limits. By embracing leadership as healing, we can navigate the future with our humanity intact, guiding organisations that are powered by care, trust and inspired service rather than fear.

Questions to reflect on

1. How can I become more visible and accessible as a leader to remote employees? What regular rituals or check-ins can I implement?
2. In what ways am I currently building personal connections and psychological safety among my hybrid team members? How could I improve in this area?
3. Do any policies or structures in my organisation unintentionally threaten employees' feelings of status, certainty, autonomy, relatedness or fairness? How might we modify them?
4. What opportunities exist for me to model and encourage vulnerability, risk-taking and learning from failure among my hybrid team?
5. How can I better attune to the emotional landscape and unspoken hurt affecting my team? How can I create safer spaces for healing?
6. Am I leading through inspiration and purpose or coercion and control? How can I appeal more to the higher aspects of human nature in my leadership?

Key points

- Leading hybrid teams is challenging as organisations undergo immense transition and change, provoking anxiety among employees.

- Leaders can minimise team anxiety by supporting the SCARF domains of status, certainty, autonomy, relatedness and fairness.
- Neuroscience shows that threats to these domains activate the brain's threat response, while supporting them activates rewards/motivation.
- Fostering psychological safety builds the trust and communication that are vital for hybrid team performance.
- Leaders should share vulnerability, listen, give feedback, and facilitate equal participation across locations.
- The 'leader as healer' paradigm focuses on serving people's emotional, spiritual and intellectual needs beyond metrics.
- Healers lead through inspiration, build deep connections and help teams find meaning.
- Leadership models overly focused on control, and outcomes don't work in times of volatility.
- Leaders as healers reintegrate fragmented parts of themselves and their organisations to unlock greater wholeness.

References

Arnsten, A. F. T. (2015). 'Stress Weakens Prefrontal Networks: Molecular Insults to Higher Cognition'. *Nature Neuroscience*, 18 (10), 1376–1385.

Clance, P. R. & Imes, S. A. (1978). The imposter phenomenon in high achieving women: Dynamics and therapeutic intervention. Psychotherapy: Theory, Research & Practice, 15 (3), 241–247. https://doi.org/10.1037/h0086006.

Coutu, D. (2002, May 1). How Resilience Works. *Harvard Business Review*. https://hbr.org/2002/05/how-resilience-works.

Duhigg, C. (2016). 'What Google learned from its quest to build the perfect team'. *The New York Times Magazine*, 26 February 26. https://centre.upeace.org/wp-content/uploads/2020/09/7.1-what-google-learnt.pdf.

Edmondson, A. (1999). 'Psychological Safety and Learning Behavior in Work Teams'. *Administrative Science Quarterly*, 44 (2), 350–83.

Edmondson, A. (2018). *The Fearless Organization: Creating Psychological Safety in the Workplace for Learning, Innovation, and Growth*. London: Wiley.

Eisenbeiss, S. A., Knippenberg, D. V. & Boerner, S. (2008). 'Transformational Leadership and Team Innovation: Integrating Team Climate Principles'. *Journal of Applied Psychology*.

Eisenberger, N. & Cole, S. (2012). 'Social Neuroscience and Health: Neurophysiological Mechanisms Linking Social Ties with Physical Health'. *Nature Neuroscience*, 15, 669–674.

Goldsmith, M. & Reiter, M. (2007). *What Got You Here Won't Get You There: How Successful People Become Even More Successful*. New York: Hyperion Books.

Goleman, D. (1995). *Emotional Intelligence*. London: Bloomsbury Publishing.

Hamachek, D. E. (1978). 'Psychodynamics of Normal and Neurotic Perfectionism'. *Psychology: A Journal of Human Behavior*, 15 (1), 27–33.

Janni, N. (2021). *Leader as Healer*. Bloomington, IN: Mantle Leadership Press.
Jung, C. G. (1989). Memories, dreams, reflections. London: Vintage.
Kohler, W. (1992). *Gestalt Psychology: An Introduction to New Concepts in Modern Psychology* (revised edition). New York: Liveright Publishing Corporation.
Lansing, A. (1959). *Endurance: Shackleton's Incredible Voyage*. New York: Basic Books.
LeDoux J. E. & Pine, D. S. (2016). 'Using Neuroscience to Help Understand Fear and Anxiety: A Two-System Framework'. *American Journal of Psychiatry*, 1 Nov; 173 (11): 1083–1093.
McKay, M. & Fanning, P. (2000). *Self-Esteem*. London: New Harbinger Publications.
Morgenstern, J. (2004). *Time Management from the Inside Out: The Foolproof Plan for Taking Control of Your Schedule and Your Life*. New York: Henry Holt and Co.
Morrell, M. & Capparell, S. (2001). *Shackleton's Way: Leadership Lessons from the Great Antarctic Explorer*. Harmondsworth: Penguin.
Pfeffer, J. (2010). *Power: Why Some People Have It – and Others Don't*. London: Harper Business.
Rock, D. (2008). 'SCARF: A Brain-Based Model for Collaborating with and Influencing Others'. *NeuroLeadership Journal*, 1 (1), 44–52.
Rock, D. and Cox, C. (2012). 'SCARF in 2012: Updating the Social Neuroscience of Collaborating with Others'. *NeuroLeadership Journal*, 4, 1–14.
Seligman, M. P. (2011). *Flourish: A New Understanding of Happiness and Well-Being – and How to Achieve Them*. London: Nicholas Brealey Publishing.
Syed, M. (2019). *Rebel Ideas: The Power of Diverse Thinking*. London: John Murray.

9 The Only Way Is Ethics
ESG and the Hybrid Organisation

Michael Drayton

Organisations do not exist in isolation from society. When a company, especially a large one, changes its way of working, those changes inevitably impact the broader community. For example, the rise of remote and hybrid work arrangements may enable some new mothers to remain in the workforce rather than leave their careers for a few years to raise children.

A law firm that previously rented six floors of an upscale downtown office tower may now require only two floors. This reduction affects surrounding businesses that cater to office workers, such as restaurants, cafés and shops. An August 2022 *Financial Times* article reported that 14 per cent of restaurants had closed in the City of London financial district over the past couple years, concluding that 'Homeworking has hobbled the hospitality sector in the financial district' (Barnes, 2022). What will happen to all that excess office space? It may get converted into much-needed housing units – who knows?

Whatever happens, hybrid organisations will reshape the society in which we live. ESG, which stands for 'environmental, social and governance', is a set of criteria used to judge how responsible an organisation is to society. At least two-thirds of investors now consider companies' ESG track records when making investment decisions, looking for companies that are poised to grow sustainably while benefiting communities (EBRD, 2018). This chapter discusses the relationship between hybrid work and ESG and how psychological principles mediate this.

ESG in Victorian Birmingham

We like to think of ESG as a modern phenomenon. But like so many things, the Victorians beat us to it. About five miles south of Birmingham city centre is Bournville, an early example of ESG in practise. In building Bournville, Cadbury's went way beyond the virtue-signalling social media campaigns that often characterise modern ESG, and constructed a place that epitomised the principles of ESG.

Bournville is an idyllic garden village built for the employees, mainly factory workers, of Cadbury's chocolate factory, which dominates the village. Construction began in 1879. It's a nice place, more typical of the Cotswolds than inner-city Birmingham. There are comfortable homes, each with its own large private garden, lots of open green spaces, a village green and a cricket pitch. There has even been a Bournville Village Festival every summer since 1902, complete with local children dancing around a maypole. The village flourished for decades and remains a thriving community today. Bournville is a great example of model town planning.

Bournville was a dramatic contrast to the housing and general environment that most Birmingham factory workers lived in. Housing conditions for the working class in late-nineteenth-century Birmingham were extremely poor. This was the era of slum housing and the Peaky Blinders. Most workers lived in cramped, unsanitary, jerry-built terraced houses. Families were often forced to share these small dwellings, with multiple people sleeping in each room. Ventilation and sanitation facilities were poor or non-existent, with many houses lacking running water and indoor toilets. Alleys behind the terraces were filled with piles of rotting waste and sewage. Disease spread rapidly in these unsanitary environments.

In contrast to working-class life in Bournville, Charles Dickens provides a fictional account of the bleak living conditions in similar industrial towns in his novel *Hard Times* published in 1854 (Dickens, 1995). In the fictitious Coketown, Dickens describes the factories consuming the sky with smoke while workers 'lodged in the little brick houses like swarms of ugly insects'. The streets are depicted as foul with mud and litter, the river polluted, and the houses cramped and decaying. Through characters like Stephen Blackpool, Dickens illustrates the desperation of the working poor, living in crowded rented rooms, where 'decent living was impossible' and disease spread rapidly. Dickens' depiction of Coketown's housing and environment is a good representation of the terrible conditions that the working class in Birmingham and other industrial cities endured during the Victorian era.

Bournville's conception reflected progressive values that predated modern CSR and ESG practices. The Cadbury factory and Bournville village were a conscious attempt to align business success with social responsibility and community well-being. The sweet aroma of chocolate fills the air, a constant reminder of Cadbury's rich heritage. But it's not just about chocolate; it's about a philosophy that has helped shape modern corporate responsibility.

George Cadbury was not content with merely following the norms of Victorian Britain. He saw his employees not as mere workers but as individuals with hopes, dreams and daily struggles. George believed that a happy worker was a good worker, and his commitment to his employees' welfare went beyond the factory floor.

This wasn't merely an act of charity; it was a strategic business decision, one that aligned perfectly with what we today recognise as ESG principles. George Cadbury understood that taking care of his community was not just morally right but also made sound business sense. By investing in his workers' well-being, he was investing in the future of his company.

Here are some ways in which Cadbury's Bournville village embodied emerging practices that we now associate with ESG:

- **Social welfare:** Providing quality, affordable housing, healthcare, education and recreation demonstrated early adoption of social responsibility and worker well-being. This went far beyond the norms of Victorian industry.
- **Sustainable business:** Cadbury's investments in the village and ethical working conditions resulted in loyal, productive employees. This evidenced how social responsibility can boost business performance through strong organisational culture.
- **Governance:** Constructing an entire village reflected a deep commitment to ethical leadership principles beyond pure profit maximisation. The way Bournville was governed exhibited Cadbury's values.
- **Stakeholder model:** Considering workers' overall quality of life showed awareness that businesses have broad stakeholders beyond just shareholders. Employees were treated as partners.
- **Philanthropy:** The educational and recreational facilities were open to the wider community, advancing public welfare. Bournville contributed to the common good.
- **Work–life balance:** Thoughtful village design integrated green spaces and recreation, exhibiting concern for mental and physical health. Cadbury's cared about quality of life.
- **Environmental:** Unlike the polluted slums of industrial Birmingham, Bournville provided clean air and green spaces. The village was built with an eye to ecological balance.

In short, Bournville displayed an early and holistic integration of key social, environmental, governance and philanthropic facets that are now grouped under ESG. It demonstrated that such factors are not only ethical necessities but prudent long-term investments as well. Bournville remains an embodiment of using business as a force for good.

ESG and the modern hybrid organisation

ESG has grown increasingly important, with leaders recognising its impact on share prices and investor reactions. According to a 2013 study, firms that behave responsibly towards the environment see significant stock price increases, while irresponsible firms see decreases (Flammer, 2013). External pressures on sustainability have also increased, such as aggressive carbon reduction targets. On top of these changes, many companies are dealing with the disruptions that hybrid work, distributed teams and remote collaboration bring. These complexities make implementing ESG initiatives within hybrid models more difficult.

This chapter examines the psychological, systemic and organisational aspects of embedding ESG policies and practices into hybrid work environments.

The 'E' in ESG: Environmental factors

The 'E' in ESG stands for environmental stewardship, which means reducing energy consumption, emissions, waste and overall environmental impact. Hybrid models provide opportunities to reduce emissions by increasing remote work. Based on typical commute lengths and vehicle emissions factors, a 100-person team working from home for two to three days per week on average could reduce annual greenhouse gas emissions by more than 200,000 pounds (EPA, 2021).

In order to fully engage employees around sustainability, leaders require psychological skills.

Psychological factors in promoting environmental sustainability

Leaders really need a basic understanding of the psychological forces that influence human behaviour in order to effectively champion sustainability. In Chapter 1, we explored the psychology of individual change. Kurt Lewin's ideas also apply when introducing ESG into hybrid organisations. Instead of using command and control tactics, leaders can inspire their employees more effectively by harnessing their intrinsic motivation and shifting cognitive biases. Elise Amel and her team argue that using the term 'environmental problem' to describe the disruptions in Earth's ecosystems misses the point (Amel et al., 2017). Human behaviour is the main problem. The internal and external forces that push people towards unsustainable lifestyles can be better understood through psychology. While psychologists have been pivotal in shaping individual behaviours for the sake of sustainability, it's now essential to understand and bolster the role of individuals in groups.

Leaders should aspire to be transformational figures, challenging the status quo, adopting ecological values and inspiring group action, for the long-term well-being of both people and the environment. Amel argues that we need to rekindle our relationship with nature if we want to raise a large group of sustainability champions, particularly in developed countries (Amel et al., 2017). Leaders play the primary role in this process.

How Patagonia uses meaning and purpose to implement ESG

The successful outdoor clothing company Patagonia engages employees in this process of positive group change by integrating sustainability into the company's culture and operations. The importance of sustainability is clearly written down in its mission statement:

> **Protect our home planet.** We're all a part of nature, and every decision we make is in the context of the environmental crisis challenging humanity. We work to reduce our impact, share solutions and embrace regenerative practices. We partner with grassroots organizations and frontline communities to restore lands, air and waters to a state of health; to arrest our addiction to fossil fuels; and to address the deep connections between environmental destruction and social injustice.
>
> (Patagonia, 2023)

This clarity of purpose helps employees feel connected to a common objective that serves as a core value guiding decisions and activities. The company reinforces this message through regular communications across multiple channels, from emails to social media to company-wide meetings. Hearing the message directly from the CEO and founder and the senior leadership team reinforces how serious the company is about sustainability.

However, Patagonia's mission statement isn't just virtue signalling or vacuous corporate management speak. The company actively puts its words into practice by, for example, giving employees paid time off to participate in sustainability initiatives. Activities like beach clean-ups and advocacy campaigns allow for hands-on participation in environmental protection. Volunteering programmes give employees the opportunity to follow personal passions related to green causes. These on-the-ground experiences make abstract concepts like waste reduction deeply resonant on an emotional level (Chouinard & Stanley, 2012).

Patagonia also offers its employees professional development focused on sustainability for those seeking to build relevant skills. Courses feature inspirational external experts who reignite motivation. Employees are also empowered to launch grassroots environmental projects within their departments, fostering autonomy and ownership. Providing resources and support for these bottom-up initiatives encourages innovation.

Patagonia further reinforces its values through internal storytelling. Sharing success stories allows employees to see first-hand how their contributions make a tangible difference, creating a sense of collective efficacy. This transparency around progress and setbacks maintains momentum.

In short, Patagonia does its best to support ESG by incorporating meaning and purpose into its organisational structures. It endeavours to engage employees' heads, hands and hearts. It provides a good case study for how to build a thriving, purpose-driven culture (Chouinard & Stanley, 2012).

The 'S' in ESG: Social factors

The letter 'S' in ESG stands for important social dimensions such as diversity, equity and inclusion (DEI), employee well-being, human rights, community development and ethical responsibilities.

DEI is not only the right thing to do, but it is also good for business, as we saw with Cadbury's. Research clearly shows that diversity improves performance. For example, a 2015 McKinsey study (Hunt et al., 2015) discovered that:

- Companies in the top quartile for ethnic diversity were 35 per cent more likely to outperform industry medians financially.
- Firms in the top quartile for gender diversity had returns 15 per cent above industry medians.
- In the US, racial/ethnic diversity displayed a linear relationship with financial performance: every 10 per cent increase in racial/ethnic diversity correlated with 0.8 per cent higher EBIT (earnings before interest and taxes).
- In the UK, every 10 per cent rise in gender diversity in executive teams was associated with 3.5 per cent higher EBIT relative to industry medians.

Professor Chad Sparber discovered that increased racial diversity increased productivity significantly in legal services, healthcare and finance. In fields requiring broad public understanding, a one standard deviation increase in racial diversity corresponded to a 25 per cent increase in productivity (Sparber, 2008).

These impressive figures demonstrate that creating a culture that promotes diversity and inclusion isn't only the right thing to do but makes sound business sense.

While most leaders agree that DEI matters, execution can feel fraught. Clumsy organisational interventions around diversity and inclusion frequently result in resistance, backlash and accusations of political correctness taking precedence over meritocracy (Dobbin & Kalev, 2016).

Employees support initiatives that feel authentically grounded in ethics and fairness, rather than those that feel externally imposed. This highlights the significance of psychological and cultural nuance.

When DEI goes horribly wrong: Alison Rose and NatWest Bank

In July 2023, Alison Rose resigned from her position as CEO of NatWest, one of Britain's most prominent banks, ending a 30-year career. Her departure was prompted by a high-profile incident involving the closure of Nigel Farage's bank account. In early 2022, NatWest subsidiary Coutts Bank had closed Farage's account due to reputational risk, sparking controversy and accusations of political bias. Despite her claims of impartiality, CEO Alison Rose faced backlash for her decision to close the account of the controversial, high-profile Brexit campaigner. She then resigned as NatWest CEO amidst speculation that she had discussed the details of Farage's bank account with a BBC journalist.

The Coutts–Farage episode offers us an opportunity to reflect on what diversity and inclusion truly mean in today's corporate world.

Throughout her tenure, Alison championed what I would suggest was a superficial, cut-down version of diversity and inclusion, focusing on physical characteristics and the 'protected characteristics' but hostile to cognitive diversity. Those holding views different from hers or deviating from the prevailing culture of NatWest were actively excluded rather than included.

Perhaps there was even an element of groupthink in the board and senior leadership team at NatWest, with leaders unconsciously recruiting people with similar views to their own. In this way the management team would have got caught up in a spiral of confirmation bias, constantly reinforcing the prevailing view as the only correct one.

Alison Rose's creation of an echo chamber at Coutts made it possible for her to make risky decisions without being challenged by her leadership team or board. When faced with a dilemma, after discussion and debate groups tend to make riskier decisions than individuals would endorse (Myers & Lamm, 1976). Several theories have been proposed to explain this effect. For example, diffusion of responsibility across the group may play a role, as individual members feel less personal accountability for potential negative outcomes of high-risk options (Wallach et al., 1964). Social comparison is also at work, as group members attempt to portray themselves as daring risk-takers in order to gain status within the group (Teger & Pruitt, 1967). Regardless of the mechanisms, the risky shift illustrates the complex dynamics involved in group decision-making, especially for the emotionally charged decisions around DEI. Discussing choices collectively rather than privately can systematically shift preferences towards higher-risk, higher-reward alternatives.

The events surrounding Alison Rose's resignation highlight the dangers of promoting DEI policies in a superficial and uncritical manner.

Diversity and inclusion extend far beyond physical characteristics or protected classes. An essential, yet usually overlooked, aspect is cognitive diversity: the variation in how individuals perceive, process and interpret information based on their backgrounds, experiences, skills and thought processes. The real power of diversity unfolds when these distinct perspectives come together, fostering innovation and shielding against groupthink.

The case of Farage's account closure exposes this blind spot in Rose's leadership. Farage and the political views he represented (which were no doubt held by many of NatWest's customers and staff) were deemed incompatible with the values NatWest espoused. However, by sidelining Farage due to his beliefs, NatWest rejected a commitment to real diversity and inclusion, excluding the cognitive diversity that Farage's views represented.

How to do DEI right

Efforts to advance social/political issues such as DEI in organisations can backfire when change feels forcibly imposed from above. Quotas, mandated training and excessive policy micromanagement can breed resentment and resistance among some employees who value autonomy (Steffens et al., 2022). Yet while heavy-handed interventions typically fail, leaders still need strategies to foster DEI in a hybrid workforce. The challenge is: how can meaningful progress be made organically?

The most effective approaches appeal to intrinsically shared values rather than imposing rules. Most employees instinctively care about fairness and helping colleagues thrive, and those innate beliefs can be activated through positive ethical messages instead of accusations or shame. For example, the outdoor apparel company Patagonia took a creative approach to retaining more new mothers. They didn't impose parental leave requirements. Instead, the leadership proactively ensured generous family bonding time was available equally to mothers and fathers. This became an organic cultural value. Turnover among female employees decreased dramatically (Chouinard & Stanley, 2012).

A similar theme emerged in an extensive review of social identification and health in organisations spanning two decades. Niklas Steffens and his team found that employees with a strong intrinsic identification to their organisation or team reported better health outcomes than employees motivated by extrinsic rewards (i.e. salary). This association was evident both in terms of mental well-being and physical health.

The benefits were more pronounced when there was a collective sense of identification within a group. They also found that, unsurprisingly, positivity and encouragement were more effective than penalty-based incentives that demanded compliance (Steffens et al., 2022).

DEI and cognitive diversity

In his book *Rebel Ideas*, Matthew Syed discusses how bringing together people with divergent thinking styles, knowledge bases and problem-solving approaches unlocks creativity and progress (Syed, 2019). He writes that the benefits of diversity come almost entirely from cognitive diversity.

When Alison Rose thought about diversity, she probably thought about disparities in gender, race, sexual orientation, age, religion and other categories. However, what makes demographic diversity powerful is not the different skin tones, genitalia or years people have lived on Earth, but the different life experiences that have led to different ways of thinking about and seeing the world.

There can be an overlap between cognitive diversity and demographic diversity, but not always. A British-born, upper-middle-class, Eton-educated, white lawyer is likely to think very similarly to a British-born, upper-middle-class, Eton-educated lawyer of Nigerian heritage. However, that upper-middle-class etc. white lawyer is likely to think very differently about life to a working-class woman, a gay working-class man or a second-generation son of Jamaican immigrant parents brought up in inner-city Birmingham. In addition, people who look and sound the same can be very diverse in their worldview. Matthew Syed puts this very well when he writes:

> Now take two white, middle-aged, bespectacled economists, who have the same number of children and like the same TV programmes. They may seem homogenous, and, from a demographic perspective, they are. But suppose that one of them is a monetarist and the other a Keynesian. These are two different ways of making sense of the economy; two very different models. Their collective prediction will, over time, be significantly better than either alone. The two economists may look the same but they are diverse in the way that they think about the problem.
>
> (Syed, 2019)

Cognitive diversity, especially when it is combined with a culture of psychological safety, dramatically improves performance in organisations. This is because a group or organisation will have a much more nuanced and comprehensive perception of the reality that they are facing.

The Japanese and American tropical fish study

Takahiko Masuda and Richard Nisbett, two social psychologists from the University of Michigan, wanted to know if cultural differences change how people see the world. By 'see' they meant what people actually experience as reality. Can culture make us blind to what is happening in front of our eyes? The researchers decided to compare two groups from very different cultures: American and Japanese.

They showed each group animated video clips of scenes of tropical fish swimming around in the sea. When the Americans were asked to describe what they saw, they tended to describe the characteristics of the individual fish. However, when the Japanese participants were asked the same question, they described the environment and the group of fish – in other words, the context.

Both groups were shown the same scene, but their descriptions (reflecting their perceptions) of the scene were radically different, as if they were describing completely different scenes. Put simply, the Americans saw individuals, and the Japanese saw groups and context.

This experiment was replicated, this time with images of wildlife. The American subjects were sensitive to changes in individual animals but almost blind to changes in the environment, whereas the Japanese subjects were almost blind to changes in individuals but were very attuned to the environment and context (Masuda & Nisbett, 2001).

This fascinating experiment demonstrates how much our upbringing and culture have an impact on how we perceive the outside world. The American subjects saw individuals in the scenes because they grew up in a society that overwhelmingly values individuality. Japanese culture places a much greater emphasis on groups and communities, and views groups as more important than just the individuals within them.

The study shows how important it is to have different ways of thinking. The Americans were unable to see certain things, but the Japanese could, and vice versa. The value would be astounding if this were used in a business setting.

Matthew Syed also discusses this:

> Suppose you were to combine a Japanese and an American in a 'team'. Alone, they might perceive only a partial picture. Alone, they each miss aspects of the scene. Together, however, they are able to recount both objects and context. By combining two partial frames of reference, the overall picture snaps into focus. They now have a more comprehensive grasp of reality.
>
> (Syed, 2019)

Cognitive diversity and the hybrid team

The research on cognitive diversity has important implications for leaders of hybrid organisations. With dispersed teams, there is an increased risk that groupthink could emerge if teams lack diversity of perspective. This is because they lack the cross-pollination of ideas that comes from meeting people from different parts of the organisation; they miss out on the 'collisions' and water cooler moments referred to in earlier chapters of this book.

Leaders of hybrid organisations should work hard to ensure that their teams include people with different thinking styles, such as by pairing detail-oriented employees with big-picture, creative types who challenge the status quo. They may mix classically trained engineers with self-taught programmers.

Diverse points of view do not always lead to better solutions; in the absence of psychological safety, junior staff or marginalised groups may self-censor. Leaders need to promote open communication so that people can respectfully argue about and combine different ideas. Different people can have different ideas about how to solve problems and see the world, but it does not help if they are afraid to say what they think; hence the need for a culture of psychological safety.

The 'G' in ESG: Governance factors

The letter 'G' stands for the governance systems that guide organisational oversight, ethics, risk management and accountability. Board composition, executive pay, internal controls, shareholder rights and transparency are all factors to consider.

Good governance requires more than formal policies, audits and control structures. The underlying organisational psychology and culture are equally crucial. Even ideal structures fail in the absence of a supportive collective mindset. This psychological dimension is especially important in hybrid organisations.

As we've seen, hybrid models introduce complex new dynamics requiring more nuanced governance to maintain cohesion and integrity across distances. Leaders who understand these psychological factors will be better able to implement effective governance.

Psychological factors in hybrid governance

At least five key psychological factors have an impact on governance:

Trust

Trust is essential for good governance because it allows for transparency, accountability and ethical behaviour. However, hybrid models offer fewer opportunities for trust to be built through daily in-person interactions and 'water cooler' bonding moments. Relationships tend to become more transactional and utilitarian, eroding trust. To counteract this, governance should include mechanisms that actively cultivate trust across distance.

Greater ambiguity in hybrid work necessitates a greater reliance on employees' good intentions. Conen et al. (2021) discovered that when leaders demonstrate benevolent trust in their employees by avoiding micromanagement, employees reciprocate with greater dedication and rule compliance. Closely monitoring remote workers signals distrust, undermining governance aims.

Psychological safety

As we already talked about, psychological safety means not having to worry about being punished for expressing worries, questions or different points of view. Because hybrid working offers fewer opportunities for informal relationship-building, leaders must take deliberate steps to foster psychological safety, such as regular check-ins, anonymous feedback channels and explicit invitations to participate (Carroll et al., 2022). Modelling openness and transparency also helps.

Organisational identification

A sense of belonging and alignment with the company's values increases intrinsic motivation to act responsibly on behalf of the organisation (Steffens et al., 2022). Weak identification puts workers at risk of becoming disengaged, lacking initiative and caring less about governance policies.

As bonds deteriorate over time and distance, hybrid working makes nurturing identification more difficult. Wiesenfeld et al. (2001) discovered that even in the absence of in-person contact, perceived social support and affiliation needs continue to drive organisational identification in remote settings. Managers should encourage social interactions and show concern for virtual employees in order to foster a sense of belonging and engagement.

Perspective-taking

Perspective-taking means looking at things from different points of view, not just your own. It helps you act more ethically by fighting narrow self-interest and biases (Galinsky et al., 2005). It provides diverse insights necessary for governance. However, because teams lack direct access to the realities of other groups, hybrid working risks fragmentation with the formation of sub-groups and silos. As a result, practices like job rotation, cross-functional projects and diversity promotion should be included in governance.

Shared mental models

Having shared mental models means that everyone understands their role and how decisions are made. Work goes more smoothly when people share their expectations. However, remote workers may not always be on the same page as office employees. As a result, hybrid team leaders must take steps to keep people's mental models aligned. Simply put, mental models are the guidelines in everyone's head. Leaders need to actively update them so that hybrid teams stay in sync. Shared mental models allow flexibility and prevent confusion. Leaders can align them by frequently showing visuals and discussing examples (Dionne et al., 2010). This clarity helps hybrid teams coordinate despite location differences.

ESG as shared vision

When implemented thoughtfully and strategically, ESG becomes a catalyst for bringing together diverse people, ideas and resources to creatively address pressing societal problems. The collective ingenuity unlocked when employees are engaged as partners in building a better future can generate technological and social breakthroughs that benefit both the organisation and the community.

ESG undertaken collectively taps into our innate human drive to make a positive difference. George Cadbury's vision for Bournville reminds us that ESG principles are not new; he built an entire village to uplift thousands through ethical business leadership over a century ago.

Today's hybrid organisations have a similar opportunity to implement comprehensive ESG strategies aimed at achieving financial success while also doing good on a social and environmental level. Adopting a purpose other than making money will be necessary to attract talent and meet societal expectations. Understanding psychology and motivation is essential for success. ESG rules that lack buy-in backfire, whereas participatory co-creation based on shared values results in real change. Just as Cadbury's legacy improved life in Bournville for generations, companies today can drive sustainable innovation that benefits all.

Questions to reflect on

1. How can you create a sense of collective purpose and ethics in your hybrid organisation?

2. What psychological insights are most important for you in your organisation to engage all employees on sustainability?
3. How can you find the best balance between business profits and social responsibility in your hybrid situation?
4. Is there any more you can do to make sure your hybrid teams have different ways of thinking and feel safe to express their different views?
5. What governance challenges arise from hybrid models in your organisation, and how can you address them through psychology?
6. What rituals and narratives could help you build shared identity and commitment across your distributed teams?
7. How can you motivate ethical behaviour in your hybrid organisation through creating cultural norms rather than just compliance?
8. What is needed for you to earn buy-in and participation for ESG initiatives in your context?
9. How can you ensure technology innovations in your organisation enhance meaningfulness rather than isolate people?

Key points

- Bournville, built by Cadbury's in the late 1800s, was an early model of ESG principles in action through good housing and facilities for workers.
- ESG factors like sustainability and diversity correlate with better business performance, but implementing ESG in hybrid models is challenging.
- Diversity brings creativity, but imposed DEI rules often backfire.
- Effective DEI appeals to shared values and requires a high level of psychological safety (feeling able to express minority views without risk of retaliation).
- Cognitive diversity – varied thinking styles and perspectives – is essential for innovation and avoiding groupthink in hybrid teams.
- Governance depends on psychological factors like trust, psychological safety, identification with the organisation, perspective-taking and shared mental models in hybrid contexts.
- Shared rituals and storytelling help remote staff develop collective identity and purpose, strengthening governance.
- Public commitments and grassroots culture tend to motivate ethical behaviour better than top-down policies and monitoring.
- Well-implemented ESG becomes a unifying call to apply ethics and compassion through collaboration on social and environmental goals.

References

Amel, E., Manning, C., Scott, B. & Koger, S. (2017). 'Beyond the Roots of Human Inaction: Fostering Collective Effort toward Ecosystem Conservation'. *Science*, 356 (6335), 275–279.

Barnes, O. (2022). 'City of London Has Lost 14% of Its Restaurants Since 2020'. *Financial Times*, 14 August. https://www.ft.com/content/f5f59e08-1dd4-41bb-a6f0-714e5c3ae47e.

Carroll, A., Conboy, K., Dennehy, D. & Morgan, L. (2022). '"It Feels Impersonal": Psychological Safety Erosion in Remote Working'. *Information Systems Frontiers*. https://doi.org/10.1007/s10796-022-10260-9.

Chouinard, Y. & Stanley, V. (2012). *The Responsible Company: What We've Learned from Patagonia's First 40 Years*. Ventura Ca: Patagonia.

Conen, W., Henkens, K. & Schippers, J. (2021). 'Making Your People Look Good from a Distance: Leader Impressions and Employee Effort in Virtual Settings'. *The Leadership Quarterly*, 32 (4), 101499.

Dickens, C. (1995). *Hard Times* (Wordsworth Classics) (K. Carabine [ed.]; New edition). Ware, Herts: Wordsworth Editions.

Dionne, S. D., Sayama, H., Hao, C. & Bush, B. J. (2010). 'The Role of Leadership in Shared Mental Model Convergence and Team Performance Improvement: An Agent-based Computational Model'. *The Leadership Quarterly*, 21 (6), 1035–1049.

Dobbin, F. & Kalev, A. (2016). 'Why diversity programs fail'. *Harvard Business Review*, 94 (7), 14.

Environmental Protection Agency. (EPA), (2021). 'Top ten ways to green your organization'. https://www.epa.gov/greenerproducts/top-ten-ways-green-your-organization

European Bank for Reconstruction and Development (EBRD) (2018). 'Sustainability Report 2017'. https://www.ebrd.com/sustainability-report-2017.

Flammer, C. (2013). 'Corporate Social Responsibility and Shareholder Reaction: The Environmental Awareness of Investors'. *Academy of Management Journal*, 56(3), 758–781.

Galinsky, A. D., Ku, G. & Wang, C. S. (2005). 'Perspective-taking and Self-other Overlap: Fostering Social Bonds and Facilitating Social Coordination'. *Group Processes & Intergroup Relations*, 8 (2), 109–124.

Hunt, V., Layton, D., Prince, S., (2015). 'Diversity Matters'. *McKinsey & Company*, 1 (1), 15–29. https://www.mckinsey.com/capabilities/people-and-organizational-performance/our-insights/~/media/2497d4ae4b534ee89d929cc6e3aea485.ashx.

Kish-Gephart, J., Detert, J., Treviño, L. K., Baker, V. & Martin, S. (2014). 'Situational Moral Disengagement: Can the Effects of Self-Interest Be Mitigated?' *Journal of Business Ethics*, 125, 267–285. https://doi.org/10.1007/s10551-013-1909-6.

Masuda, T. & Nisbett, R. E. (2001). 'Attending Holistically Versus Analytically: Comparing the Context Sensitivity of Japanese and Americans'. *Journal of Personality and Social Psychology*, 81 (5), 922.

Myers, D. G. & Lamm, H. (1976). 'The Group Polarization Phenomenon'. *Psychological Bulletin*, 83 (4), 602.

Patagonia (2023). 'Our Core Values'. https://eu.patagonia.com/gb/en/core-values.

Reich, A., Ullmann, E., Van der Loos, M. & Leifer, L. (2020). 'Igniting Innovation Power through Design Thinking and Effective Team Management'. *The Journal of Modern Project Management*, 7 (3).

Sparber, C. (2008). 'A Theory of Racial Diversity, Segregation, and Productivity'. *Journal of Development Economics*, 87 (2), 210–226.

Steffens, N. K., Yang, J., Jetten, J., Thai, H., Haslam, S. A., Yin, J. & Zheng, X. (2022). 'Control Deprivation Motivates Endorsement of Conspiracy Beliefs, Collective Narcissism, and Political Extremism: Evidence from China and Australia'. *Group Processes & Intergroup Relations*, 25 (2), 337–361.

Syed, M. (2019). *Rebel Ideas: The Power of Diverse Thinking*. London: John Murray.

Teger, A. I. & Pruitt, D. G. (1967). 'Components of Group Risk Taking'. *Journal of Experimental Social Psychology*, 3 (2), 189–205.

Wallach, M. A., Kogan, N. & Bem, D. J. (1964). 'Diffusion of Responsibility and Level of Risk Taking in Groups'. *The Journal of Abnormal and Social Psychology*, 68 (3), 263.

Wiesenfeld, B. M., Raghuram, S. & Garud, R. (2001). 'Organizational Identification Among Virtual Workers: The Role of Need for Affiliation and Perceived Work-based Social Support'. *Journal of Management*, 27 (2), 213–229. https://doi.org/10.1177/014920630102700205.

10 The Future of Hybrid
How to Make a Hybrid Company Where You Want to Work

Michael Drayton

This final chapter summarises the main ideas, plans and thoughts presented in this book. Its purpose is to build on the main points we have already talked about in order to give us a bigger picture and a look ahead.

This chapter is built around a set of questions designed to make you think about the main ideas in a way that is both interesting and useful. The purpose of these questions is to get you to think more deeply about how you can use the strategies described in this book when planning for the future of your own organisation.

It is time to think about the book's main ideas again from the point of view of what you can do. The questions and answers are both a review of what we have already discussed and a set of guidelines for successfully building and running a hybrid organisation.

While definitive answers are not always possible in the volatile, uncertain, complex and ambiguous landscape of hybrid working, the following questions are an opportunity to synthesise the research, models and examples presented in previous chapters.

The questions and answers that follow provide pathways, rather than prescriptions, for dealing with common hybrid leadership challenges. They are meant to make you think, give you direction, and give you the confidence to make smart choices when you are facing uncertainty. With these ideas in mind, you can shape the future of your hybrid organisation.

The leadership mindset

What is the best way to think about being a leader in a hybrid organisation?
'Leading a hybrid organisation requires a different mindset than leading a traditional organisation.'

In Chapter 1, I proposed that the key to effective leadership in a hybrid organisation is having the right mindset – a mindset that recognises the new problems and opportunities that come with the hybrid organisation. The way you think now might be better suited to running a traditional office-based business. This traditional approach to your changing organisation is suboptimal. It will probably keep things ticking along, but that's about all.

As a leader, your mindset is made up of the assumptions and beliefs you have about work that you have formed from leading traditional office-based teams in the past. This traditional mindset may have served you well in the past, but it may not be appropriate for leading hybrid teams today. To be successful, you must consciously change your mindset to accommodate the new realities of hybrid working.

You should consider changing three important things about the way you think as a leader of a hybrid organisation:

- Recognise that the prospect of change creates ambivalence. People have mixed feelings about the transition to hybrid working. There is excitement about the increased flexibility and autonomy. However, there is also apprehension about the unknown and disruption to established ways of working. As a leader, you must do your best to recognise, acknowledge and understand these conflicting emotions in your teams. Don't just list the benefits of hybrid working. Allow people to express their worries and do your best to address their concerns.
- Consider the change to hybrid working as a continuous, dynamic process. It's usually a case of 'two steps forward, one step back'. A variety of driving forces, such as improved work–life balance, influence the staff's attitude towards hybrid working, but these are hampered by resisting forces, such as concern about being out of sight and out of mind. As a leader, using Kurt Lewin's Force Field Analysis to look at these forces on a regular basis will be very helpful. Consider how you can strengthen forces that drive positive change while decreasing resistance.
- Use a more interactive, Theory Y-style of leadership to build trust. Traditional command-and-control management (Theory X) erodes trust between leaders and teams. This trust is essential for hybrid teams to function effectively. Adopt a more empowering, involving leadership approach aligned to Theory Y. Allow your employees autonomy, include them in the development of new processes and trust them to deliver without micromanagement. This gives employees a greater sense of control during the transition.

Additionally, you need to remain future-focused in your mindset. Look at the new opportunities that hybrid working opens up, like access to talent unrestricted by geography. Consider what capabilities your organisation will need to develop to capitalise on these opportunities. Avoid becoming fixated on old ways of doing things, as Kodak was with film.

In summary, successful leadership of hybrid organisations requires making some key mental shifts towards being more flexible, empowering and focused on the future. Leaders who consciously shift their mindset will be best positioned to help their organisations and people thrive in this new environment.

Creating a cohesive culture

What can I do to instil a strong sense of belonging and identification in my employees?
'Your team needs to meet in person on a consistent and predictable basis. It is best to do this once a week, but any regular, planned face-to-face meeting will be very helpful. When you do get together, avoid activities that can be done just as easily from home and instead do things that need to be done in person, like coming up with ideas, making plans or putting together teams.'

Chapter 2 explored identity and belonging in hybrid organisations. John Bowlby's ground-breaking research in attachment theory showed that people have an innate need to form attachments not just to other people but also to groups and places. Leaders who understand this attachment process can purposefully create a culture in which employees can form bonds with both their team and the larger organisation. This sense of belonging unlocks discretionary effort, creativity and performance. Chapter 2 discussed how this process of attachment can be applied to organisations, particularly hybrid organisations, to build a sense of belonging and minimise employee attrition.

The case study, cited in Chapter 2, clearly demonstrated this. New hires who received 'personal identity socialisation' during onboarding to reinforce their sense of belonging were 250 per cent more likely to stay long term than new recruits who received standard onboarding procedures.

In line with Bowlby's attachment theory, MIT's Thomas Allen discovered that the most important factor in team performance is the quantity and quality of communication in the team. The teams that communicated frequently and well delivered high-quality results on time. Those that communicated less frequently and less effectively delivered work that was not only late but also contained errors.

Allen also found that physical proximity is the most important factor in good team communication. He studied R&D teams and plotted communication frequency versus distance on his famous Allen Curve. Communication (and performance) quality declines rapidly when colleagues are more than six metres apart.

Allen discovered that remote teams benefit from proximity as well. Those who met in person on a regular basis worked better together online afterward because their bonds were stronger.

Ben Waber, an MIT researcher, used the lessons from Allen's Curve about proximity at Bank of America, with dramatic results. He was brought in to investigate chronic employee burnout and high turnover rates of around 40 per cent. Waber discovered that a lack of positive social connections at work was the root cause. He suggested that the office layout and schedules be optimised in order to increase daily interpersonal interactions.

For example, he suggested better positioning of coffee machines to make them gathering points during breaks. He also suggested aligning break times so that employees could take regular 15-minute coffee breaks together. He proposed that the tables in the staff restaurant be changed from four-person to ten-person tables. These seemingly minor changes to allow for more employee 'collisions' and social time had a significant impact. Employee burnout significantly decreased. Turnover dropped from 40 per cent to 12 per cent. Furthermore, team productivity increased by more than 20 per cent.

If you want to instil a strong sense of belonging and identification in your employees, try the following:

- When teams do meet, ensure your office layout gets them collaborating shoulder to shoulder, not isolated. Use Allen's six-metre rule to bring people physically close together. Clustering desks sparks the communication and camaraderie that Allen uncovered.
- Consider the type of work that people do when they are in the office. Use the valuable face-to-face time to carry out tasks that require a high level of communication and creativity, such as strategic planning or team building. Bringing people into the office and asking them to do work that they could easily do at home is pointless and will most likely irritate them. One possible work structure would be to gather people in the office to plan a new initiative and then divide up and assign tasks that can be completed while working from home.
- Establish hubs and spaces for employees to congregate and socialise during in-person time. Set up focal points, such as good-quality coffee machine stations, as Waber suggests, to turn breaks into bonding events. Also, make it a habit to take breaks together rather than separately.
- Make sure that teams have regular and frequent offsites/meetups to encourage bonding in remote teams. Thomas Allen found that even occasional face-time significantly improve collaboration and performance. So budget for regular get-togethers.

- Build bonding into onboarding, like WIPRO. Allow new employees to speak about themselves and their roles. Give them branded merchandise that connects them to the company's identity.

In summary, thoughtfully designed physical proximity and social rituals foster the interpersonal closeness that leads to attachment. People make friends and feel a sense of belonging and identify with the organisation. This pays dividends in discretionary effort and performance. It is critical for a leader to cultivate a sense of belonging.

Change management

What is the most effective way to manage change in my hybrid organisation?
'When you approach change, don't just address the reasons to change – focus on the reasons why people don't want to change and address those.'

Organisational change is never easy. We talked about this in the first chapter. The prospect of change is frequently met with opposition. Many employees prefer what they know and are apprehensive about what they do not know. So how do you lead effective change?

Do you remember Peter's story from Chapter 1? Despite the CEO's demands, Peter refuses to come into the office for a couple of days a week. Why? The social psychologist Kurt Lewin would say that Peter probably has mixed feelings. Part of him understands the importance of face-to-face collaboration. However, the restraining forces – his comfort with working from home, his desire not to waste time commuting – are currently influencing his behaviour.

Lewin would no doubt advise Peter's manager to figure out and address Peter's objections to coming in rather than bombarding him with reasons to come in. In other words, remove the restraining factors.

According to Kurt Lewin, behaviour is influenced by two opposing factors: driving forces that push for change and restraining forces that resist change. This is his force field theory of change.

Lewin also found that successful change happens through a three-step process: unfreezing the current equilibrium state, making the desired change and then refreezing into a new equilibrium. Understanding the complex balance of forces and nudging them in the direction of the desired change is the key.

The sad story of Kodak's demise exemplifies this process. Despite the fact that Kodak invented the first digital camera in 1975, the company's leadership remained firmly committed to their legacy product – film photography. Their underlying mindset never unfroze. They persisted in viewing Kodak as a film and photographic chemicals company rather than a 'memories' company. The *restraining forces* of legacy systems, old habits and short-term profits outweighed the *driving forces* towards digital transformation. Kodak is a cautionary tale of what happens when leaders cling to outdated legacy mindsets rather than adapting to a rapidly changing society and market.

Here are some ideas based on Kurt Lewin's work to help you manage change in your hybrid organisation:

- Identify driving and restraining forces. What factors encourage change? What's holding people back?
- Strengthen drivers. Add incentives, promote benefits, align processes.
- Reduce restraints. Address concerns, modify policies, provide resources.
- Communicate clearly. Explain the what, how and why of changes.
- Allow time for refreezing. People need time to adjust to a new equilibrium.

The key point is to try your best to deeply understand the forces driving and restraining change. Superficial initiatives will fail.

Adaptation to hybrid work

Why do some people thrive on hybrid work while others struggle?
'Remember, everyone is different. Some people like working in groups, others like working alone. Some people hate change, other people hate being bored. Try to fit people's hybrid work tasks to their personality.'

Chapter 3 explored individual personality differences and hybrid working. People's reactions to hybrid work arrangements are heavily influenced by their individual personalities. According to the big five model, our personality is made up of five factors: openness, conscientiousness, extraversion, agreeableness and neuroticism. Our overall personality style, and thus how we adapt to change, is determined by whether we are 'high' or 'low' on each factor.

Those with a high level of openness thrive on variety and novelty. They like the change of pace that hybrid schedules provide. Those who are less open prefer predictability and routine. They dislike the disruption of changing locations during the week.

Conscientious people are well-organised and diligent. They like how the office gives them structure and limits. People who are not very conscientious do not like rules and being watched. They may take advantage of the flexibility of working from home.

Extroverts feel energised when they are around other people. When they work from home, they feel alone and isolated. Going back to work gives them a chance to recharge. Introverts find constant interaction stressful and exhausting. They flourish with the peaceful focus that home offers.

People with a high level of agreeableness enjoy collaborating. When working from home, they miss their office's social connections. Disagreeable employees like having freedom. They might fight against rules that require them to be at work at certain times.

People with high neuroticism become anxious when things are uncertain or changing. Their already high level of anxiety will be exacerbated by hybrid arrangements. Individuals who are emotionally stable cope well with ambiguity and transition.

As organisations transition to hybrid models, people's personalities serve as either driving or restraining forces. Leaders can provide flexibility and support by understanding how each employee is affected. This helps everyone on the team to do their best, even if they have different wants and needs.

Here is some advice on how to improve performance by matching personalities to task and environment:

- Try to understand and think about the personalities of your team members when you consider what they will do in a hybrid workplace.
- Be flexible when assigning office versus remote days based on what you have seen. For example, give extraverts more days to work in the office to meet their need to work with others. Give introverts and autonomous employees more remote days for focused work.
- Be clear about what you want. Highly conscientious and high-neuroticism employees need structure to do their jobs well. Set clear ground rules and guidelines for both office and remote work, such as when to start, take breaks and end work. Check in frequently.
- Try to accommodate preferences whenever possible. Look for ways to accommodate a highly introverted employee who excels at working remotely. Give an extravert first dibs on in-person activities if they enjoy the office.

Watch out for things that could lead to conflict. Employees who are not very agreeable may not follow the rules. Avoid conflicts by meeting to discuss issues openly. Reframe issues as solving challenges together.

Finding the right balance between being consistent and being able to adapt to different personalities is key. Encourage a culture of trust in which employees can do their best regardless of work location.

Communication strategies

What are the most effective methods of communication in a hybrid organisation?
'Keep online or virtual meetings short. If the meeting's purpose is to develop strategy and teams, try to hold it in person. Prioritise actual work over virtual meetings. Recognise, understand and build on the cultural differences in international teams. Let people focus on their work without being interrupted by email and messaging services.'

Chapter 4 discussed how best to communicate in a hybrid organisation. As we saw in Thomas Allen's work, good communication is critical for organisational performance, but hybrid working presents significant challenges. While virtual tools such as Zoom make remote collaboration easier, they fall short of replicating the creative spark of in-person interactions. Leaders have to find an artful way to combine online and offline communication methods in a way that optimises the quantity and quality of team communication.

For online communication, Chapter 4 presented compelling evidence that 'bursty' exchanges outperform drawn-out meetings. People can share their ideas quickly when they talk to each other in short, focused bursts. This speeds up work and gets it done faster. On the other hand, people can do mentally demanding tasks (called 'deep work') without being interrupted when they spend more time in silence and all forms of communication are turned off. This pattern fits the natural rhythms of office communication better than back-to-back video conferences.

Leaders can encourage deep work by limiting the number of online distractions. If there are fewer pings and notifications, employees can focus for long periods of time on tasks that require a lot of mental effort. Try to schedule online meetings sparingly, clustering necessary discussions into targeted bursts while preserving long stretches for independent work. Give people permission to turn off alerts and close unnecessary browser tabs during independent work.

When teams meet in person, the power of unplanned 'collisions' for sparking innovation and strengthening bonds is unleashed, as ex-Zappos CEO Tony Hsieh knew. As employees converse casually at the water cooler, these chance meetings spread ideas. We have already explored the ideas of Thomas Allen and Ben Waber about designing workplaces to optimise these employee collisions.

A major issue in many global organisations is that their hybrid teams are dispersed globally and include people of various nationalities and, of course, cultures. These teams can struggle to perform at times due to conflicts caused by misunderstandings about different cultural norms and communication styles. This problem, as I described in Chapter 4, was studied by Joe DiStefano and Martha Maznevski. They identified three types of global teams in their research:

- **Creator teams** use their diversity as a positive attribute to solve hard problems and develop creative solutions. They are good at acknowledging differences, managing conflict and generally creating an atmosphere of psychological safety.
- **Equaliser teams** adopt a 'we are all equal' mentality that emphasises commonality while minimising differences among members. These groups are in denial about their differences. They get along fine in general, but they tend to produce boring, mediocre work.
- **Destroyer teams** are dysfunctional because they frequently dismiss or ridicule each other's cultural norms. This causes withdrawal and paralysis as a result of unresolved conflicts over differences. They spend more time arguing about differences and diversity than they do on the job. Instead of creating value, these teams actively destroy it.

To guide global teams in journeying from destructive to generative, DiStefano and Maznevski put forward the Map-Bridge-Integrate framework:

- **Map** involves objectively describing differences in abilities between team members, allowing complementary strengths to be identified.
- **Bridge** focuses on communicating across cultural divides, building trust through empathy and mutually adjusting communication patterns.
- **Integrate** involves vigilantly monitoring participation to ensure inclusion, bringing to light and resolving disagreements, and synthesising novel solutions that incorporate diverse perspectives.

This ongoing process necessitates dedication, but it allows diverse teams to view their multinational makeup as an asset rather than a liability.

Implications for hybrid teams include explicitly acknowledging cultural differences in communication, actively managing speaking patterns to equalise contribution, and remaining vigilant of conflict hotspots that can stymie progress.

Here are three key things you can do to improve communication in your hybrid team:

- Use rapid online 'bursts' for coordination. Brief, focused messaging exchanges outperform long virtual meetings. Quick back-and-forths keep work moving.

- Optimise face-to-face time. Through accidental 'collisions', in-person interactions generate more ideas. Bring team members together in person whenever possible.
- Bridge cultural divides. Recognise and adapt to differences in communication styles. Make sure everyone feels heard.

Allocating work

How can I best allocate tasks to maximise performance, taking into consideration the varying attributes/strengths/weaknesses of the home and office workspace?

As discussed in Chapter 5, the workplace has evolved dramatically from the private offices of 1960s advertising firms to today's open, collaborative designs, influenced by technological advancements, cultural shifts, and shifting workforce priorities. For example, the rigid hierarchy and formality of the 1960s *Mad Men* era gave way to more informal, creative layouts, such as the German "Bürolandschaft" model. The introduction of computers in the 1980s revolutionised workflows, and in the 2000s, companies such as WeWork captured the gig economy's desire for flexibility.

However, while superficial elements such as space configuration and dress codes have evolved significantly, the fundamental human need for connection and community remains. Because the pandemic and lockdown suddenly spread out the workforce, leaders need to think carefully about how to boost productivity, creativity and a sense of belonging in a model that uses both real and virtual spaces.

In a hybrid working model, the best way to assign tasks is to match each task to the optimal environment – home or office – for that task. Tasks that require concentration or deep thought, such as data analysis or report writing, are usually better suited to the controlled, quiet environment of a home workspace. On the other hand, collaborative, creative tasks like brainstorming and planning benefit from the energy and direct interaction of an office setting.

To determine the best task allocation, first create a comprehensive list of all organisational tasks and responsibilities. Next, assess the skills, competencies, and working style required for each task. Finally, assign tasks to the workspace that best meets these requirements, such as individual concentration-based work to home offices and team-based creative tasks to company workspaces. Furthermore, recognise that some complex projects may include both independent and collaborative components, and plan for a hybrid approach accordingly.

Approaching task allocation in this deliberate, methodical way allows you to strategically harness the unique attributes and strengths of both the home and office. Workers can access the optimal environment to increase their productivity for each assignment. This thoughtful distribution of responsibilities encourages employee autonomy while maintaining connection through shared in-office collaboration. Overall, consciously matching tasks to workspaces allows for optimal execution, which drives organisational success.

Ensuring security

How can I reduce the risk of security breaches in my hybrid organisation?
'To reduce security risks, businesses should have strict hiring procedures, constant monitoring, helpful interventions, and strong onboarding and off-boarding systems. These should all be part of a trust-based security culture.'

We discussed security in hybrid organisations in Chapter 6. The shift to working from home caused by the pandemic has created new data-security problems. The more employees access sensitive information from home on personal devices, the more vulnerable those employees become.

The Critical Pathway model shows the steps that many insiders take before breaching security procedures. Rule-breaking is preceded by personal predispositions, stressors and concerning behaviours. People can then be pushed further down the path by bad responses from organisations.

In the chapter, we discussed the story of Nick, a software engineer who leaked and sold his company's confidential data after a rejected job application stressed him out. Even though Nick's colleagues had complained about him before, leaders turned a blind eye because they valued his expertise. This emboldened him in his wrongdoing.

If leaders want to lower the risk of security breaches, they should follow these suggestions:

1. Begin by thoroughly screening new employees, particularly for remote positions. Do not just rely on background checks, which only show past behaviour. Ask deep questions to find out what someone is really thinking and how loyal they are.
2. When someone first starts working for the company, make them aware of the rules about ethics and security, as well as what will happen if these rules are broken.
3. Always be on the lookout for strange or odd behaviours, such as downloading files without permission, working odd hours or mood changes. Keep an eye out for things that do not seem to fit with what you normally do at work or online.

4. If employees exhibit warning signs, respond with support rather than punishment. Health and morale-boosting programmes show that you care about their success.
5. Finally, manage exits proactively. Implement comprehensive offboarding procedures, such as revoking network credentials. Also, keep in mind that even after the person has left the organisation, inside knowledge still poses risks.

Overall, addressing the human factors that contribute to insider threats is critical. Technical controls cannot prevent all intentional or unintentional data breaches. The best prevention is to cultivate a security-conscious culture based on trust and care.

Employee well-being

What can I do in my hybrid organisation to boost well-being and reduce burnout?
'Burnout is usually caused by problems in the organisation (inefficient organisation of work, poor boundaries around start/finish times, frequent interruptions) rather than by personal weakness. Leaders should set clear rules about working from home, help people who get tired of working online, make sure home offices are set up correctly, and encourage people to take frequent breaks, take time away from their screens and do some exercise. Workloads must be monitored on a regular basis, roles must be aligned with individual strengths and a sense of purpose must be fostered to create a sustainable hybrid work culture that benefits both employees and the organisation.'

In Chapter 7, we discussed how to build a healthy hybrid organisation. Remote work allows for greater flexibility, but it can also lead to isolation and blurred work–life boundaries. If you do not take the right precautions, these things can cause stress, workaholism and finally burnout, which is a state of being so tired that you cannot do anything and you feel cynical and less effective.

It is important for leaders to understand that burnout is more often caused by problems within the company than by weakness in individuals. Your employees can do well if you give them the right tools, like Tim, the lawyer in Chapter 7. When the managing partner at Tim's law firm implemented some relatively simple and easy changes, stress levels decreased and productivity increased for everyone.

If you want to do this, make clear policies about remote work. Set up regular times for working together and having meetings. Ban people from sending emails after work hours and reinforce this by not doing it yourself – be a good role model.

Watch out for 'Zoom fatigue', which is exhausting and often wastes time. Follow Christoph Riedl's 'bursty work' model by alternating periods of intense online teamwork with quiet time to work alone.

Make sure that every employee has a proper home-office setup. Offer technical support and training in cybersecurity. Laptops and ergonomically designed furniture can help people work from home and avoid stress.

Bring together remote workers in person to help them make friends, feel connected and avoid feeling alone. Get people to pair up for virtual coffee breaks. Host online social events. Rewarding people for their hard work boosts morale and draws people together.

Check in often to look at the workload and warn of the risk of burnout. Adjust responsibilities before overload becomes chronic. Offer empathy, rather than judgement, if employees struggle. Provide access to confidential counselling.

Cultivate meaning and purpose in work. Craft roles aligned with individuals' strengths and passions. Remind teams of their contributions to organisational goals. According to Antonovsky's theory, comprehension, manageability and meaning bolster resilience.

Essentially, employee wellness is a shared duty. Individuals must care for themselves through self-care practices and setting boundaries. But leaders play the bigger role in making hybrid models humane and sustainable.

Remember, burned-out employees are symptomatic of a diseased organisation. Healing requires systemic change to foster psychologically safe cultures. This ultimately benefits both employee health and the bottom line.

Leadership style

How could I adapt my leadership style to best lead my hybrid organisation?

'To lead hybrid teams effectively, adopt an adaptive, empowering style like Ernest Shackleton – set a vision, but allow flexibility in reaching goals. Attend to psychological needs building trust and safety. Take a "healer" approach – unify teams by revealing purpose, making space for emotions and compassionately processing change.'

Chapter 8 examined the challenges that leaders face when guiding organisations through the transition to hybrid working. A lot of employees are worried about how this ongoing process of change might affect their day-to-day work life and their future. Leaders need to deal with these fears by understanding and focusing on the basic psychological needs of people going through this transition.

The chapter began by looking at Ernest Shackleton's 1914 Antarctic expedition to demonstrate the difficulties of leading during uncertainty. The crew was marooned in bitterly cold conditions after his ship became trapped in ice floes, seemingly without hope. But Shackleton kept all 27 men alive for months and eventually led them to safety. He accomplished this by remaining positive, being creative and being genuinely concerned about their well-being. His adaptability, open communication and hands-on leadership style were effective and remain so today.

Shackleton encouraged collaboration and publicly acknowledged and praised hard work and accomplishments. He also worked hard to get to know each man on a personal level by having casual conversations with them one on one while working with them on the ice. Shackleton talked to his crew a lot about the situation, the plan and what was expected of them so that everyone knew what the priorities were. He also actively asked everyone on the team, no matter what rank they were, to give input and take part in decisions. His forward-thinking adaptability and preference for flexible backup plans over strict adherence to protocol allowed him to quickly change course when things suddenly got worse. Despite their being marooned, Shackleton inspired his crew's grit, tenacity and sense of belonging by leading by example, showing compassion and encouraging mutual loyalty.

To maintain cohesion and effectiveness in today's disrupted, anxious hybrid teams, similarly enlightened leadership is required. The chapter discussed David Rock's SCARF model, which shows how ambiguity activates the brain's natural threat response in areas like status, certainty, autonomy, relatedness and fairness. This impairs higher cognitive functions, narrows focus, causes unhelpful emotional reactions such as blame or withdrawal, and reduces overall performance. Improving and supporting these SCARF domains, on the other hand, elicits counter-reward emotions like safety, trust and motivation, which act as enablers of openness and change.

According to David Rock's neuroscience research, leaders of hybrid organisations must ensure that remote employees have the same status and recognition as office employees, reduce uncertainty by over-communicating context and plans, foster autonomy by avoiding micromanagement, proactively build interpersonal connections both virtually and in person, and emphasise fairness in policies and opportunities across locations. Taking each of these steps helps to reduce anxiety among employees while also activating engagement, creativity and performance.

The chapter also focused on the critical role that psychological safety plays in enabling hybrid teams to collaborate across distance and digital barriers by reducing what David Rock would see as the threat response.

For instance, Google's two-year Project Aristotle showed that psychological safety was the most important factor in predicting how well a team would work together, even after looking at a lot of other structural, skill and resource factors. Leaders who want to optimise hybrid teams must set an example of openness, listen attentively without judgement, facilitate equal participation across locations and provide developmental feedback. This builds trust and communication channels that help to connect people in different places and over different technologies.

Finally, the chapter introduced the emerging 'leader as healer' paradigm developed by organisational consultant Nicholas Janni. This holistic approach to leadership recognises that today's leaders must address the deeper psychological and spiritual disconnections and organisational fragmentation exacerbated by the pandemic and consequent disruptions of hybrid working.

Instead of 'command and control', healer leaders lead through inspiration, emotional awareness, ethics and purpose. They strive to bring together fractured, siloed teams by revealing shared purpose and creating environments where people feel safe to be authentic and vulnerable.

Such leaders create space for difficult emotions, compassionately bringing to light hidden conflicts, championing transparency and guiding groups to process grief mindfully when losses occur. This reintegrates fragmented parts of the organisation, creating a renewed sense of individual and collective wholeness.

Ethical considerations

How can I ensure that my hybrid organisation is both environmentally and socially responsible, as well as well-governed?
'Inspire your team to engage in sustainability through purpose and meaning by tapping into their intrinsic motivation to do the right thing. This is far more effective than rules and corporate virtue signalling. By embracing cognitive diversity, you can create an organisation where different ways of thinking and seeing things can thrive, making sure that everyone's voice is heard and valued. Finally, strengthen the bonds between your remote and on-site teams by using rituals and stories. These not only help to create a sense of shared identity and commitment, but they also help to make sure that ethical standards are deeply ingrained in the company culture.'

Chapter 9 explored how organisations exist within an interconnected social ecosystem. When businesses adopt new business models, such as hybrid working, there are ripple effects on communities.

The chapter described how, towards the end of the nineteenth century, the chocolate manufacturer Cadbury's built an idyllic garden village called Bournville south of Birmingham to house factory workers. The concepts that led to the construction of Bournville were similar to what we would call environmental, social and governance (ESG) today. Bournville provided employees with far better living conditions than Birmingham's crowded, unsanitary slums. Workers enjoyed pleasant cottages with gardens, plenty of green space, recreation facilities and an overall healthy environment.

This wasn't only a philanthropic gesture. Cadbury's saw that taking care of their employees' health and happiness made them more loyal, motivated and productive. Long before the term 'corporate social responsibility', the company linked profit and social responsibility. George Cadbury and Bournville exemplified ESG values.

Chapter 9 discussed how today's leaders have a once-in-a-lifetime opportunity to implement comprehensive ESG strategies. However, disruption from hybrid models has complicated matters. Leaders must be psychologically and culturally sensitive in this unique situation.

The chapter discusses environmental protection. Remote work in hybrid organisations could reduce emissions, but mandates alone will not inspire engagement. Leaders must tap into intrinsic motivations by linking sustainability to a common goal and meaning.

For example, the outdoor clothing company Patagonia integrated environmental values into its culture through strategies like:

- Giving employees training focused on sustainability
- Giving people paid time off to do green voluntary work
- Publicly stating its goals and accomplishments
- Empowering employees to launch grassroots initiatives.

By putting principles into action, Patagonia transformed abstract concepts like waste reduction into meaningful and practical initiatives.

The next part of the chapter talked about social factors, mainly diversity, equity and inclusion (DEI). Extensive research has shown that diversity led to higher performance. Yet heavy-handed DEI initiatives frequently backfired due to psychological and emotional resistance.

Effective leaders did not impose rules; instead, they appealed to core values such as fairness and created a psychologically safe environment for people with opposing viewpoints to speak up. This is where 'cognitive diversity' comes into play – diversity in thinking styles as well as demographic diversity. Leaders needed to actively encourage different points of view in order to foster innovation and avoid narrow-minded groupthink.

Psychological safety meant that all employees felt safe expressing minority views without fear of retaliation. The benefits of diversity can only emerge if people are willing to express and listen to different points of view.

The chapter talked about how important psychology is in governance. Hybrid models destroyed the shared identity and casual connections that made people act in an ethical way. Using rituals and stories can reverse this erosion and bring remote and office-based teams back together with a common goal. Ethical social norms are not just imposed from the top down; they are formed through relationships between peers.

In summary:

- Engage people in sustainability through purpose and meaning, not just policies.
- Embrace cognitive diversity; actively nurture varied thinking styles and perspectives. Ensure psychological safety for all views.
- Strengthen social connections. Use rituals and storytelling to reignite shared identity and commitment across distributed teams. Shape ethical norms through culture.

Conclusion

The future of work is hybrid.

Transitioning from a conventional to a hybrid model is challenging and complex, but its potential is vast with proper leadership and management. This final chapter has synthesised the essential lessons on leading hybrid organisations effectively.

Change always starts from within. Before trying to change your organisation, you have to change yourself. Leaders should shift their mindset and perspectives towards openness to new ways of working, adaptability, empowerment and forward-thinking, understanding both the drivers and resistors of change.

With careful planning, hybrid work has the potential to significantly humanise work by giving people more autonomy and opportunities. Leaders must, however, stay alert. Blind reliance on technology or establishing rules without due consideration can result in pushback and disengagement. Ethical considerations, wellness and sustainability should take precedence over pure utility in technological applications.

What kind of future do you want to create? Try not to let the pursuit of perfection get in the way of your progress. Most of time, 'good enough' is better than 'perfect'. Navigating the hybrid landscape is a team journey, but one that requires you, the leader, to be fully present in the moment. The path forward is shaped by your attentive listening and flexibility, and the quality of your team's relationships. In forging ahead, always remember that your choices and presence set the tone, guiding your team towards a successful, high-performance hybrid organisation.

Index

Note: Information in figures and tables is indicated by page numbers in *italics* and **bold,** respectively.

acceptance 49
adaptability, leadership and 138–139
adaptation, to hybrid work 177–178
agreeableness 47, 50, 178
Allen, Thomas 28–30, 174–175, 179
Allen Curve 29, 30, 32–33
Amazon 149–150
Antonovsky, Aaron 128–129
anxious-preoccupied attachment style 52
Apple (company) 17
assessment, personality 44–45
assumptions, in organisational culture 64
attachments: group identity and 20–23; to groups 22–23; hybrid team and 26–28; to places 22–23; to workplace 27
attachment style 51–53
attachment theory 21–24, 26–30, 51
authoritarian management style 12
authority, leadership and 145–146
autonomy, in SCARF model 143–144

background checks 112
Bakewell, William 139
Bannister, Don 43
Barker, Pat 120
behaviour change 13–14
belonging, sense of 23–26, 174–175
Berne, Eric 51–52
big five model of personality 43–44
Bowlby, John 21–22, 24

brainwriting 69–70, 149
bridging 68, 180
bring your own device (BYOD) 91–92
Bunn, Matthew 112
burnout 118–119, 183–184; defining 122–124; as gradual process 124–125; in hybrid workplace 121–122; organisational context of 123–124
Bürolandschaft 76–78
BYOD *see* bring your own device (BYOD)

Cadbury, George 157–158, 168
Capparell, Stephanie 137
certainty, in SCARF model 143–144
change: in behaviour 13–14; Lewin and 5–7; in people 4; process of 7–10; psychology of 5; SCARF model and 142; success with 10; trust and 14
change management 176–177
cognitive diversity 164, 166
coherence theory 128–129
Cold War 28
communication: brainwriting and 69–70; bursty 65–66, 179; challenges of hybrid work 58–59; diversity and 66–69; genuine 152; in hybrid organisations 56–71; interpersonal collisions and 60–62; leadership and 139, 141; open 139, 141; optimal online 65; organisational culture

Index

and, importance of 63–65; over-communication 139; psychological safety and 148; social norms and 62–63; strategies 179–181; *Titanic* disaster as lesson in 56–58
commutes 118
comprehensibility 129
confidence, lack of 146
connectedness, well-being and 127–128
conscientiousness 46, 48–49, 177
conspiracies, insider 112
corruption 97
COVID-19 pandemic 2, 92–93
Coyle, Daniel 25, 34
creators 67, 180
crime script 104, **104**
Critical Pathway 97–99, *98*, 182–183
cross-cultural teams 66–69
cubicles 77
culture, organisational 63–65, 112–113, 174–176
Culture Code, The (Coyle) 25

data retention 110–111
data theft 97
DEI *see* diversity, equity, inclusion (DEI)
demotions 110
destroyers 67, 180
Dickens, Charles 157
Diderot, Denis 77
disclosures, unauthorized 97
disconnection 150–151; *see also* isolation
dismissive-avoidant attachment style 52
DiStefano, Joe 67–68, 180
distractions, well-being and 127
diversity 66–69
diversity, equity, inclusion (DEI) 161–164, 187
due diligence, in risk management 108

Eastman, George 15
Edmondson, Amy 61–62
Ellis, Kevin 59

empathy, psychological safety and 148–149
enabling environment 84–86
environment: enabling 84–86; hybrid work, as mixed blessing 118; supportive work 109
environmental, social, governance (ESG) 187; environmental aspect of 159–161; governance factors in 166–168; in hybrid organisations 158–159; psychological factors and 159–160; as shared vision 168; social factors in 161–166; in Victorian period 156–158
equalisers 67, 180
ESG *see* environmental, social, governance (ESG)
extraversion 46–47, 49–50

failure, fear of 145
fairness, in SCARF model 144
Farage, Nigel 162
fearful-avoidant attachment style 52–53
fear of failure 145
Ferriss, Tim 78
Force Field Analysis 13, 16–17
forming, with teams 35
4-Hour Work Week, The: Escape the 9–5, Live Anywhere, and Join the New Rich (Ferriss) 78
fraud 97
freeze, in change process 8
Freud, Sigmund 42–43
Freudenberger, Herbert 122

Gestalt theory 136
gig economy 78
Godin, Seth 32
Goldsmith, Marshall 3, 136
Google 146–147
group identity: attachments and 20–23; in hybrid organisations 20–36; teams and 27–28

Hanssen, Robert 97–98
Hard Time (Dickens) 157
Hemingway, Ernest 8
Hobsbawm, Julia 58–59

Holmes, Jeremy 22
Hsieh, Tony 34, 60–62, 82, 179
Human Side of Enterprise, The (McGregor) 11
hybrid organisations: burnout in 121–122; communication in 56–71; employee engagement in 130; environmental, social, governance in 158–159; evolving workplaces and 73–87; future of 172–188; group identity in 20–36; healing in 152; interpersonal collisions and 60–62; leadership mindset in 2–3; mindset and 17–18; risk management in 105–113, *107*; security in 89–113; task allocation in 86; well-being in 125–127
hybrid working: adaptation to 177–178; attachment theory and 26–28; communication challenges of 58–59; communication effects of 59–60; as important issue 1–2; return to office and 4–5; symbolic meaning of 81

imposter syndrome 145
individualism 165
insider trading 97
integrating 68, 180
isolation 118, 126–127; *see also* disconnection

James, Reginald 140
Jobs, Steve 17
Jung, Carl 78–80, 151–152

Kodak 14–18

leadership: adaptability and 138–139; of anxious hybrid team 142–144; authority and 145–146; communication and 139, 141; by example 137–138, 141, 148; as exploration 136–137; fear of failure and 145; flexibility and 141; as healing 150–153; in hybrid organisation 135–153; mindset 2–3, 14–18, 172–174; modeling healthy 152; morale and 140; motivation and 140–141; optimism and 140–141; perfectionism and 145; principles 141; SCARF model and 142–144; style *130*, 130–131, 184–186; technology and 141; trust and 11–12; vision and 141; well-being and *130*, 130–131
leaks, media 97
Lewin, Kurt 5–7, 16–17, 129
life-cycle model, in risk management 106

Machiavelli, Nikolai 5
Mad Men 75–76
manageability 129
management style: authoritarian 12; participative 13
Manning, Chelsea 91
mapping 68, 180
Masuda, Takahiko 165
Maznevski, Martha 67–68, 180
McGregor, Douglas 11
meaningfulness 129
media leaks 97
morale, leadership and 140
Morrell, Margot 137
motivation, leadership and 140–141
move, in change process 8–9

NatWest Bank 162–163
neuroticism 47, 50–51
NIMO (not in my organisation) 112
Nisbett, Richard 165
norming, with teams 35
norms, social 62–63
Nowhere Office, The (Hobsbawm) 58–59

office: in 1960s Manhattan 75–76; Bürolandschaft and 76–78; gig economy and 78; history of 75–84; open-plan 76–78; as symbol 78–81
onboarding 108–109
openness 46–48, 177
optimism 140–141
Ortis, Cameron 103

Index

pandemic 2
participation, psychological safety and 148
participative management style 13
Patagonia 160–161
perfectionism 145
performance, proximity and 28–30, *29*
performing, with teams 35
personality: big five model of 43–51; defining 40–42; in Freud 42–43; history of thought on 42–43; in Plato 42; self-assessment 44–45
personality theory 40–41
perspective-taking 167–168
places, attachment to 22–23
Plato 42
Project Aristotle 146–147, 186
promotions 110
Propst, Robert 77
proximity, performance and 28–30, *29*
psychological energy 84–86
psychological safety 146–150, 167
psychology, of change 5

Rebel Ideas (Syed) 164
red flags 112
reflection, well-being and 127
refreeze, in change process 9–10
Regeneration (Barker) 120
relatedness, in SCARF model 144
resistance 49
return to office 4–5, 38–40, 53–54
reward response 142–143
risk management 105–113, *107*
Rock, David 135, 142
Rose, Alison 162–163

safety, psychological 146–150, 167
Sagan, Scott 112
SCARF model 142–144, 185
secure attachment style 51–52
security: coerced insiders and 95–96; corruption and 97; COVD-19 pandemic and 92–93; crime script and 104, **104**; data theft and 97; ensuring 182–183; fraud and 97; history of organisational 90–91; in hybrid organisations 89–113; infiltrators in 96; insider risk and 97–99, *98*; insider threats and 91–105; insider trading and 97; intentional insider threats and 95; media leaks and 97; mitigating factors in 104–105; organisational culture and 112–113; personal predispositions and 99–100; problematic organisational responses and 102–104; rule breakers in 96–97; sabotage and 97; stressors and 100–101, **101**; unauthorised disclosures and 97; unintentional insider threats and 95; workplace violence and 97
self-assessment, personality 44–45
self-limiting beliefs 145
self-reflection 105–106, 127, 152
Seligman, Martin 140
Sellers, Laura 98
Shackleton, Ernest 135–137
Shackleton's Way: Leadership Lessons from the Great Antarctic Explorer (Morrell and Capparell) 137
shared mental models 168
Sharp, Nick 93–94
Shaw, Eric 98
social activities, with teams 27
social media 92
social norms 62–63
Sorkin, Andrew Ross 57–58
sourcing, risk management and 107–108
Staats, Bradley 24
status, in SCARF model 143–144
Steffens, Niklas 163
storming, with teams 35
stressors, security and 100–101, **101**
structure, well-being and 127
Syed, Matthew 164–165
symbolism, of office 78–81

task allocation 86, 181–182
teams: Allen Curve and 30; attachment theory and 26–28; cognitive diversity and 166; cross-cultural, communication in 66–69; developing group of individuals into 34–36; face time with 26–27; informal social activities with 27; leadership of anxious 142–144; psychological safety in 146–150; shared identity and 27–28
technology: leadership and 141
temperaments theory 42
Tett, Gillian 1
Theory X 11–12, 173
Theory Y 11–12, 173
threat response 142–143
Titanic disaster 56–58
Too Big to Fail (Sorkin) 57–58
Transactional Analysis 51–52
tripartite soul theory 42
trust: change and 14; governance and 166–167; leadership and 11–12
Tuckman, Bruce 34–36

Ubiquiti 93–94
understanding, psychological safety and 148–149
unfreeze, in change process 8

values, in organisational culture 63–64
violence, workplace 97
vision 141

Waber, Ben 33, 175, 179
well-being 183–184; in hybrid environment 125–127; leadership and *130*, 130–131; organisational environments for 127–128
WIPRO 23–26, 176
work-life balance 146
work tasks 84–86
Worst Practices Guide to Insider Threats, A: Lessons from Past Mistakes (Bunn and Sagan) 112

Zappos 60–62
Zoom 2, 19n1

Printed in Great Britain
by Amazon

44746367R00115